*The Phenomenon of Teilhard*
*Prophet for a New Age*

# The Phenomenon of Teilhard
## Prophet for a New Age

by
David H. Lane

⁓

MERCER UNIVERSITY PRESS

ISBN 0-86554-498-0                    MUP/P131

⁓꜅⁓

*The Phenomenon of Teilhard: Prophet for a New Age*
Copyright ©1996
Mercer University Press, Macon, Georgia 31210-3960 USA
Produced in the United States of America
First edition June 1996

⁓꜅⁓

The paper used in this publication meets the minimum requirements
of American National Standard for Information Sciences—
Permanence of Paper for Printed Library Materials, ANSI Z39.48-1984.

⁓꜅⁓

*Library of Congress Cataloging-in-Publication Data*

Lane, David H., 1955–
The Phenomenon of Teilhard: prophet for a new age /
by David H. Lane.
xvi+192pp. 6x9" (15x23cm.).
Includes bibliographical references and indexes.
ISBN 0-86554-498-0 (alk. paper).
1. Teilhard de Chardin, Pierre. 2. New Age movement.
I. Title.
B2430.T37L36    1996
194—dc20    96-8777
CIP

# Contents

# Foreword

The New Age movement is rooted in pantheism (All is God). However, one neglected and very important modern source of New Age thinking is a form of panentheism (All in God) stemming from Alfred North Whitehead and Teilhard de Chardin. Whitehead was the son of an Anglican minister and Teilhard was a Roman Catholic Jesuit priest.

New Age writer of the popular *Aquarian Conspiracy* Marilyn Ferguson observed that many of the leading lights of the New Age movement claim Teilhard as one of the most influential persons in their lives. Other influences acknowledged include C. G. Jung, Aldous Huxley, Swami Muktananda, Thomas Merton, Werner Erhard, and Maharishi Yogi. Indeed, of the 185 New Age leaders surveyed, Teilhard was the most frequently mentioned of any person who had most influenced their thinking. If this is the case, then if we are to understand the New Age movement properly it behooves us to take a careful and critical look at Teilhard de Chardin. David Lane has done precisely this in a clear, well documented, and penetrating way.

While Teilhard claims to be Catholic, orthodox Catholics disown him. In fact, in the final analysis his philosophy is not even theistic, but pantheistic, denying both *ex nihilo* creation and God's ultimate transcendence over the cosmos. God is reduced to the universal evolutionary process. Teilhard himself is a noted evolutionary paleontologist, though not of the strict Darwinian variety. Darwin tried to prove that animals developed into humans. Teilhard, however, attempts to show how humans (and the world) will develop into Godhood. In brief, Darwin taught biological evolution, but Teilhard and his New Age followers believe in spiritual evolution.

In this crucial book David Lane lays bare the philosophical, theological, and scientific failures of Teilhard's New Age enterprise. In a highly documented and insightful scrutiny of Teilhard's cosmic evolution, Lane unveils the apostate Christian roots of one of the most important forerunners of the New Age movement. This is one of the most significant and serious treatments of the modern roots of the New Age in print.

Charlotte, North Carolina                    *Norman L. Geisler*, Ph.D.
Academic Dean, Southern Evangelical Seminary

# Dedication

This book is dedicated
to my wife Soogi
and my parents Rex and Ruth Lane.

# Preface

The first comprehensive analysis of the goals, direction, and composition of what has come to be called the New Age Movement appeared in 1980: Marilyn Ferguson's *The Aquarian Conspiracy: Personal and Social Transformations in the 1980's*.[1] As Ferguson pointed out in this best-seller, the movement (which she called the "Aquarian Conspiracy") is a loosely linked network of organizations "conspiring" to bring about a "global shift in consciousness." Aquarius the Water Bearer is the zodiac sign under whose influence those in the movement believe man will discover his infinite potential. Ferguson refers to the "pervasive dream in our popular culture," that with the closing of a dark, violent age, the Piscean, there will be the dawning of the Age of Aquarius. It is believed that this millennium of love and light and global spirituality-consciousness, will quench mankind's innermost longings. Many New Agers believe we are about to enter this Age; some believe we have recently entered it.

In the course of research for her book, Ferguson interviewed 185 New Age leaders. She asked them to identify the people who had most influenced their thinking, leading to their involvement in the movement. The name most frequently mentioned was that of the French Jesuit paleontologist Pièrre Teilhard de Chardin.[2] (He is referred to throughout this present work as Teilhard—the name he preferred.)

The year 1995 marked forty years since the death of this remarkable man who died in relative obscurity in New York City on Easter Sunday, 10 March 1955. Following the posthumous publication of his largely religiophilosophical writings (banned from publication in his lifetime by the Roman Catholic Church) and his personal correspondence, Teilhard's thought has gained prominence worldwide. It is this published work that forms the basis of the present analysis.

My main objectives are to provide a preliminary critique of Teilhard's religiophilosophical writings and relate his influence on the development of New Age thought. I provide a more comprehensive critique of his theological and philosophical thinking in works to be published shortly.

---

[1]Marilyn Ferguson, *The Aquarian Conspiracy: Personal and Social Transformations in the 1980's* (Los Angeles: J. P. Tarcher, 1980). The 1987 version of the book contains some updated material.

[2]Ibid., 420.

In 1984 Ursula King, former president of the Teilhard Center for the Future of Man (London), wrote: "Teilhard was really a pioneer of what is today called 'new age thinking,' one of the early observers of our planet Earth who clearly saw its need for a profound transformation, for an entirely new culture which cannot come about without a new spirituality."[3] He "pleaded for technicians and engineers of spiritual energy resources who can help to develop the sense of one world, of one human family." Dr. King is professor of Theology and Religious Studies at the University of Bristol, a specialist on Teilhard de Chardin, and a leading figure in the field of interfaith religious dialogue. Her comment is therefore significant, for she confirms the link between Teilhard and the New Age Movement. As yet scholars have not gone on to examine in any detail the basis of the link.

Although numerous articles and books have been written on Teilhard's work, there are very few critiques of his work that include all of the following: (1) an examination of the entire corpus of his religiophilosophical writings; (2) extensive documentation from his writings; (3) a detailed examination of the vast body of work already published on Teilhard; and (4) a comprehensive analysis of the metaphysical and theological aspects of his work in the light of the Bible. It is my hope that the present work and those that follow it, will go some way towards providing such a comprehensive critique.

Most published critiques have been written by those who largely agree with Teilhard's philosophical position and a comprehensive critique of his position is well overdue. This position may differ on a number of points from the "Teilhardism" or "Teilhardianism" expressed by those within the so-called Teilhardian movement. The latter ideology, fabricated by Teilhardian initiates and presented as a doctrine, has been given wide circulation in the popular press.[4] On some points it may well be a distortion of Teilhard's thought.[5]

---

[3]Ursula King, "Science and Mysticism: Teilhard de Chardin in Religious Thought Today," *Teilhard Review* 19/1 (Spring 1984): 10. (N.B.: Publication suspended end of 1994.)

[4]Jacques Maritain, *The Peasant of the Garonne: An Old Layman Questions Himself about the Present Time* (London: Geoffrey Chapman, 1968; orig. in French in 1966 by Desclée de Brouwer) 120: "While it is true that Teilhardism—I say *Teilhardism*, the ideology fabricated by the initiates and given circulation by the popular press—presents itself as a doctrine (which we must describe for what it is); on the contrary, what matters essentially in Teilhard himself is a personal experience, and, truly speaking, incommunicable, although he never ceased looking for ways to communicate it."

[5]Henri de Lubac, a leading expositor and supporter of Teilhard's ideas, has pointed out that Teilhard and "Teilhardism" are not to be confused. By "Teilhardism" he means views shared by those within the Teilhardian "movement." He claimed that apparent apostles of Teilhard's theories were actually propagandizing for their own quite different theories.

I have quoted extensively from Teilhard's published writings and provided full documentation for all quotes. I hope that in doing so I will encourage readers to examine Teilhard's writings for themselves. I have endeavored to provide extracts that represent fairly the full range of his expressed views. Extensive documentation is also provided from a large range of scholarly works on Teilhard's writings and personal life. The detailed footnotes are provided to allow scholars to gain full benefit from my own research work, details of which would not be suitable to include in the main text.

To understand the full implications of Teilhard's writings demands much careful thought and contemplation. Those with backgrounds in philosophy, theology, or science, will find such studies of great help in appreciating his work. The reader will be faced with coming to terms with a number of Teilhard's neologisms, for example, *cosmogenesis, hominization, noosphere,* and others. These terms are defined when they first appear and it is important for the reader to pause and grasp the concepts associated with the terms.

Teilhard was one who saw the dawning of a "New Age." He saw in the "Cosmic Christ" the source of the unifying energy that would bring human history to what he called "Omega Point." He called the "Christification" of evolution *cosmogenesis*[6]—a process involving the progressive spiritualization of the material elements of the cosmos leading to a fullness of being (or Pleroma[7]) of the Cosmos—the Cosmos aware of its own innate divinity. Deeply committed to the view that God was a Person, Teilhard related his cosmic vision of evolution to his Roman Catholic faith. He argued that evolutionary progress was at the very center of God's plan for the universe. He sought to show that Christian doctrines such as the Incarnation, Redemption, and Original Sin, could be reinterpreted within an evolutionary framework and given a transhistorical dimension.

The present study is written by a biologist who finds the scientific "evidence" put forward in support of the Neo-Darwinian explanation ("mechanism") of the General Theory of Evolution[8] (molecules-to-man evolution), to be unconvincing. Furthermore, I have yet to be convinced by any of the alternative explanations of "mechanism" offered in support of this General Theory. The claim that this theory is a *fact* of science has no basis. Those who indulge in such claims

---

[6]Letter of 1 February 1954, cited in Claude Cuénot, *Teilhard de Chardin: A Biographical Study* (London: Burns & Oates, 1965) 368.

[7]In Christian theology the Pleroma is defined to include the consummated mystical body of Christ. Teilhard used the term to mean the whole of creation in its union with Christ.

[8]The theory that "all the living forms in the world have arisen from a single source which itself came from an inorganic form." See Gerald A. Kerkut, *Implications of Evolution* (Oxford: Pergamon, 1960) 157. Kerkut stated that the general theory of evolution can only be considered "a working hypothesis."

fail to recognize that they use circular reasoning to substantiate their claim, by *assuming* that the General Theory is a *fact* and the *only* explanation of the diversity of living organisms. I reject the doctrine of evolutionary theism, which teaches that God used evolution to create the first life form, the first man, and the rest of the biological world. *I reject it, not on the basis of an a priori accep-tance of a particular interpretation of the Bible, but on strictly metaphysical grounds.*[9]

The writings on comparative religions by Islamic scholar and metaphysician Frithjof Schuon and the work of Islamic scholar Professor Seyyed Hossein Nasr have greatly influenced me towards this position. My own understanding of the biblical doctrine of creation has also clearly played a role in the formulation of my basic philosophical position. Whether God exists is a question the empirical sciences cannot answer. Furthermore, the Bible was clearly never written to pro-vide a mechanism of creation which could be studied by the empirical sciences. (Readers interested in my biblical understanding of creation can examine my published papers on this subject.)[10]

It was the breadth of Teilhard's interests that attracted me to his writings. He spanned many fields which I have been actively researching for many years, in-cluding paleoanthropology (human evolution), paleontology, geology, entomolo-gy,[11] theology (including apologetics), and philosophy. It was the reading of the following statement in a the book *Evolution the Great Debate* (1989), that effectively launched me into the present study of Teilhard's writings:

> Teilhard was right to focus on evolution as the new perspective of the twentieth century. *He was also realistic in believing that the church needs to express its deeper truth concerning human destiny within that framework* [of evolution].[12]

---

[9]The metaphysical problems are dealt with more comprehensively in my second book.

[10]David H. Lane, "A Critique of Theistic Evolution," part 1 (of 2 parts): "Special Cre-ation or Evolution: No Middle Ground," *Bibliotheca Sacra* (January–March 1994): 11-31; part 2: "Theological Problems with Theistic Evolution," *Bibliotheca Sacra* (April–June 1994): 155-74. Reprinted in *Vital Apologetic Issues: Examining Reason and Revelation in Biblical Perspective*, ed. Roy B. Zuck (Michigan: Kregel Publications, 1995) 123-57.

[11]My own major in my M.Sc. (Hons.) Zoology course, completed in 1984 (Victoria University, Wellington), was entomology. For a summary see David H. Lane, "The Recognition Concept of Species Applied in an Analysis of Putative Hybridization in New Zealand Cicadas of the Genus *Kikihia* (Insecta: Hemiptera: Tibicinidae)," in David M. Lambert and Hamish G. Spencer, eds., *Speciation and the Recognition Concept: Theory and Application* (Baltimore and London: Johns Hopkins University Press, 1995) 367-421.

[12]Vernon Blackmore and Andrew Page, *Evolution—The Great Debate* (London: Lion, 1989) 169. Vernon Blackmore is editor with Lion Publishing Co. (Oxford, U.K.) and Andrew Page, is senior lecturer in biology at Sheffield City Polytechnic.

The authors are both professing Christians who believe that the deeper truth of Christian theology should be expounded "with full recognition of science's understanding of humanity based on evolution and anthropology."[13] I found it disturbing that Christian scholars were prepared to concede that Teilhard's "synthesis" of evolutionism and theology provided the new "foundation" for communicating the deeper Christian truths about humanity and its relationship to God. I discovered that this view is now widespread within large areas of Christendom. The writings of Teilhard are seen to provide a "shining beacon" and a "ray of hope" in a largely post-Christian Society.

As I pursued the research, I was surprised to discover how many people had been deeply influenced by Teilhard. Many had such a warm affection for his writings that they spoke of their first encounter and absorption of his ideas as though it had been a kind of "conversion experience." Secular humanists, atheists, agnostics, and those from a range of non-Christian faiths, testified to the far-reaching impact of his work on their personal beliefs. Without exception, those who had been outside the Christian faith before encountering his work had not gone on to embrace the faith. Rather they had been steered away from accepting the fundamentals of the faith, embracing a form of monism, pantheism, or secular humanism.

I witnessed firsthand the esteem with which Teilhard is held by New Agers during a lecture to about 500 people delivered by "New Age" leader Dr. Jean Houston in August 1992. Her presentation climaxed with her recollection of her meetings and talks with "Mr. Teilhard" in Central Park, New York, when she was a young girl. An audible gasp of excitement and the tingle of deep "resonance" (to use a New Age "buzz word") swept across the crowd at the mention of Teilhard's name. The question of why he has been exalted to a position as guru, prophet, and a "patron saint" of the New Age Movement has intrigued me. What is it about his writings that harmonizes so well with "New Age" thought? Why is it that such a wide range of people with very different philosophies find a common bond in and through the Teilhardian faith? These are the sorts of questions that helped provoke my own research efforts.

My analysis of Teilhard's work is highly critical. By exposing what I believe to be serious flaws in his methodology, his worldview, and theological speculations, I have no desire to detract from the many positive aspects of his work. He wrestled with issues with which I have struggled myself for many years—the relationship of science to faith. The intensity of focus involved in such a study of his writings, has meant that at times I have felt I have "touched" in some spiritual sense, the very "heartbeat" of the writer.

---

[13]Ibid.

Because Teilhard was gripped by the same passages of Scripture that have inspired me for many years, I have felt very privileged to share his insights, even when they have appeared to conflict with what I considered to be Christian teaching. The breadth of his cosmic vision has been described by many scholars as exhilarating. However, by attempting to graft evolutionism onto the Apostle Paul's teachings on the Fall of man, the Incarnation, Redemption, and the glorified, risen Christ, Teilhard produced a perverse "theological" perspective which strikes at the very heart of Christianity.[14]

There are many passages in Teilhard's works that are profoundly Christian, and which I have found deeply moving. However, when his entire works are analyzed, one finds a philosophical framework being advanced that cannot be reconciled with biblical Christianity. This conflict will be dealt with more fuller in forthcoming publications.

From Teilhard's own writings and the testimony of his friends, it is clear he was totally committed to promoting his religiophilosophical ideas to the public, despite Rome's ban. All his "suppressed" work was in wide circulation during his lifetime in mimeographed copies, with his knowledge and without his hindrance. He saw himself as an "Apostle of Evolution" spearheading a new world religion, a form of "Christian humanism" and "Christian pantheism," incorporating science (evolutionism) and "mysticism." Pantheism is the theory that All, or the Whole, and God are identical. It is my contention that Teilhard's theology/philosophy is best described as evolutionary pantheism—a philosophical position that undergirds much of New Age thinking.

The ease with which much of his thinking has been absorbed into "New Age" thought, which has its roots in gnosticism, evolutionism, and scientism, raises the question: What is the true relationship between Teilhard's thought and the New Age Movement? I trust that in the process of attempting to answer this question readers will gain new insights from the research I have undertaken.

---

[14]For a full discussion of these problems see my second book.

# Acknowledgments

I am indebted to theologian and philosopher Dr. George H. Duggan S.M. for carefully reading the entire manuscript in its final draft and providing detailed comments and suggestions on every chapter. He kindly examined earlier drafts and gave generously of his time to allow for discussions on a number of points. He has shown a great interest in the work and I have benefited greatly from his detailed knowledge of many areas the study impinges on. His critique has proved invaluable, particularly in the areas of metaphysics and scholastic matters of Church doctrine and practice. His own published essay *Teilhardism and the Faith* provided me with a masterly insight into the flaws in Teilhard's metaphysics. While we share similar concerns over the damaging impact of Teilhard's writings on Christian faith, the lines of enquiry I have followed up are entirely my own work.

I am grateful to Dr. Norman L. Geisler for his interest in the work. He read one of the earlier drafts of the work and wrote a response which I have included as a foreword. His commitment to the task of Christian apologetics has been an inspiration to me, as have a number of his books dealing with the New Age Movement.

The reading of Prof. John Morton's books *Redeeming Creation* and *Man, Science, and God* alerted me to his interest in Teilhard de Chardin. Prof. Morton has shown great interest in the present work and I have enjoyed the opportunity to discuss many aspects of the manuscript with him. He has written an introductory chapter to my forthcoming book on Teilhard.

I wish to pay a special tribute to my friend Allan Dewar, B.Theol. (Otago), Dip. Tchg. who has offered many helpful suggestions and much encouragement during the course of the study. He has provided a number of invaluable references and generously given of his time to discuss many aspects of the work. His extensive knowledge of the literature on Islamic mysticism and philosophy has been invaluable. He has given many helpful suggestions relating to style and grammatical points in the course of proofreading the manuscript. Other friends who have assisted include Dr. Jonathan Sarfati, Justin Cargill, John Elsbury, and Michael Townsend.

I sincerely thank Scott Nash, managing editor of Mercer University Press, and Edd Rowell, senior editor, for their patience as I have prepared the manuscript for publication. I am also very grateful to my parents, Rex and Ruth Lane, and my wife Soogi for their encouragement.

The full responsibility for the accuracy of all quotations, references, and other details of the text, is mine. All emphasis (italics) in quotations is my own unless otherwise stated in the notes. On occasion, additional points of clarification have been added to the quotations using brackets. All biblical quotations are taken from the New American Standard Bible, Reference Edition (copyright 1973, The Lockman Foundation).

Finally, I would welcome comments, criticisms, and suggestions from readers, and trust that, having read the present work, they will find my forthcoming publications on Teilhard de Chardin and the New Age Movement of value. Readers may contact me through the publisher.

# Teilhard de Chardin: The Man and His Message

> In a concrete sense there is not matter and spirit: All that exists is matter becoming spirit. There is neither spirit nor matter in the world; the "stuff of the universe" is *spirit-matter*. No other substance but this could produce the human molecule.[1]
>
> Properly speaking, God *does not make*: He *makes things make themselves*.[2]
>
> Christ is the term *of even the natural* evolution of living beings; evolution is holy.[3]
>
> . . . if a Christ is to be completely acceptable as an object of worship, he must be presented as the savior of the idea and reality of evolution.[4]
>
> —*Teilhard de Chardin*

## 1.1 The United Nations Honors a "Visionary of World Peace"

From 20 to 21 September 1983 at the United Nations headquarters in New York, in conjunction with the opening of the thirty-eighth meeting of the United Nations General Assembly, an international colloquium was held in honor of the French Jesuit scholar Pièrre Teilhard de Chardin (1881–1955). It focused on the life and writings of this priest-scientist whose thinking on human and cosmic evolutionary development has had an enormous impact worldwide. The proceed-

---

[1]Teilhard de Chardin, *Human Energy*, trans. J. M. Cohen (London: Collins, 1969) 57-58. Italics in original. N.B.: italics in quotations are my own unless otherwise stated.

[2]Teilhard de Chardin, *Christianity and Evolution*, trans. René Hague (London: Collins, 1971) 28. Italics in original. Cf. Teilhard de Chardin *The Vision of the Past*, trans. J. M. Cohen (London: Collins, 1966) 25: "God . . . does not so much 'make' things as 'make them make themselves'."

[3]Teilhard de Chardin, *Writings in Time of War*, trans. René Hague (London: Collins, 1968) 59. Italics in original.

[4]Teilhard de Chardin, *Christianity and Evolution*, 78.

ings of the colloquium[5] were published in 1985 to celebrate forty years of the
United Nations and to mark the International Year of Peace. The colloquium was
the first in a series of conferences and events organized by the University for
Peace under the title *Visionaries of World Peace.*

The colloquium was the first ever to be held by the University, a multidis-
ciplinary academic institution which enjoys full autonomy and academic freedom
and was approved in 1980 by the thirty-fifth United Nations General Assembly.
According to the University's Chancellor Robert Muller, it aims to "give all other
universities the global views, inspirations, and curricula needed for a peaceful
society and right human relations."[6] Chancellor Muller is also the former assistant
secretary-general of the United Nations and a former vice president of the
Teilhard Center (now called the British Teilhard Association).

In a message to participants in the colloquium, H. E. Javier Pérez de Cuéllar,
secretary-general of the 179-member United Nations stated:

> [T]wo of my eminent predecessors as secretary general of the United
> Nations, Dag Hammarskjöld and U Thant, once indicated that Teilhard
> de Chardin was one of the contemporary thinkers who exercized great
> influence upon them. I share their profound admiration for the universal,
> humanitarian, and spiritual thinking of this philosopher, this visionary
> of peace. . . . Today we lack a new, global, and essentially human
> vision of peace, fraternity, and universal cooperation. The analysis and
> the dissemination of the vision of Teilhard de Chardin thus appears to
> me of great importance. This vision merits ample discussion on the
> threshold of the new global era which is opening before us.[7]

The colloquium included contributions by more than twenty Teilhardians,
from Canada, Europe, South America, and the United States of America, experts
in a variety of scientific disciplines, as well as philosophy, politics, sociology,
and theology. During the first plenary session the International Teilhard Foundation Award Ceremony was held. The recipient of the award was Robert Muller
who entered the United Nations in 1980 as an economist. He holds a doctorate
in law and economics from the University of Strasbourg and degrees in
economics from Heidelberg and Columbia universities. His most characteristic
quality is his ebullient optimism, which many found remarkable while he worked

---

[5]Leo Zonneveld, ed. *Humanity's Quest for Unity: A United Nations Teilhard Colloquium* (The Hague: Mirananda, 1985).

[6]Robert Muller, *New Genesis: Shaping a Global Spirituality* (Garden City NY:
Doubleday, 1982) 22.

[7]Zonneveld, ed., *Humanity's Quest for Unity*, 15. The message was delivered in
French. U Thant wrote that Teilhard and Albert Schweitzer were the two Western philoso-
phers who had most influenced his thinking. See U Thant, *Views from the UN: The
Memoirs of U Thant* (Garden City NY: Doubleday, 1977) 24-25.

for the United Nations, in view of his daily involvement with questions of poverty, illiteracy, disease, and abuses of human rights on the global scale.

In the award ceremony he was recognized as a "true Teilhardian" and the award was made to him with the words: "for the tremendous contribution you have offered as a devoted United Nations servant to foster its course. You are also known to have given your work the extra dimension of global and divine wholeness and stressed an ever more universal interdependence. Your world-affirmative and positive outlook on the future of mankind has been an important element in your shaping the institution that functions so specifically in the spirit of the Noosphere."[8]

The term "Noosphere" (Greek *Noos*, spiritual intellect) is perhaps the best known of Teilhard's many neologisms. He defined noosphere as the "thinking envelope of the biosphere," and "the conscious unity of souls."[9] This "ultimate envelope," in his view, was "the very Soul of the Earth,"[10] woven around the earth from the contributions of the totality of mankind. He believed that it was a present reality and that its density was constantly increasing through the rise in the human population, its interrelations, and its spiritual quality.[11]

Like Teilhard, many Teilhardians believe the United Nations is a vital organ—"a noospheric structure"—essential to mankind's evolutionary progress and "creative evolution." For example, Muller has stated:

> While there are no cellular particles in the human body that are suffi-
> ciently "intelligent" to detect or determine the direction of biological
> evolution and then change themselves accordingly, such a system *is*
> being developed for the human species as a whole. In my view, the
> United Nations and its specialized agencies, together with the mass

---

[8]Zonneveld, ed., *Humanity's Quest for Unity*, 60; "Report: Visionaries of World Peace: Teilhard de Chardin," *Teilhard Review* 19/1 (Spring 1984): 25-26.

[9]Teilhard de Chardin, *Vision of the Past*, 63.

[10]Teilhard de Chardin, *The Heart of Matter*, trans. René Hague (London: Collins, 1978) 32.

[11]Teilhard de Chardin, *Let Me Explain* (texts selected and arranged by Jean-Pierre Demoulin) trans. René Hague et al., (London: Collins, 1970) 17-18. Dr. King points out that "the Greek *nous*, on which *noosphere* is based, does not denote the ordinary mind with its faculty of reasoning, but a faculty of direct intuitive vision, a spiritual faculty which in its *noèsis* transcends the multiplicity of discursive reasoning and overcomes the subject-object differentiation in a vision of unity. For the Greeks, the *nous* was the spiritual intellect, which primarily serves as an instrument of self-transcendence." See Ursula King, *The Spirit of One Earth: Reflections on Teilhard de Chardin and Global Spirituality* (New York: Paragon House, 1989) 81.

media and many international efforts, are becoming this collective brain or macrocephalus of humanity."[12]

In 1989 Muller was awarded the Peace Education Prize by UNESCO, one of some thirty-two specialized agencies and world programs of the United Nations he once administered. It was when he discovered that Teilhard had viewed the United Nations as the progressive institutional embodiment of his philosophy that he first decided to investigate his work. He ranked this discovery as the first of what he calls "Five Teilhardian Enlightenments."[13] It took place in 1973 when he was asked to speak to the American Association of Systems Analysts on the subject "Can the United Nations Become a Functional System of World Order?" He spoke of the United Nations framework as representing "Pascal's genial view of the universe, from the infinitely large to the infinitely small." He records that he realized for the first time that the framework was "typically Teilhardian." "It was universal in scope and covered every aspect of our planetary home." It was a "formidable enterprise" and a "world organization reflect[ing] accurately the unified system of planetary concerns, aspirations, convergence, and consciousness [Teilhard] had conceived."[14]

During the same year Muller spoke to the American Institute of Biological Sciences at Amherst University on "Biological Evolution and the United Nations." He described the United Nations as the "collective brain and warning system of the human species."[15] He reports that after his address Professor Ernst Mayr, arguably the world's leading evolutionary biologist, commented that the speech had come as a "total surprise" to him, for he had never heard the work of the United Nations presented as a living part of the evolutionary process. Muller records him as stating:

> I felt as if I were witnessing a rare moment in evolution—namely, the birth of a collective organ to a species, a moment similar to that when the first protozoa developed into a metazoa. Perhaps indeed, the human race is entering a new period of evolution, a period of global life, an event that will only be fully understood by future generations."[16]

---

[12]Robert Muller, *Most of All They Taught Me Happiness* (Garden City NY: Doubleday, 1978) 183. Italics in original.

[13]Muller, *New Genesis*, 159-68. Muller's heading for his first "enlightenment" is "From the Infinitely Large to the Infinitely Small." Muller was first exposed to the ideas of the philosophy of Teilhard through Father Emmanuel de Breuvery, a companion of Teilhard, when working for the National Resources Division of the UN. See Muller, *Most of All They Taught Me Happiness*, 113-17.

[14]Muller, *New Genesis*, 160-61.

[15]Muller, *Most of All They Taught Me Happiness*, 187.

[16]Ibid., 188. Cf. Muller, *New Genesis*, 161-62.

In 1975 Muller spoke at a joint conference of the Audubon Society and the Sierra Club on the subject "Interdependence: Societies' Interaction and Ecosystems." That speech, which he recorded in his book *New Genesis: Shaping a Global Spirituality*, "brought [him] one step closer to Teilhard's theory of evolution, to his view of the earth as a 'living cell' as well as his outcry for responsible earth management."[17]

Muller has exalted the "vastness of the cooperation" he has seen develop over the thirty years of his service to the United Nations. The growth of the organization, in his view, "is a response to a prodigious evolutionary march by the human species towards total consciousness, an attempt by man to become the all-understanding, all-enlightened, all-embracing master of his planet and of his being."

> Something gigantic [is] going on [he wrote], "a real turning point in evolution, the beginning of an entirely new era of which international cooperation at the United Nations [is] only a first outward reflection. . . . the result [is] now clearly here, glorious and beautiful like Aphrodite emerging from the sea. This [is] unprecedented and full of immense hope for man's future on his planet. Perhaps after all, we [will] be able to achieve peace and paradise on Earth.

The United Nations, he added, provides evidence that we are "approaching Teilhard's point of convergence."[18]

According to Teilhard the process of convergence involved the coming together of the human community and the energy resources available for this within our global religious heritage. At the upper term or summit of cosmic convergence he postulated a transcendent center of unification, "Omega Point" (see §2.3 below for full discussion of this term). He identified this supreme center of evolution with the final, full revelation of God in Christ. "Christ coincides . . . with what I earlier called Omega Point."[19] "The revealed Christ is identical with omega . . . 'Omnia in omnibus Christus'—the very definition of omega"[20] In Scripture, Alpha and Omega, the first and last letters of the Greek alphabet are denoted to Christ, who is the final goal of all creation.[21]

---

[17]Muller, *New Genesis*, 163.

[18]Robert Muller, "A Copernican View of World Cooperation," *Teilhard Review* 13/2 (Summer 1978): 80-81.

[19]Teilhard de Chardin, *Science and Christ*, trans. René Hague (London: Collins, 1965) 164.

[20]Ibid., 54.

[21]See Rev. 1:8, 11; 21:6; 22:13.

Further testimony to the pervasive influence of Teilhard's thinking both within and outside the United Nations, was the holding of a UNESCO colloquium on Teilhard de Chardin in 1981 in Paris, on the centenary of his birth. The 1981 event was accompanied by a paleontological exhibition at the Museum of Natural History. The late French president François Mitterand gave an address at the commemorative ceremony on 18 September at which about a thousand were in attendance. The participants signed a petition urging UNESCO to organize a dialogue of world religions, an objective that was central to Teilhard's vision for world peace. The 1983 United Nations Teilhard colloquium delegates endorsed a similar proposal by calling for the University for Peace to provide a forum for the study of convergence in intrareligious cooperation.[22]

A special symposium in honor of Teilhard was held on 13 June 1981 at the Center Sèvres, the Jesuit conference center in Paris. More than 200 participants (mainly from France) heard contributions by some thirty speakers from many countries. French and Canadian television networks broadcast films on Teilhard and a special stamp issue was produced in France. In 1982 the French celebrations were completed with a further exhibition and the naming of a square in Paris after him.

In the same year Robert Muller wrote:

[A]fter a third of a century of service with the UN I can say unequivocally that much of what I have observed in the world bears out the all-encompassing, global forward-looking philosophy of Teilhard de Chardin. . . . I have come to believe firmly today that our future peace, justice, fulfillment, happiness and harmony on this planet will not depend on world government but on divine or cosmic government, meaning that we must seek and apply the "natural," "evolutionary," "divine," "universal" or "cosmic" laws which must rule our journey in the cosmos. Most of these laws can be found in the great religions and prophecies, and they are being rediscovered slowly but surely in the world organizations. Any Teilhardian will recognize in this the spiritual transcendence which he [Teilhard] announced so emphatically as the next step in our evolution.[23]

By transcendence Teilhard meant a type of relationship in which one term constitutes the other without being limited by it (for example, the soul transcends the body; God transcends the world). It is noteworthy that Muller published his article "My Five Teilhardian Enlightenments" under the heading "My Personal Global *Transcendence*" in his book *New Genesis*. This book is described on its

---

[22]Zonneveld, "Report: Visionaries of World Peace," 26.

[23]Muller, *New Genesis*, 160, 164.

cover as containing "his blueprint" and "framework for an ever-evolving humanity, reaching toward fulfillment and happiness, grounded in the enlightened pragmatism of Teilhard de Chardin."

Leo Zonneveld, co-organizer of the 1983 United Nations Teilhard colloquium and editor of the 1985 publication on Teilhard based on it, also coedited with Muller, an international compendium of essays in honor of Teilhard, published in 1983.[24] In the preface of the 1985 publication, Zonneveld, a former council member of the Teilhard Center (London), summed up the accolades bestowed on Teilhard by the colloquium participants:

> Pierre Teilhard de Chardin, one of the greatest thinkers of the twentieth century . . . in a sense can be seen as the developer of a *cosmology of peace*. . . . No more appropriate environment for the discussion of Teilhard's ideas could be thought of than the very heart of the United Nations. No more appropriate organization could be chairing the colloquium on Teilhard's thought than the University for Peace.[25]

In his report on the colloquium he referred to Teilhard as one of "the world's greatest peace prophets and visionaries," and "one of the greatest and most influential thinkers of the twentieth century."[26]

Teilhard's perception of peace involved a concept of "planetization" whereby the supposed ascending forces of evolution shifted from divergence to convergence, with a consequent transformation of humanity's consciousness. The double thrust toward unification and ascent was summed up in one of his favorite aphorisms: "Everything that ascends must converge."[27] He considered the emergence of the great world religions as having played a vital role in this transformation, a period of transformation which the eminent philosopher Karl Jaspers called the "the first axial period."[28]

Teilhard considered Christianity the most evolved religion to have emerged in this period of transformation. The second phase of its evolution during the second axial period, in his view, would involve the awakening of "global con-

---

[24]Leo Zonneveld and Robert Muller, eds., *The Desire to Be Human: A Global Reconnaissance of Human Perspectives in an Age of Transformation Written in Honor of Pierre Teilhard de Chardin. International Teilhard Compendium* (The Hague: Mirananda Uitgevers, 1983). The main theme running through the whole of the Compendium is the state of the art of Teilhardian thinking, its value for today's world and its future.

[25]Zonneveld, ed. *Humanity's Quest for Unity*, 10.

[26]Zonneveld, *"Report: Visionaries of World Peace,"* 25.

[27]Claude Cuénot, *Teilhard de Chardin: A Biographical Study* (London: Burns and Oates, 1965), 390.

[28]Karl Jaspers, *The Origin and Goal of History*, trans. Michael Bullock (New Haven CT: Yale University Press, 1953).

sciousness."[29] The American theologian Ewert H. Cousins sees this global development as having two aspects: it is global in that it encompasses the entire human community and all its historical experience around the globe; it is also global in that it is a consciousness recovering its rootedness in the earth.[30] Teilhardians consider the role of the United Nations to be central to the planetization process and consider it an external structure reflecting the emerging complexified and planetized consciousness. They envisage the earth becoming a totally integrated organism. As Teilhard expressed the vision:

> *The age of nations has passed. Now, unless we wish to perish we must shake off our old prejudices and build the earth.*[31]

For those still unmoved by the Teilhardian message, it may be hard to appreciate the passionate feelings his writings have aroused in so many people. Many speak of a "conversion experience to faith" initiated by the reading of his works. This passion is captured in a statement made by Jerome Perlinski to participants at the 1983 United Nations Colloquium on Teilhard. Perlinski, who has been the secretary-general of the International Teilhard Foundation (founded in 1980) and editor of *Noosphere*, the Foundation's news journal, called for a moment of reflection at the colloquium and then said:

> I would suggest that each of us try to return for a moment to the days when we first discovered the Teilhardian message. I know (and so do many of you) the personal histories of many here present and of those who will hear of these proceedings later. Almost to a person, Teilhard's vision was a liberation; a breathless, exhilarating confirmation, a light which at once transformed us "as a precious stone by a ray of the proper light." We became invigorated. I remember the heady emotions which swirled about the Paris Foundation Teilhard in the 1960s when it was crowded with Spanish, Portuguese, and anti-Peronista dissidents; when the theologians of the reforming Second Vatican Council paid visits; when the activist "red" bishop of Recife, Dom Helder Camara, or Tanzania's then young president Julius Nyerere, spoke out for social renewal in the name of Teilhard.

---

[29]See Frederic C. Copleston SJ, "Teilhard de Chardin and a Global Outlook," in *The Spirit of the Earth: A Teilhard Centennial Celebration*, ed. Jerome Perlinski (New York: Seabury Press, 1981) 5-18. Copleston states: "What I term a global consciousness is conspicuously exemplified in the thought of Teilhard de Chardin" (8).

[30]King, *The Spirit of One Earth*, 76.

[31]Teilhard de Chardin, *Human Energy*, 37. Italics in original.

> This is . . . a reminder of the alert passion which Teilhard aroused in so many of us, a passion enhanced as we studied and continue to study the complex intellectual structure built upon it.
>
> If we focus then not on the intellectual content of the "Teilhardian" message, but on its feeling content . . . I think we will find that, far from brushing it aside as inconsequential, poetic or embarrassing, the joy and anger which can come from the experience of a vitalizing vision of its strength, its guide, its purity and its rootedness in matter.[32]

Teilhard's ideas have provided a ray of hope for many seeking an understanding of man's place in the evolution of the cosmos and a reconciliation between Christian faith and the theory of evolution. Who exactly then is this man whose thinking has had such a profound influence on not only leaders within the United Nations, but twentieth century thought?

## 1.2 The Jesuit Prophet, Scientist, and Seer

Marie-Joseph-Pièrre Teilhard de Chardin was born on 1 May 1881 in the small village of Sarcenat a few kilometers from the ancient city of Clermont-Ferrand, in the province of Auvergne, France. He was nurtured in the Roman Catholic faith in a patrician home by pious parents and was the fourth of eleven children. His father was an antiquarian, an ornithologist, and a gentleman farmer, as well as being a keen student of history. His mother was a great-grandniece of the famous French scholar Voltaire, the paragon of the Enlightenment.

On 20 March 1890 Teilhard entered the Jesuit novitiate at Aix-en-Provence and was ordained a priest on 2 August 1911 by Monsignor Amigo, Bishop of Southwark, in the chapel at Ore Place, the Jesuit house in Hastings on the Sussex coast. On 26 May 1918 he made his perpetual vows as a Jesuit at Sainte-Foy-lès-Lyon.

Teilhard was also a professional geologist and paleontologist who established a long and distinguished career which took him to many parts of the world.[33] He became world famous for his involvement with the excavation of the so-called "Peking Man"[34] (*Sinanthropus pekinensis*) from an ancient limestone quarry at Chou-kou-tien, some thirty miles south west of Peking. He did not discover the fossils but was merely involved in describing them. For many years these ape-

---

[32]Jerome Perlinski, "Hoping for Peace: Teilhard in the History of Ideas," in *Humanity's Quest For Unity*, ed. Zonneveld, 119-20.

[33]For a concise summary of his career see Teilhard de Chardin, *The Heart of the Matter*, 152-64.

[34]See Jia Lampo and Huang Weiwen, *The Story of Peking Man* trans. Yin Zhigi (Hong Kong: Oxford University Press, 1990); Harry L. Shapiro, *Peking Man* (NY: Simon & Schuster, 1974).

like fossils, now classified as *Homo erectus*, were touted as man's oldest ancestors, allegedly proving man's ancestry from ape-like creatures.

It was probably through Teilhard that the cultural activities of "Peking Man," including fire utilization and tool making, were first brought to light.[35] As a result, the hypothesis of the fossil bones being those of the animal prey of still-unidentified men operating the limestone quarry in which the fossils were found, was thought to be ruled out.[36] However, Teilhard's conclusions, which were never accepted by the world's authority on early man at the time, Professor Marcellin Boule, still remain highly questionable today.

The complete loss of all these fossils in December 1941, during the time of the Japanese occupation of China in the Second World War, has not helped resolve this controversy. Teilhard declared that "the discovery of *Sinanthropus* represents an important victory for those who uphold the extension of transformation to the human zoological form."[37]

Teilhard was also involved in another highly controversial excavation of "early man," the Piltdown fraud, which brought the subject of human origins into disrepute for many years, following the exposure of the hoax in 1953. More recently, he has gained some notoriety in America because of paleontologist Stephen Jay Gould's oft-repeated charge that he was a conspirator in the fraud. However, there appears to be no prima facie evidence to incriminate him in the affair.[38]

In 1912 he applied to study for a doctorate under Marcellin Boule (d. 1992) who was Professor and director at Institut de Paléontologie Humaine in Paris from 1902 to 1936. At that time Boule was engaged in studying the celebrated La Chapelle-aux-Saints Man (Neanderthal Man). Through Boule, Teilhard was brought into contact with such eminent prehistorians as Abbé Henri Breuil and Hugo Obermaier.

In 1920, when Teilhard turned thirty-nine, he became professor of Geology at the Catholic Institute of Paris where he taught for three years. In the same year he was elected president of the French Geological Society and made Chevalier of the Légion d'Honneur for his war service and gallantry on the battlefield,

---

[35]Helmut de Terra, *Memories of Teilhard de Chardin*, trans. (from the German) J. Maxwell Brownjohn (London: Collins, 1964) 71. Teilhard reported on these findings, which aroused much interest, in a lecture dealing with the Quaternary period in China.

[36]Cuénot, *Teilhard de Chardin*, 113. Also see Teilhard de Chardin, *Man's Place in Nature: The Human Zoological Group*, trans. René Hague (London: Collins, 1966) 83n.: "on the hypothesis (which is by far the most probable) that Peking Man is indeed the originator of the industry found in association with the bone remains in the archaeological deposits."

[37]Nicolas Corte, *Pierre Teilhard de Chardin: His Life and Spirit*, trans. (from the French) Martin Jarrett-Kerr (New York: MacMillan, 1960) 40.

[38]For the charge made against Teilhard see S. J. Gould, "The Piltdown Conspiracy," *Natural History* 89/8 (August 1980): 8-28.

where he served as a stretcher bearer (1915–1918). He saw frontline action at the Somme, the Chemin-des-Dames, and Verdun, and his bravery gained him two citations in divisional orders (1916), as well as the awards of Croix de Guerre (1915) and Médaille Militaire (1917). A medical major wrote of him as having two striking personality features: courage and humility. He was promoted to the rank of corporal while serving at the war front. In 1922 he was awarded a doctorate degree in paleontology from the Sorbonne.

On 25 June 1927, at the request of the Foreign Affairs Ministry, he was promoted to the grade of officer of the Légion d'Honneur, for his scientific contributions. In the same year he became director of research at the National Center for Scientific Research and was elected a corresponding member of the Académie des Sciences (mineralogical section), in recognition of his scientific work completed in the Far East. In 1923 he had been invited to collaborate on geological and prehistoric research in China by Père Emile Licent, a fellow Jesuit who had established a museum at Tientsin. He accepted the invitation and spent many fruitful years researching in the Far East.

In 1928 he was asked to offer himself as a candidate for the prestigious chair of Prehistory at the Collège de France, when it became vacated by Henri Breuil. Although he had a firm assurance that he would be elected unanimously if he agreed to stand, he could not stand without permission from the Jesuit authorities. Eventually he had to decline the invitation as a result of orders from his religious superiors.[39] On 22 May 1951 Teilhard was elected to full nonresident membership of the Institut de France (Academy of Sciences).[40] At about the same time he was elected to the Linnean Society of London.

While Teilhard was not a philosopher in the strict sense, he has been described as an "evolutionary natural philosopher,"[41] a "process philosopher,"[42] and a "metaphysician in the inductive sense."[43] Few philosophers of evolution of the twentieth century can match Teilhard's extensive scientific training, research, and

---

[39]Cuénot, *Teilhard de Chardin*, 275.

[40]*Letters from My Friend Teilhard 1948–1955*, collected and intro. by Pierre Leroy, trans. Mary Lukas (New York: Paulist Press, 1976) 42.

[41]Jane Mathison, "Paley, Darwin, Teilhard: A Paradigm Change in Natural Theology," *Teilhard Review* 14/1 (Spring 1977): 31.

[42]Anthony Hanson, ed. *Teilhard Reassessed* (London: Darton, Longman & Todd, 1970) 176.

[43]See Philip Hefner, *The Promise of Teilhard: The Meaning of the Twentieth Century in Christian Perspective* (Philadelphia/New York: J. B. Lippincott, 1970) 38. Cf. Henri de Lubac, *The Religion of Teilhard de Chardin*, trans. René Hague (London: Collins, 1967) 85: "Still less was Père Teilhard a metaphysician, and still less did he wish to be one, at least in his general habit of thought, so that he can hardly be called one at all. It was not that he denied the value of all metaphysics—although he was somewhat mistrustful of what he called 'abstract metaphysics'."

experience. During his career he published around 200 scientific research papers in the fields of geology and paleontology, which represent more than double the theological texts from Teilhard's pen.[44]

In his day, his professional colleagues considered him an expert of international standing in the field of Asian prehistory, geology, and vertebrate paleontology.[45] Professor Helmut de Terra, a geologist of German origin attached to Yale University, accompanied him on a number of expeditions. He wrote: "Teilhard had all the enthusiasm of a detective who is permanently aware of his responsibility to some higher authority. There was a restlessness about him, as though he were determined to deduce the leitmotiv of human evolution and the impulse of psychical energy toward fuller consciousness from geological occurrences."[46]

In the *Cambridge Encyclopedia of Human Evolution* published in 1992, he is included among the "Who's who of historical figures"[47] and listed as a possible coconspirator in the Piltdown forgery.[48] The *Encyclopedia* even notes that a group of "primitive' monkeys have been named in honor of Teilhard's contribution to paleontology.[49]

However, his importance in the field of paleoanthropology has been exaggerated by many of his followers. On the occasion of the one hundredth anniversary of the publication of Darwin's principal work, a three-volume collection of articles on evolution was published in Chicago with contributions by leading biologists and anthropologists worldwide, but particularly from the United States and Britain. Teilhard's name is not mentioned in any of the treatises on natural science that deal with evolution in general and the problem of the genesis of man.[50]

In 1947 Teilhard received a letter from his superior general forbidding him to publish anything whatsoever of a philosophical or theological nature. His

---

[44]Karl Schmitz-Moormann, "The Scientific Writings of Teilhard," *Teilhard Review* 13/3 (Winter 1978): 124. The author considers that this estimate is still correct even if one regards all the texts published in the "Oeuvres-Séries" (Ed. du Seuil, Collins) as not scientific. Some of them are bordering on scientific works and were first published in scientific journals.

[45]De Terra, *Memories of Teilhard de Chardin*, 16.

[46]Ibid., 38.

[47]Steve Jones, Robert Martin and David Pilbeam, eds., *The Cambridge Encyclopedia of Human Evolution* (Cambridge: Cambridge University Press, 1992) 446-53. See 452 for details on Teilhard.

[48]Ibid., 448.

[49]Ibid., 203. The tarsier-like primates (omomyids) include *Teilhardina*, an anaptomorphine.

[50]Sol Tax, ed., *Evolution after Darwin*, vol. 2, *The Evolution of Man* (Chicago: University of Chicago Press, 1960).

writings on these topics were considered so harmful that they were banned outright by the Roman Catholic Church and he was forbidden to lecture on these subjects in France.

At this time, as René d'Ouince SJ, his religious superior noted, Teilhard's "moral authority" had never been so great and "the halo of persecution added still further to his prestige."[51] He seemed to delight in seeing himself as something of a modern-day Galileo. He was fond of quoting the apocryphal dying words of Galileo "E pur si muove" ("The Earth Turns!"), combining them with his catch-cry "Humanity Converges!"

In his essay entitled "Faith in Peace" he wrote: "wherever I look I am forced to the same conclusion: that the earth is more likely to stop turning than is Mankind, as a whole, likely to stop organizing and unifying itself."[52]

René d'Ouince described Teilhard as a "paradoxical blend of audacity and fidelity."[53] In an address he gave at the "service for the repose of the soul of Père Pierre Teilhard de Chardin," he spoke of him as "of the blood of the great missionaries . . . eager to win the earth for Jesus Christ; of the blood of the seventeenth-century educationists who aimed to bring up the whole of Europe's youth in faith in Jesus Christ: . . . [and whose] dream it was to realize upon earth our image of the kingdom of heaven.[54]

Teilhard's posthumously published works have made him a household name throughout much of the world. Professor Jean Piveteau of the Paris Faculté des Sciences, referred to his "masterly works" as produced by "one of the greatest minds the world has known,"[55] "written with fearlessness and put forward with humility."[56]

Professor George B. Barbour, a Scottish geologist, who worked in the field with Teilhard on four continents, regarded Teilhard's contribution as "comparable" to the "prophetic leadership" displayed by Darwin.[57] He described Teilhard

---

[51]René d'Ouince, prologue in Teilhard de Chardin, *Letters to Two Friends 1926–1952* (London: Rapp & Whiting, 1970) 11.

[52]Teilhard de Chardin, *The Future of Man*, trans. Norman Denny (London: Collins, 1964) 152.

[53]Teilhard de Chardin, *Letters to Two Friends*, 18.

[54]Address given in the Chapel of the Rue de Sèvres, 27 April 1955. See De Lubac, *The Religion of Teilhard de Chardin*, 268.

[55]Jean Piveteau, in his preface to *Le Groupe zoologique humain* (Paris, 1956). Cited in Teilhard de Chardin, *Letters from a Traveller*, trans. René Hague et al. (London: Collins, 1962) 60.

[56]Edouard Boné SJ, "Pierre Teilhard de Chardin," *Revue des questions scientifiques*, Louvain, 20 Jan. 1956. Cited by Claude Aragonnès (Mlle Teillard-Chambon) in *Letters from a Traveller*, 60-61.

[57]George B. Barbour, "A Geologist in the Field," in *Teilhard de Chardin: Pilgrim of the Future*, ed. Neville Braybrooke (London: Darton, Longman & Todd, 1964) 36.

as "the noblest man I ever lived with."[58] The late Dr. Joseph Needham (d. 1995), ex-president of the Teilhard Center (London), who first met Teilhard in Paris in 1947 and got to know him while they both worked in New York, wrote:

> I should say without any hesitation that Father Teilhard was called to be the greatest prophet of this age. That will become more and more clear, I believe, as time goes on. . . . I found him a charismatic as well as a lovable person. . . . [He] is the prophet of this age, a prophet not for the Western world alone but for all men everywhere, so that his insights will need translation into the idioms of the Eastern nations.[59]

Henry de Monfreid, one of Teilhard's intimate friends, wrote:

> In humanity, in purity of soul, Teilhard was an extraordinary being. Not a shadow ever disturbed his calm. He had the limpidity of a diamond, flooded with divine light. The man himself was a light, surpassing measurement. The words of this sublime man made clear and understandable to me the ineluctable eternity of the human soul . . . [he] knew how to bring dead consciences to life, just as Jesus of Nazareth brought Lazarus back from the dead.[60]

In his comprehensive biography of Teilhard, Claude Cuénot (1911–1992) said that Teilhard "by himself personifies, in a certain way, on the spiritual plane, a mutation of *homo sapiens*."[61] Cuénot has been described as one of the first generation of Teilhardian polemicists who saw their task to defend and promote the thought of Teilhard.

A number of Teilhardians promote the erroneous view that Teilhard was a theologian. For example, in a letter to the editor of the *Times*, Needham describes him as a "great theologian."[62] This letter was published in the *Teilhard Review*[63] without any disclaimer, yet in other issues of the journal, those outside the close-

---

[58]Barbour, letter of 6 May 1958, cited in Cuénot, *Teilhard de Chardin*, 156.

[59]Joseph Needham, foreword in King, *Towards a New Mysticism*, 7-8, 10. Needham got to know Teilhard while he was working to establish the National Sciences Division of UNESCO. Needham also wrote more recently: "Teilhard . . . turned into one of the greatest prophets of our times." See his foreword in Allerd Stikker *The Transformation Factor: Towards an Ecological Consciousness* (Rockport MA: Rockport Pub., 1992) ix-xi.

[60]*La Table Ronde*, June 1955. Cited in Robert Speaight, *Teilhard de Chardin: A Biography* (London: Collins, 1967) 161.

[61]Cuénot, *Teilhard de Chardin* (Ed. Il Saggiatore) 67. Cited in Zonneveld, ed., *Humanity's Quest for Unity*, 113.

[62]Letter to editor of the *Times*, 8 January 1982.

[63]*Teilhard Review* 17/1 (Spring 1982): 29.

knit Teilhardian network who have referred to him as a theologian have been criticized.[64]

In the judgement of Professor Georges Crepsy, "Teilhard never developed a theological system in and for itself. A Teilhardian catechism does not exist. Indeed in the technical sense the term a Teilhardian theology does not exist."[65] Teilhard never gained any advanced degree in theology, but he passed all his religious exams in his training under first-rate Jesuit teachers. He also established many friends among his peers who went on to become leading theologians and philosophers.

Professor of Theology Anthony Hanson considers that it is in the "category of prophet"[66] that Teilhard "shines most brightly." "It is as a prophet that he points towards the solution of the problem . . . [namely] how to set Christian theologians on a course which allows for both openness and fundamental Christian belief."[67]

René d'Ouince recognized that on his arrival in France from China in May 1946, Teilhard "was welcomed by a crowd of strangers, as a prophet."[68] However, according to Professor Helmut de Terra, "even among his intimates he did not . . . behave like a prophet of political or social change, but contented himself with looking at things in perspective and thinking constructively where others could only express doubts."[69]

Many scholars have referred to Teilhard in glowing terms, such as "genius,"[70] "apostle of evolution,"[71] "mystic visionary,"[72] a Christian humanist who was a "true mystic,"[73] and as a "seer."[74] Eric Doyle argues: "If Teilhard can be fitted into any category at all it is that of Christian mystic."[75] One scholar de-

---

[64]E.g., in a review of J. L. Simmon's book *The Emerging New Age* (1990), Alison Williams criticizes the author for referring to Teilhard as a "visionary theologian." See *Teilhard Review* 27/3 (Winter 1992): 88. Williams writes: "Teilhard was not a theologian."

[65]Georges Crepsy, *From Science to Theology: An Essay on Teilhard de Chardin* (Nashville: Abingdon Press, 1968). Cited in Hefner, *The Promise of Teilhard*, 8.

[66]Teilhard did not consider himself a prophet: "I am no politician and still less a prophet." See "Faith and Peace" (1947) in *The Future of Man*, 149.

[67]Hanson, ed., *Teilhard Reassessed*, 177.

[68]René d' Ouince SJ, prologue in Teilhard de Chardin, *Letters to Two Friends*, 10.

[69]De Terra, *Memories of Teilhard de Chardin*, 106.

[70]*Times Literary Supplement*, 25 May 1962, 366.

[71]Cuénot, *Teilhard de Chardin*, 383.

[72]William H. Thorpe, *Science Man and Morals* (London: Methuen, 1965) 56.

[73]Hefner, *The Promise of Teilhard*, 5, 17.

[74]Charles Raven, *Teilhard de Chardin: Scientist and Seer* (London: Collins, 1962).

[75]Eric Doyle, "Teilhard and Theology," *Teilhard Review* 20/1 (Spring 1985): 2; repr. from *Irish Theological Quarterly* 38/2 (April 1971).

scribes him as "perhaps the first technological mystic, the first to be transformed by the laboratory into an enlightened being."[76] By calling him a "mystic" scholars generally mean one who gained incommunicable knowledge of God through direct experience (see §1.3 below for a fuller discussion of the term).

Thomas Berry, a historian of religion and former president of the American Teilhard Association for the Future of Man, maintains that Teilhard is primarily a cosmologist, an interpreter of the universe, with special reference to the planet earth and to its human expression. Teilhard once described himself as "a geobiologist" who had "looked hard and long at the face of Mother Earth."[77] On another occasion he said, "I am neither a philosopher, nor a theologian, but a student of the "phenomenon," a physicist in the ancient Greek sense."[78]

He expressed regret once to a friend, for not having any aptitude for music or poetry (his greatest regret), or the talent or art of a novelist. Nevertheless, his ideas found expression in what he described as "philosophicoliterary essays," which during his lifetime, were "read only by a limited group of friends."[79]

Many of these essays defined the successive stages of the development of his "faith" and were built on his apologetics or his dialectic. (Christian apologetics is the reasoned defence of the Christian faith against objections, but also includes the setting forth of positive grounds for Christianity). Referring to the whole body of his work, completed or projected, he wrote: "All together, in short, they constitute my Apologetics."[80] He stressed unashamedly in his writings that he felt his Christian duty was to be an apologist.[81]

In his biography on Teilhard, Robert Speaight describes Teilhard as "a passionate apologist" who "brought many people to a belief in Christ who would otherwise have had no belief in him at all."[82] He argues that "it cannot be too strongly insisted that the foundation of [Teilhard's] thought and his apologetic was St. Paul."[83]

---

[76]Francis Tiso, "Love's Conspirators: Builders of Earth-House-Hold," in *The Spirit of the Earth*, ed. Perlinski, 89.

[77]Teilhard de Chardin, "Faith in Peace" (1947), *The Future of Man*, 149.

[78]*Les nouvelles littéraires* (11 January 1951). Cited in De Lubac, *The Religion of Teilhard de Chardin*, 85.

[79]Teilhard de Chardin, letter of 12 October 1926. *Letters to Two Friends*, 43.

[80]Letter of 22 August 1925. Cited in De Lubac, *The Religion of Teilhard de Chardin*, 231.

[81]E.g., "La pensée du Père Teilhard de Chardin" (by Teilhard himself), in *Les Etudes philosophiques* (1955): 57-81.

[82]Speaight, *Teilhard de Chardin: A Biography*, 13.

[83]Ibid., 71.

Teilhard was fascinated by Cardinal John Henry Newman's *Apologia* and his attempt to reconcile the love of God and the love of life in all its natural forms.[84] The Jesuit scholar Henri de Lubac, who has been a leading champion of Teilhard's thought, is of the view that his writings do not derive in their principal order from apologetical motives, but were initially prompted by the desire to illuminate his own mind (in which, indeed, they resemble all serious apologetics).[85] De Lubac wrote of him: "One of the chief signs of Père Teilhard's originality—one of the marks, we might say, of his genius—is that he was a generation ahead of his contemporaries."[86]

In the introduction to one of his better-known essays, "My Universe," Teilhard wrote: "All I wish to do is to explain how I personally understand the world to which I have been progressively more fully introduced by the inevitable development of my consciousness as a man and a Christian." He explained that the special value of "the system" he was "putting forward [was] that it provided "an incontestable psychological witness." He indicated that he had found "balance" for his "interior life" in a "unitary concept, based upon physics, of the world and Christ."[87]

His successive essays each completed and corrected one another and his intention was never to present, as he put it, "any fixed and self-contained system" of thought. Rather, he sought to define a possible line of approach to one of the aspects of the truth. In 1916 he wrote to his cousin: "I am making notes and I am doing all I can to open up my mind to contact with God. A little more responsiveness to his influence, a little more union with him!"[88] In 1919 he wrote: "the rather hazardous schematic points in my teaching are in fact of only secondary importance to me. It's not nearly so much ideas that I want to propagate as *a spirit*: a *spirit* can animate almost all external presentations."[89]

Teilhard has been widely recognized as a master of the French language, and his gift of expression enabled him to popularize both his scientific ideas and his religious visions. He was articulate in both his native French and in English. He considered himself a "freelance thinker" and a solitary, in whom change was the product of "an internal evolution, beyond any influence of persons."[90]

---

[84]Ibid., 71-73.

[85]De Lubac, *The Religion of Teilhard de Chardin*, 231.

[86]Henri de Lubac SJ, *The Eternal Feminine*, trans. René Hague (London: Collins, 1971) 134.

[87]Teilhard de Chardin, *Science and Christ*, 37-38.

[88]Teilhard de Chardin, *The Making of a Mind: Letters from a Soldier-Priest 1914–1919*, trans. René Hague (London: Collins, 1965) 91. Letter of 22 January 1916.

[89]Letter of 1 February 1919, in ibid., 281. Italics in original.

[90]Cuénot, *Teilhard de Chardin*, 256.

He also described himself as a sort of John the Baptist "on a much reduced scale . . . that is, . . . one who presages what is to come. . . . perhaps . . . called . . . simply to help in the birth of a new soul [of the world] in that which already is."[91] There is a hint in some of his writings that he saw himself as a prophet who was seeking to make plain to man the mystery and true meaning of the "nascent human faith" that was emerging in his day.[92] On New Year's Eve 1926 he wrote to his friend Valensin of the need for another Christian leader of the stature of St. Ignatius or St. Francis of Assisi to emerge:

> What a wonderful dream—to follow a man of God along a free, fresh road, impelled by the full force of the religious life-sap *of his own* time. Often I pray to God that I may be the ashes from which will arise, for other generations, the great blaze that our own looks for in vain.[93]

Less well known is the fact that Teilhard was an astute observer of his times and was deeply interested in all facets of human endeavor, including politics and international relations. The scope of his work has been compared with that of the philosopher of history Oswald Spengler (1880–1936),[94] who interpreted the events of his time as proof that Western civilization was degenerating; and Arnold Toynbee (1889–1975),[95] who has detected the basic rhythm of civilizations in their rise and decline. However, it is arguable whether his work is in the same class as this scholarship.[96]

Teilhard was a prolific reader and letter writer, who revelled in the exchange of ideas relevant to his areas of research on man's place in the cosmos. In a letter to a close friend written in 1927 he confirmed that geology provided the stimulus for his interest in Man: "For me, geology is like a root that pushes me with its sap toward the human questions: . . . I cannot live outside this realm."[97] In another letter written in 1937 he wrote: "geology must continue to be my root in the real as well as my platform."[98]

---

[91]Ibid., 244.

[92]Eg. Teilhard de Chardin, *Activation of Energy*, trans. (from the French) Réne Hague (London: Collins, 1970) 178.

[93]Cited in De Lubac, *The Religion of Teilhard de Chardin*, 20. Italics in the original.

[94]Oswald Spengler, *The Decline of the West*, 2 vols., trans. (from the German) Charles Francis Atkinson (London: George Allen & Unwin, 1932).

[95]Arnold Toynbee, *A Study of History* (New York: Oxford University Press, 1972); *Surviving the Future* (London: Oxford University Press, 1971).

[96]G. H. Duggan (personal communication) does not consider Teilhard's writings to be in the same class as Spengler or Toynbee.

[97]Teilhard de Chardin, letter of 6 April 1927, in *Letters to Two Friends*, 66.

[98]Letter of 28 June 1937, in ibid., 93.

Paleontology and geological research served as the basis of his evolutionary speculations and vision for the future, but it was geology that provided him with scientific standing. In letters to friends he wrote:

> It is almost as though, for reasons arising from the progress of my own science, the past and its discovery had ceased to interest me. *The past has revealed to me how the future is built,* and preoccupation with the future tends to sweep everything else aside. It is precisely that I may be able to speak with authority about the future that it is essential for me to establish myself more firmly than before as a specialist on the past.[99]

> I have a distinct feeling that I am losing the thrill of geology. And yet geology is my real platform.[100]

For Teilhard, the future and the past history of life are inextricably bound together. This was a central theme of his vision which he described to a friend in the following terms:

> I am a pilgrim of the future on my way back from a journey made entirely in the past."[101]

This strange paradox can be understood when one recognizes that between 1935 and 1937 he disengaged himself from a preoccupation with the science of man's past, and became engrossed in the question of man's future. His vision for man's future arose from his studies of man's past, and he pioneered work in the field of anthropogenesis: the science that deals with man as an extension of a science of life.

Teilhard's spoken words have been described as "going straight to your soul, with the persuasive force of an apostle. . . . "[102] Many feel this is also true of his written words. Even the spiritual writer Thomas Merton (1915–1968), who became alert to what he termed "grave errors" in Teilhard, once wrote two very positive essays on him. He noted that his writings "point to a new and important horizon in Christian spirituality."[103] For him "the real importance of Teilhard is

---

[99]Teilhard de Chardin, letter of 8 September 1935, in *Letters From a Traveller*, 207-208. Italicized by the French editor as being a cardinal expression of Père Teilhard's thought.

[100]Teilhard de Chardin, letter of 7 May 1939, in *Letters to Two Friends*, 131.

[101]Letter of 23 October 1923 written from Tientsin to Abbé Breuil, in *Letters from a Traveller*, 101.

[102]Henry de Monfreid, *Charas*, cited in ibid., 124.

[103]Thomas J. King, "The Milieux Teilhard Left Behind," *Teilhard Review* 24/3 (Autumn 1989): 92.

his affirmation of the 'holiness of matter'" and he praised his book *The Divine Milieu*. Of one of its pages he wrote: "No finer and more contemplative page has been written in our century."[104] The reviewer for the *Times* commented that this book "will certainly take its place among the rare spiritual classics of the twentieth century." Claude Cuénot describes Teilhard's lyric works as ranking "with the finest of the world's religious poetry," incorporating the elements of the mystical, the epic and the eschatological.[105] As one scholar wrote: "The grandiose eschatology of Teilhard inspired some of his most profound pages of lyrical beauty."[106]

Henri de Lubac described his thought as "essentially eschatological," a perspective that "never varied" right up until the year of his death.[107] Fr. Robert Faricy SJ, who has taught at the Gregorian University in Rome, currently a vice president of the British Teilhard Association, also describes Teilhard's thought as "fundamentally eschatological." He defines eschatology (from Greek *eschaton*, the ultimate goal of all things studied) as dealing with "the polar tension between things-as-they-are and things-as-they ought-to-be, between the present and the ultimate future."[108] As a result of this future-directedness, Faricy considers the central Christian mystery in Teilhard's writings is the Parousia—the second coming of Jesus Christ.[109] In Christian theology the *eschaton* ("the last things") involves the last and final consummation of the human being in God. Teilhard saw Christ as universal redeemer who is closely related to a "cosmic emergence of the Spirit." He tried to interpret the data of evolution in the light of revelation and together they gave him the basis for his great eschatological hope.

Bernard Towers, professor of Pediatrics and Anatomy at the University of California (Los Angeles) and the first chairman of the Teilhard Center (London), has referred to Teilhard as a "genius" who "writes like a visionary" and whose "vision . . . marks the most significant achievement in synthesis since that of Aquinas."[110] However, other scholars, like New Zealander G. H. Duggan, consider that Aquinas achieved a genuine synthesis of faith and reason, while Teilhard did not.[111]

---

[104]Ibid.

[105]Cuénot, *Teilhard de Chardin*, 42.

[106]Claire Huchet Bishop, "Teilhard and the Cosmic Christ," in *The World of Teilhard*, ed. Robert T. Francoeur (Baltimore: Helicon Press, 1961) 39.

[107]De Lubac, *The Religion of Teilhard de Chardin*, 30.

[108]Robert Faricy SJ, "Teleology, Prophecy, and Apocalyptic in Teilhard's Eschatology," *Teilhard Review* 15/1 (Spring 1980): 2.

[109]Robert Faricy SJ, "The Heart of Jesus in the Eschatology of Teilhard," *Teilhard Review* 13/2 (Summer 1978): 82.

[110]Bernard Towers, *Concerning Teilhard and Other Writings on Science and Religion* (London: Collins, 1969) 43.

[111]George H. Duggan, *Teilhardism and the Faith* (Cork: Mercier, 1968).

Some scholars view the difference between the two perspectives as paralleling that between a pre-Copernican view of matter and the universe, and the dynamic evolutionary worldview issued in by Charles Darwin's *The Origin of Species*, published in 1859. Professor Hemut de Terra described Teilhard as having "a brilliant capacity for proceeding straight to a synthesis from carefully sifted details."[112]

Most of Teilhard's French apologists provide long lists of the distinguished scholars in many fields that he visited and impressed.[113] While he never put himself forward as a theologian, Professor of Theology Anthony Hanson ranks him as a theologian whose works are well worth studying.[114]

Theodosius Dobzhansky, a leading evolutionist who was a vice president of the Teilhard Center (London), referred to him in 1968 as "one of the foremost thinkers of our time."[115] He considered the Teilhardian synthesis to be the work of one who was indisputably a scientist and a theologian, but "moreover of someone who had the gifts of prophetic vision and of poetic inspiration."[116] According to Dobzhansky, he was "too much a scientist to set forth his conclusions in a manner wholly to please the theologians, and too much a theologian to make himself altogether a scientist."[117]

Other authors consider him one of the leading thinkers in the twentieth century on the intersection of Christianity and evolution.[118] The claim that he was a theologian is hard to sustain. He was not temperamentally disposed towards biblical exegesis and he displayed no special orientation towards biblical studies. This approach may have stemmed from a lack of scriptural and exegetical emphasis in his education.[119]

Teilhard wrote influential books promoting "spiritual evolutionism," a theory, as he described it, that "places the true future of the world's development and being on the side of spirit, that is to say synthesis,"[120] and "everything becomes,

---

[112]De Terra, *Memories of Teilhard de Chardin*, 24.

[113]Many of these claims have been discounted. See Ian G. Barbour, "Five Ways of Reading Teilhard," *Teilhard Review* 3/1 (1968): 3-20.

[114]Hanson, ed., *Teilhard Reassessed*, 177.

[115]Theodosius Dobzhansky, "Teilhard de Chardin as a Scientist," in *Letters to Two Friends*, 222.

[116]Ibid., 224-25.

[117]Ibid., 221.

[118]Eg. William R. Fix, *The Bone Peddlers: Selling Evolution* (New York: Macmillan, 1984) 247.

[119]Cuénot, *Teilhard de Chardin*, 12. In an undated letter from Paris to a friend he noted that he was not in the habit of quoting scripture. *Letters to Two Friends*, 86. Etienne Gilson and Jacques Maritain have expressed their surprise at Teilhard's ignorance of the philosophy of St. Thomas Aquinas.

[120]Teilhard de Chardin, *The Vision of the Past*, 138n.

if not spirit, at least distant preparation, spiritized 'matter'."[121] "The true evolution of the world," he wrote, "takes place in souls and in their union. Its inner factors are not mechanistic but psychological and moral."[122] To Teilhard's mind, God was a self-evident fact.

His many works including *The Divine Milieu*,[123] and *The Phenomenon of Man*,[124] promoted the view that there was "a higher pole or center" of the universe,[125] a theory he called "an evolutionism by convergence."[126] Bernard Wall held that in *Le Milieu Divin* one can "hear the voice of St. Ignatius of Loyola, St. John of the Cross and (a non-Jansenist) Pascal expressed in a terminology of twentieth-century man."[127] Teilhard described this work as containing "the sort of ascetical and mystical doctrine that [he had] been living and preaching so long . . . [it] include[s] nothing esoteric and the minimum of esoteric philosophy."[128]

Even E. L. Mascall, an Anglican theologian, writing in 1965, referred to *Le Milieu Divin* as expressing Teilhard's "magnificent vision of the function of the scientist and the technician as the transformation of the created world in accordance with the purposes of God."[129] He also described *The Phenomenon of Man* as providing "perhaps the most famous example" of a work that argues "not merely that Christianity and science are compatible, but also that it is only in the light of Christian doctrine that the scientific exploit and achievement can be seen to make sense."[130]

In 1961 Cardinal Konig of Vienna said that "Teilhard went further than anyone else in dedicating himself to the task of finding positive evidence of agree-

---

[121]Ibid., 134.

[122]Teilhard de Chardin, *Science and Christ*, 48.

[123]Teilhard de Chardin, *The Divine Milieu* (New York: Harper & Row, 1968).

[124]Teilhard completed the bulk of the manuscript to *Le Phénomène Humaine* (Paris: Editions du Seuil, 1955) in June 1940. In April 1944 the completed manuscript reached Rome and on 6 August that year he learned that ecclesiastical permission to publish the work had been refused. Despite revisions it was never accepted for publication by the authorities in Rome. The vision of the work was fundamentally identical to the solution presented in "La Vie Cosmique" which was completed in April 1916. He had already written two brief outlines of *Le Phénomène*, the first in 1928, the second in 1930. See J. Needham, "Cosmologist of the Future: A Review of *The Phenomenon of Man* by Teilhard de Chardin," *New Statesman* 88 (1959): 632.

[125]Teilhard de Chardin, *The Vision of the Past*, 78.

[126]Ibid., 138.

[127]Bernard Wall, introduction to Teilhard de Chardin, *Man's Place in Nature*, 2.

[128]Letter of 8 November 1926. Cited in M. Barthélemy-Madaule, *Bergson and Teilhard de Chardin* (Paris: Editions du Seuil, 1963).

[129]E. L. Mascall, *The Secularization of Christianity* (London: Darton, Longman & Todd, 1965) 44.

[130]Ibid., 193.

ment between science and religion."[131] Edouard Boné SJ, emeritus professor of the faculty of Theology in the Catholic University of Louvain, considered that Teilhard was an enormous help to "a whole generation undermined by scientism" and helped them "to listen to the message of faith." By the integrity of his scientific effort, his sincere religious belief, and avoidance of "untimely proselytizing" and "indiscreet zeal"; he "lit the flame of hope in the modern world" of academia in particular. He raised hopes "of reconciling Christian thought with the claims of research and the autonomy of science."[132]

Professor Robert J. O'Connell SJ summed up his contribution well: "Teilhard . . . strove to open a way to bridging the chasm between 'scientific' and more humanistic, poetic, and religious modes of envisaging our evolving world, a way in which those seemingly inimical views could converge without becoming confused."[133] The question of whether or not he succeeded in achieving this convergence is a matter of great debate among scholars.

It was in fact the doctrine of evolution that he sought to reconcile with Christianity and he promoted what he called "Christian superevolutionism."[134] In 1946 he wrote: "Christianity and evolution: not two irreconcilable points of view, but two ways of looking at things that are designed to dovetail together, each completing the other."[135] Teilhard wrote that "Christianity is an exemplary ["and necessary"] form of the religion of science."[136] He viewed it as "the only form of religion currently viable" that "corresponds to an essential and continually growing function of evolution."[137]

He wrote of the uniqueness of Christianity: "no other type of faith that has so far been developed in mankind is equally able to make the world around us (in spite of its immensity and apparent blindness and ruthlessness) sweet and *warm* inside (because it is personal, lovable, and loving at its upper term and in its essence)."[138] He saw Christianity "emerg[ing] as the only spiritual current

---

[131]Cited in Christopher F. Mooney, *Teilhard de Chardin and the Mystery of Christ* (London: Collins, 1966) 199.

[132]Edouard Boné, "Revue des questions scientifiques," Louvain, (20 January 1956). Cited in *Letters From a Traveller*, 362.

[133]Robert J. O'Connell, *Teilhard's Vision of the Past: The Making of a Method* (Bronx NY: Fordham University Press, 1982).

[134]Teilhard de Chardin, "Introduction to the Christian Life," (1944) in *Christianity and Evolution*, 157.

[135]Teilhard de Chardin, *Science and Christ*, 189-90.

[136]Teilhard de Chardin, *Human Energy*, 180.

[137]Teilhard de Chardin, 3 April 1930, *Letters to Léontine Zanta*, trans. Bernard Wall (London: Collins, 1969) 103.

[138]Teilhard de Chardin, letter of January 3 1948, in *Letters to Two Friends*, 179. Italics in original.

capable of developing in souls the sense of the Absolute and the Universal, conceived above all as personal, in other words the true 'mystical sense'."[139]

Teilhard is often presented by his supporters as a radical pioneer who
attempted to deal with the doctrine of evolution as a theologian and to develop
a new conspectus of understanding in the fields of theology and natural science.
However, he was a European latecomer to this field. He only brought Catholic
theology up to date with a "task" which Anglo-Saxon and North American theology had performed immediately after the appearance of Darwin and of the philosophers and natural scientists who were influenced by him. German Protestant
theology had dealt with this subject in great detail since the beginning of the
twentieth century. As Professor Ernst Benz points out:

> [T]here is not a single idea of Teilhard's which had not already been
> raised in the theological discussion at the turn of the century. This
> statement does not say anything about the rank of his ideas nor about
> their value for us today. But it helps to clarify his position within the
> total development of modern theology and in the meeting and confronta-
> tion of theology with modern science. It also protects us from overrating
> him improperly.[140]

For Teilhard, Christianity occupied "a privileged central axis—around a
Christ who is incommensurable (in cosmic dignity) with any other prophet or any
Buddha." He considered the exclusivity of this claim to be "the only possible
Christian and biological concept."[141] He considered Roman Catholicism to be the
only true form of Christianity: "to be a Catholic is the only way of being fully
a Christian and a Christian through and through."[142]

In his view, the Roman Catholic Church with the supreme pontiff as Vicar
of Christ at its head, was the only possible focus of unity. Acting as the axis of
evolution itself, it alone could mold a fragmented humanity into a unified and for-
ward-thrusting collectivity destined ultimately to converge upon God as its true
and predestined Center. Furthermore, he wrote: "during historic time the principal
axis of anthropogenesis has passed through the West. It is in this ardent zone of
growth and universal recasting that all that goes to make man today has been
discovered, or at any rate *must have been rediscovered*."[143] The "proof" of this,

---

[139]Letter of 4 May 1931, in *Letters From a Traveller*, 177-78. These considerations
were the basis of the essay *Esquisse d'un univers personnel* (1936).

[140]Ernst Benz, *Evolution and Christian Hope: Man's Concept of the Future from the
Early Fathers to Teilhard de Chardin* (London: Victor Gollancz, 1967) 222.

[141]Teilhard de Chardin, "Ecumenism" (1946) *Science and Christ*, 197.

[142]*Energie* (1937); *Introduction* (1944). Cited in De Lubac, *The Religion of Teilhard
de Chardin*, 15.

[143]Teilhard de Chardin, *The Phenomenon of Man*, trans. Bernard Wall (London:

he maintained, "lies in the fact that all peoples, [in order] to remain human or to become more so, are inexorably led to formulate the hopes and problems of the modern earth in the very same terms in which the West has formulated them."[144]

Many Teilhardians today reject these views. They consider Teilhard's beliefs in the cultural supremacy of the West and the religious supremacy of the Roman Catholic Church as products of the historical and cultural situation in which he lived. Many Jesuits would insist that today, with our deeper knowledge of Eastern religions and the unity underlying all religious belief and practice, Teilhard's partisan positions on these matters are unacceptable.[145]

## 1.3 The Rise of the New "Mysticism"

Those who do not hear the fundamental harmony of the Universe which I try to transcribe (fortunately, many do) look in what I write for some kind of narrowly logical system, and are confused or angry. Fundamentally, it is not possible to transmit directly by words the perception of a quality, a taste. Once again, it would be more to my purpose to be a shadow of Wagner than a shadow of Darwin. Taking myself as I am, I see no better course than to strive by all means to reveal Humanity to Men.[146]

There is a communion with God, and a communion with earth, and a communion with God through earth.[147]

Lord, it is you who, through the imperceptible goadings of sense-beauty, penetrated my heart in order to make its life flow out into yourself. You came down into me by means of a tiny scrap of created reality; and then, suddenly, you unfurled your immensity before my eyes and displayed yourself as Universal Being. Lord, in this first image, so close at hand and so concrete, let me savor you at length, in all that quickens

---

Collins, 1960) 211. Italics in original. For details on anthropogenesis, see 42, 50, 138, 241.

[144]Ibid. 212.

[145]Christianity does not hold that "there is a unity underlying all religious belief and practice." The Apostle Peter, with reference to "the name of Jesus Christ the Nazarene" declared: "And there is salvation in no one else, for there is *no other name* under heaven that has been given among men, by which we must be saved" (Acts 4:12). Jesus himself affirmed: "I am the way, and the truth, and the life, no one comes to the Father but through Me" (Jn. 14:6).

[146]Teilhard de Chardin, letter to Ida Treat, 14 February 1927, in *Letters to Two Friends 1926–1952*, 59.

[147]Teilhard de Chardin, "Cosmic Life" (1916), in *Writings in Time of War*, 14.

and all that fills to overflowing, in all that penetrates and all that envelops—in sweetness of scent, in light, and love, and space.[148]

Mystics often find language inadequate to communicate when they seek to express a perception of a quality, a taste of the divine presence they have felt in their souls. The reality of the experience of God in the human soul is affirmed throughout Scripture. For example, the Psalmist declares "O *taste* and *see* that the Lord is good!" (Ps. 3:8). The New Testament writers affirm that all true Christian believers can "become partakers of the divine nature" (2 Pet. 1:4). The path to fuller participation in the life of God and the experiences accompanying it, cannot be defined by some narrowly logical system. It is by God's grace alone and through faith (Eph. 2:8-10) that the believer becomes a recipient of the divine life and is marked out by God's Spirit (Eph. 1:13) as one who has passed from spiritual death to spiritual life (Jn. 5:24; 1 Jn. 3:14).

Teilhard held that the mystic is the true animator of the world: "Nothing in the world is more intensely alive and active than purity and prayer, which hang like an unmoving light between the universe and God. Through their serene transparency flow the waves of creative power charged with natural virtue and with grace."[149] He credited his mother as the source of his own "Christian mysticism" when he wrote:

> That spark, through which "my Universe," as yet but *half* personalized, *was to attain centricity by being amorized*, that spark undoubtedly came to me through my mother: it was through her that it reached me from the current of Christian mysticism and both illuminated and inflamed my childish soul.[150]

Broadly speaking, mysticism[151] teaches that all things are one in God who is the Transcendent Center on to which all other "centers" converge. The *Concise Catholic Dictionary* defines it as "the experience of direct communion with God; the interior communion and intercourse of a fervent soul with God; the highest form of mental prayer; the subject of mystical theology; the understanding of the mysteries of faith."[152] Both these definitions fail to focus on the element of mys-

---

[148]Ibid., 120.

[149]Teilhard de Chardin, *Writings in Time of War*, 144.

[150]Teilhard de Chardin, *The Heart of the Matter*, 41.

[151]For a comprehensive discussion of the term mysticism see Steven T. Katz, ed., *Mysticism and Philosophical Analysis* (London: Sheldon Press, 1978). A Symposium of ten invited contributions of scholars from England, the USA, and Switzerland, published as vol. 5 of the series Studies in Philosophy and Religion (P. R. Baelz, gen. ed.). For a detailed discussion of Teilhard's "mysticism" see Thomas M. King, *Teilhard's Mysticism of Knowing* (New York: Seabury Press, 1981).

[152]*The Concise Catholic Dictionary*, comp. by Robert C. Broderick (St. Paul MN:

ticism that sets it apart from other aspects of Christian experience, namely, the element of the "incommunicable" and "ineffable." In his book *What Is Mysticism?*, David Knowles defines "mystical theology" as "an incommunicable and inexpressible knowledge and love of God or of religious truth received in the spirit without precedent effort or reasoning."[153] It is imparted through God's grace and is not irrational. The metaphysician Frithjof Schuon has highlighted the problems associated with the definitions:

> The terms "mystical" and "mysticism," . . . lend themselves readily to misuse by being applied to everything inward or intuitive at whatever level. In reality these words denote all inward contact (other than the purely mental), with realities that are directly or indirectly Divine; and it is only right that they should suggest above all a spirituality of love because they are European terms and Europe is Christian. Their associations with the idea of the "irrational" is clearly false; spiritual intuition is not irrational but suprarational. In any case it seems to us that the only legitimate meaning one can give to the word "mystical" is, first, that traditionally given to it by theology and, second, the meaning proposed above, which compels acceptance by extension, or rather by considerations of etymology; the usage clearly cannot be associated with ill-intentional attempts to devalue the word or with cases of simple misuse of language.[154]

Mascall has noted that the Christian doctrine that God is both immanent and transcendent has produced a tension which has seemed to many to be paradoxical and even inconsistent. The believer seeks communion with God by leaving behind all created things, while striving to pierce the "cloud of unknowing" which separates him or her from the ineffable superessential Deity. On the other hand, he notes, the one and only place in which the believer can find Him is in the "apex" or "depth" or "fine point" of his or her soul. Christian mystics who have described these apparently entirely opposite movements do not seem to feel that they involve any contradiction. While the descriptions of the movements are different, both are in relation to the one Object who is the one transcendent and immanent God.

Mascall notes: "their difference is much less than might be expected. For the transcendent God who is sought in the cloud of unknowing is present already in the depth of the soul; while the immanent God who dwells in the center of our

---

Catechetical Guild Education Service, 1944) 230-31.

[153]David Knowles, *What Is Mysticism?* (London: Burns and Oates, 1967) 13.

[154]Frithjof Schuon, *Logic and Transcendence* (London: Perennial Books, 1984) 2-3.

being is infinite, perfect and self-existent." He describes the essence of Roman
Catholic mysticism as follows:

> God is immanent in the depth of the soul and it is there that he is to be
> found. But he is immanent there, not as contained in it, but rather as
> containing it; not in the sense that he is limited and restricted by man,
> but in the sense that man, at the very root of his being, is altogether
> dependent upon God. . . . the general theory of Catholic mystical
> theology, with its two fundamental doctrines that God is both trans-
> cendent and immanent and that mystical union is achieved not by any
> human effort, but by the pure and unconditioned act of God himself,
> who elevates the soul into a participation of his own divine life.[155]

Teilhard sought to resolve what he called the "unhappy war between science
and religion." He considered it "a struggle between two rival mysticisms for the
mastery of the human heart" and argued that "this state of war" needs to be
"resolved in a higher synthesis."[156] He once described mysticism as "the science
of Christ running through all things" and he criticized Christian theology for its
tendency "to give the word mystical a minimum of organic or physical meaning."
For him science was an integral part of his "mysticism"—"the Science of
Sciences"; the "great science and the great art, the only power capable of synthe-
sizing the riches accumulated by other forms of human activity."[157] In his view,
"the mystical vibration is *inseparable* from the scientific vibration."[158] Such a
statement is clearly wrong, for true mystics like St. John of the Cross were outstanding scholars, but did not owe their insights to their knowledge of science.

The "new mysticism" of which Teilhard spoke so often, meant for him the
"sanctification of all human efforts, all sufferings, all joys." It was the pursuit of
"some spiritual Reality" in and through all of life's efforts to find "the heart of
the unique greatness of God."[159] However, true mysticism is the pursuit of the
One transcendent Divine Reality, not "*some* spiritual Reality," and sanctification
is a natural concomitant of such a pursuit.

---

[155]E. L. Mascall, *He Who Is: A Study in Traditional Theism* (1943; repr. London:
Longmans, 1962) 147-48.

[156]Teilhard de Chardin, *Human Energy*, 177.

[157]Letter to the Abbé Henri Breuil, 9 September 1923, in *Letters From a Traveller*,
87. Cf. Letter of 13 December 1918 in *The Making of a Mind*, 268: "I've almost made
up my mind to write something on 'mystical science,' to defend from such abuses and
place in its real light . . . this science of sciences which is also the supreme art and
supreme work."

[158]Teilhard de Chardin, *Letters from a Traveller*, 152-53.

[159]Ursula King, "Science and Mysticism: Teilhard de Chardin in Religious Thought
Today," *Teilhard Review* 19/1 (Spring 1984): 7.

Teilhard rejected the "mysticism of progress" born from positivism, which he felt led to "a sort of worship of science" and "strayed off into the worship of matter."[160] He predicted the rise of a new mysticism—"a hitherto unknown form of religion"[161] based on evolution. This implies that Christianity is destined to disappear, yet Christ taught the very opposite.[162]

Furthermore, revealed religion is not based on evolution but on the Word of God. Teilhard stated: "science, in all probability, will be progressively more impregnated by mysticism (*not* in order *to be directed*, but in order *to be animated*, *by it*)."[163] "Far from tending to discover a new god, science only goes on showing us matter, which is the footstool of the divinity. One does not draw near to the Absolute by travelling, but by ecstasy. Such is the final intellectual lesson of transformism and its final moral and religious teachings."[164] In a report to his society in 1947 Teilhard said:

> We priests, we Jesuits, must do more than interest ourselves and occupy ourselves in research. We must *believe* in [research], because research (undertaken "with faith") is the very ground on which may be worked out the only humano-Christian mysticism that tomorrow can bring about unanimity of man.[165]

Teilhard believed that the "worship of the concrete Real" or "preoccupation with and love for *all* the earth" in all its "prodigious greatness" was needed before mankind could "regain its passion for God."[166] For him, mysticism constituted the synthesis and the unified peak of all mental activities. In a chapter entitled "The Ultimate Earth" in *The Phenomenon of Man* he states: "in the conjunction of reason and mysticism, the human spirit is destined, by the nature of its development, to find the uttermost degree of its penetration with the maximum of its vital force."[167]

Teilhard defined this new mysticism as that "Resonance to the All," that "fundamental vibration" experienced by the mystics "in the expectation and awareness of a great Presence."[168] Teilhard was very taken by the writings of Dante, in which mysticism and poetry were allied. He was also charmed by

---

[160]Teilhard de Chardin, *Human Energy*, 172.
[161]Teilhard de Chardin, *Activation of Energy*, 382-83.
[162]See Matt. 24:35; 28:20.
[163]Teilhard de Chardin, *Science and Christ*, 83. Italics in original.
[164]Teilhard de Chardin, *The Vision of the Past*, 132.
[165]Teilhard de Chardin, *Science and Christ*, 205. Italics in original.
[166]Teilhard de Chardin, *Letters to Léontine Zanta*, 72. Letter dated 15 October 1926.
[167]Teilhard de Chardin, *The Phenomenon of Man*, 285.
[168]Ibid., 266.

Robert Hugh Benson's description of the pantheist *mystique* and the conceivable unification of the human *monade*.[169]

Henri de Lubac holds that "an element of ambiguity" or essential paradox evident in some of Teilhard's writing, is typical of the language of the mystics, who seek to express "the dialectic of an interior spiritual world which is foreign to pure intellect."[170] Speaight has stated: "People will always debate whether Teilhard himself was a mystic or merely a mystical writer, and even whether his mysticism was of the natural or supernatural kind."

A number of scholars like Eric Doyle OFM[171] and R. C. Zaehner[172] argue that Teilhard should be primarily classified as a Christian mystic. Ursula King, former president of the Teilhard Center for the Future of Man, agrees. In the introduction to her book *The Spirit of One Earth: Reflections on Teilhard de Chardin and Global Spirituality* (1989), she states: "Teilhard truly was a great Christian mystic, a contemporary mystic in the best tradition of Christian mysticism, but also a mystic in search of a new mystical way, a new spirituality open to the rhythm of the world and deeply involved with its development."[173]

In her book *Towards a New Mysticism: Teilhard de Chardin and Eastern Religions*, King traces the development of Teilhard's alleged "mysticism" from his early years, through his experiences in Egypt and his study of mysticism, to his travels in India, Indonesia, Burma, and Japan. She notes the absence of references to Teilhard's thought "in contemporary works on mysticism,"[174] which suggests that his status as a "great Christian mystic" is questionable. Teilhard always distinguished between two basic types of mysticism as fundamental alternatives or even opposites. King states that he defended a "mysticism of unification" which she defines as:

> the concentration and unification of each and all "through a peak of intensity arrived at by what is most incommunicable in each element" . . . This type of mysticism represents "an ultrapersonalizing, ultradetermining, and ultradifferentiating UNIFICATION of the elements within a *common focus*; the specific effect of LOVE" . . . [This is] a *transtheistic*

---

[169]Speaight, *Teilhard de Chardin: A Biography*, 70-71.

[170]De Lubac, *The Religion of Teilhard de Chardin*, 89.

[171]Eric Doyle OFM, "Teilhard and Theology," *Irish Theological Quarterly* (April 1971): 103-104.

[172]R.C. Zaehner, *The Convergent Spirit* (London: Routledge & Kegan Paul, 1963) 16. Zaehner remarks that Teilhard's position is an essentially Christian mysticism—a mysticism of affirmation and solidarity as against a mysticism of negation and isolation.

[173]King, *The Spirit of One Earth*, 7.

[174]King, *Towards a New Mysticism*, 153.

mysticism towards which Christianity tends but which has not been fully worked out yet.[175]

Elsewhere King has written that this type of mysticism "is not strictly identical with theistic forms of mysticism."[176] Teilhard described it as "a road not yet described in any 'book' (?!) . . . the true path 'towards and for' oneness."[177] He therefore distanced himself from the wealth of literature documenting authentic Christian mystical experience and claimed that he alone had discovered the "true path." He called his unique brand of "mysticism" the new "road of the West," a path of unification which has only become possible through the contact of Christianity with the modern world.[178] He thereby effectively ruled all other forms of Christian mystical experience prior to the advent of modern science outdated and irrelevant to the modern world. However, the locus of traditional Christian mystical experience is a union of love in a higher supernatural life by the grace of Christ the Savior. It is not tied to a particular understanding of modern science and it is certainly not grounded in the evolutionary pantheism espoused by Teilhard.[179]

Philosophical pantheism has been defined as "the pseudophilosophy that teaches that all reality is substantially divine and constitutes one being: God."[180] Etymologically, pantheism means "everything [is] God." The philosopher Nicolas Berdyaev's assessment of it is correct: "As a rational system it is a form of acosmism, a denial of the reality of the world and of man; or again, a form of atheism, a denial of Divine Reality, an affirmation of the divinity of the natural world."[181]

The other basic type of mysticism Teilhard discussed and rejected—"mysticism of identification"—King describes as essentially monistic and distinguished by the absence of love in the *ultra*personal. The crucial point is that Teilhard's

---

[175]Ibid., 199.

[176]King, *The Spirit of One Earth*, 89.

[177]Teilhard de Chardin, *Toward the Future*, trans. René Hague (London: Collins, 1975) 210.

[178]Ibid. Patrick Grant, in his book *Literature of Mysticism in Western Tradition* (London: Macmillan, 1983), claims that mysticism cannot be discussed separately from a framework of faith. As King notes: Other recent studies take a different approach by "recogniz[ing] the pluralism of mystical experience and analyze its occurrence in a wider social, psychological, linguistic, philosophical, and theological context." See King, *The Spirit of One Earth*, 83-84.

[179]Many scholars sympathetic to Teilhard's philosophy would dispute the fact that he was a pantheist. A comprehensive analysis of the pantheism implicit in his writings is provided in my second book.

[180]Arnold J. Benedetto SJ, *Fundamentals in the Philosophy of God* (New York: Macmillan, 1963) 147.

[181]Nicolas Berdyaev, *Spirit and Reality* (London: Geoffrey Bles, 1939) 136.

"mysticism" was strongly orientated towards pantheism and monism, philosophical positions he admitted on many occasions to holding (*Monism* is the philosophical theory that all being may ultimately be referred to one category). Although he always used these terms in a qualified sense, the "system of thought" he expounded only makes sense within a pantheistic/monistic framework. Even King concedes that for Teilhard there was no abyss separating pantheism and theistic forms of mysticism:

> [Teilhard's] powerful vision of the universal and cosmic Christ . . . remains inseparable from the mystical quality of his nature experiences, but the monistic pantheism of earlier years had gradually been prolonged and transcended into what he occasionally referred to as "pan-Christic monism," and what might also be called a person-centered theistic mysticism or pantheism. . . .
> . . . he links mysticism to a continuum of progressively more "centered" experiences, ranging from pantheistic to monistic to theistic forms. . . . It was his comparatively wide reading which, . . . made him aware of the variety of phenomena designated by the term *mysticism.* But Teilhard did not argue for a sharp break between natural pantheism on the one hand and religious mysticism of a monistic, or theistic, kind on the other. He saw these different experiences as continuous and organically interrelated although each possesses a distinctive element of its own.[182]

The term "'pan-Christic' monism"[183] Teilhard uses, is a term taken over from the philosopher Maurice Blondel, who spoke of "pan-Christism."[184] Monism is incompatible with Christian faith, and one can only conclude that Teilhard's terminology is self-contradictory.

In the second section of King's book *Towards a New Mysticism*, entitled "Eastern and Western Religions in a Converging World," she repeatedly stresses the need for developing Teilhard's ideas for a new spirituality, to combine the active and contemplative components of human spirituality. Teilhardians actively promote the revival of what they term the "Christian mystical tradition" or "New Mysticism," since they believe that this form of spirituality will lead humanity towards Omega Point—"the supreme focus point of evolution."[185] King claims that Teilhard drew on aspects of this tradition studying the Christian mystics such

---

[182]King, *The Spirit of One Earth*, 87.

[183]Teilhard de Chardin, *Christianity and Evolution*, 171.

[184]See Henri de Lubac, ed., *Blondel et Teilhard de Chardin, correspondence commentée* (Paris: Beauchesne, 1965) 52-53.

[185]Teilhard de Chardin, *Activation of Energy*, 111.

as Meister Eckhart and his disciple John Tauler.[186] It is important to note that neither of these mystics were pantheists or monists.

Teilhard championed the view that there is no domain and no point in which science and revelation encroach on one another, and that the relationship between the two is both dynamic and complementary.[187] He respected the distinction between these different disciplines and sought to avoid "an illegitimate contamination of the phenomenal plane by the metaphysical."[188] He was equally resolute in refusing to let them stand in isolation, thereby destroying the unity of man.

He recognized that the Christian in "drawing upon an added source of knowledge [scriptural revelation], may advance yet another step" beyond the insights based on science.[189] "By its mechanical determinism, and . . . illogical worship of self-sufficient, or even all-powerful man, the 'religion of science,' . . . closed the very future into which it thought it was launching itself."[190] He felt it contained within it "seeds which would soon produce a dangerous crisis for man's activities."[191]

Teilhard called the "higher synthesis" he formulated, "a new faith: the religion of evolution."[192] He also referred to it as a "'pan-Christic' mysticism," a position he felt was best exemplified in his essays "The Mass on the World" (1926) and "*Le Milieu Divin*" (1927).[193] He argued that there are two opposed Christianities: a Christianity of disdain or evasion of the world, and a Christianity of development, or Evolution.[194]

It is the "Religion of Evolution" that he espoused which has found favor at the highest level in the leadership of the United Nations[195] and among leading intellectuals. As one contributor to the 1983 United Nations colloquium on Teilhard stated:

> Either mankind will find a *new religion* corresponding to the new evolutionary stage that is now approaching, and with this mankind will find a new viable expression of human wholesomeness and peace, or mankind will more and more be fossilized inside its present struc-

---

[186]King, *Towards a New Mysticism*, 51.

[187]Teilhard de Chardin, *Activation of Energy*, 404-405.

[188]Teilhard de Chardin, *The Vision of the Past*, 134. Metaphysics is the theoretical philosophy of being and knowing.

[189]Teilhard de Chardin, *The Future of Man*, 223.

[190]Teilhard de Chardin, *Human Energy*, 173.

[191]Ibid.

[192]Teilhard de Chardin, *Christianity and Evolution*, 240.

[193]Ibid., 47.

[194]Cuénot, *Teilhard de Chardin*, 259.

[195]Zonneveld, ed. *Humanity's Quest for Unity.*

tures—with the danger of exploding one day or of being left behind in the march of evolution that will continue.

Such pronouncements indicate that many Teilhardians seem to think Christianity in its present form is obsolete. They appear to consider both its doctrines and form only fit to be consigned to the evolutionary trash can.

## 1.4 A Controversial Thinker

Much controversy has been generated by Teilhard's life and work. As noted earlier, his writings on theological and philosophical matters were considered so harmful that they were banned outright by the Roman Catholic Church and he was forbidden to lecture on those topics in France. The renowned geneticist Theodosius Dobzhansky noted that only a minority of those who read his works "remain indifferent, neutral, or even judiciously impartial. More usual reactions are either glowing admiration, often bordering on hero worship, or angry rejection and sometimes abuse."[196] As Philip Hefner notes, Teilhard's critics treat his writings as a scientific and theological "disease" while those on the other extreme regard them with what amounts to veneration.[197]

In the foreword to his biography on Teilhard, Robert Speaight wrote: "While Teilhard's thought continues to be examined from every angle, the man behind it is hidden. Between the smoke raised by his critics and the smoke raised by his thurifers his true stature tends to be obscured."[198] Speaight addresses the criticisms of Teilhard relating to his professional competence and personal integrity. His concern is with Teilhard "in his habit as lived."[199] He believes that if Teilhard has suffered from his opponents, he has also suffered from his more uncritical advocates. "A bold exponent of the Gospel has been treated as if he were the Gospel itself. This is the last thing he would have wanted."[200]

In 1965 Joseph Collignon, in an article on *The Phenomenon of Man*, described Teilhard as "perhaps the most controversial figure in the Christian world" of that day.[201] Professor Anthony Hull, a theologian and editor of the symposium *Teilhard Reassessed* (1970), stated that he found it most difficult to make a cool assessment of Teilhard's work. This was because he found that his work "seems to invite hostility or partisanship." Hull feels that because Teilhard

---

[196]Theodosius Dobzhansky, "Teilhard de Chardin as a Scientist," in *Letters to Two Friends*, 221.

[197]Hefner, *The Promise of Teilhard*, 15.

[198]Speaight, *Teilhard de Chardin: A Biography*, 11.

[199]Ibid., 12.

[200]Ibid.

[201]Joseph Collignon, *Christian Century* (7 April 1965): 426.

never had the benefit of his contemporaries' criticisms of his work, he "was bound to be a bit of a Narcissus."[202]

In 1984 Miller and Fowler described Teilhard as "a scientist whose science was questionable, a theologian whose theology was suspect [because he] has been charged with scientific fraud, theological heresy, and cosmological anthropocentrism."[203]

The French evolutionary biologist Jean Rostand argued that Teilhard did not cast the slightest light on the great problem of organic evolution:[204] "Teilhard deliberately ignores embryology and genetics; he is not interested in chromosomes, in genes, in nucleic acids, and he leaves aside all the specific questions which face all biologists who care, using modern methods, to clarify the mechanisms of evolutionary phenomena."[205]

The simple truth, as Dobzhansky has pointed out, is that he did not touch on these questions for good reason, he had nothing to contribute to these specialist areas of biology. He lived in relative isolation as an exile in China for seventeen years, cut off from the mainstream of biological endeavor which gave birth to the modern synthetic theory of evolution.[206] From 1939 to 1946 he remained a virtual prisoner in Peking.

Rostand was far from a detractor of Teilhard's reputation, for he conceded that "the work of Teilhard, in which are strangely mixed scientism and mysticism, respect toward things of the earth and aspirations toward heaven, has given splendor in French literature to a curious spiritual compound that was hitherto unknown."[207] However, he did not share Teilhard's optimism concerning explanatory powers of the doctrine of evolution. In 1954 Teilhard requested permission from his superiors to rebut Rostand's published work, but was denied the chance. He was ordered by Rome to leave France and return to New York.[208]

Professor Helmut de Terra notes Teilhard's "patent neglect of environmental factors in the evolutionary process," but suggests that it "is conceivable . . . that when writing about this subject in Peking he was without the requisite specialized literature, which has been substantially augmented since then by more recent research."[209] Elsewhere he argues that his "determinist interpretation of the

---

[202]Hanson, ed., *Teilhard Reassessed*, vii.

[203]J. Miller and D. Fowler, "What's Wrong with the Creation/Evolution Controversy?," *CTNS Bulletin* (Autumn 1984): 1, 9.

[204]Jean Rostand, *Fiagro Littéraire* (September 1965): 23-29.

[205]Jean Rostand, cited by Theodosius Dobzhansky in "Teilhard de Chardin as a Scientist," *Letters to Two Friends 1926–1952*, 226.

[206]Ibid., 226.

[207]Ibid..

[208]Speaight, *Teilhard de Chardin*, 321-22.

[209]De Terra, *Memories of Teilhard de Chardin*, 30. On p. 48, De Terra records his

origin of man also explains why Teilhard bestowed such scant attention on environmental factors."[210]

De Terra concludes that "anyone who overlooks [the ecological factor] must, of necessity, attribute the development of consciousness to psychical forces about whose nature science is wholly incapable of supplying precise information."[211] The Jesuit scholar Emile Rideau, writing as a confrère of Teilhard stated:

> In every circle of society, in every nation that respects culture, among unbelievers and Christians, a keen interest has been aroused by the personality and writings of Pièrre Teilhard de Chardin . . . however [he] is also a symbol of contradiction. The attitude he adopted towards some of the most fundamental of problems, arouses violent opposition, bitter controversy, and contradictory interpretations. In consequence, *many minds are at a loss to know what they should think about him, and are looking for information and a decisive judgement of his position.* . . . Whatever may be said about any shortcomings in his thought, they are outweighed by the great value of his positive contributions. *Teilhard clears the way for a restatement of the philosophy of science and religion. . . . Teilhard stands on a level with the greatest thinkers in history.*[212]

The claim that Teilhard "clears the way for a restatement of the philosophy of science and religion," suggests that all that has gone before Teilhard's "synthesis" is deficient and needs replacement. Many scholars would find such a suggestion preposterous. G. H. Duggan considers the claim that Teilhard ranks "with the greatest thinkers in history" to be "extravagant nonsense."[213]

Bernard Towers was quite correct when he stated that Teilhard's influence "increases year by year, and despite the abuse that is sometimes levelled at him (or perhaps obviously because of it), he is clearly not someone that an educated person can afford to ignore."[214] As we will shortly see, Teilhard cannot be ignored if one is seeking to understand the thinking behind the New Age Movement phenomenon. Central to New Age thought are the concepts of creative evolution, transformism, and cosmogenesis—all the subject matter of the next chapter.

---

surprise in finding that Teilhard makes no mention of the Ice Age in his discussion of anthropogenesis.

[210]Ibid., 46.

[211]Ibid.

[212]Emile Rideau, *Teilhard de Chardin: A Guide to His Thought*, trans. René Hague (London: Collins, 1967) 9-10, 12.

[213]G. H. Duggan, personal communication August 1993.

[214]Towers, *Concerning Teilhard*, 20.

# Creative Evolution

Let us be done once and for all, therefore, with the naive conception of the "evolutionary hypothesis"; it has long been out-of-date. No, taken sufficiently broadly, evolution is no longer, and has not been for a long time, a hypothesis—nor merely a simple method. It is in fact a new and common dimension of the universe, and consequently affects the totality of elements and relations of the universe. Not a hypothesis, therefore, but a condition which all hypotheses must henceforth fulfil. The expression for our minds of the world's passage from the state of "cosmos" to the state of "cosmogenesis."[1]

— *Teilhard de Chardin*

## 2.1 Transformism and Cosmogenesis

During the period 1912 to 1923, Teilhard's thinking underwent a fundamental change: from a belief in fixed species he became fully converted to the doctrine of evolutionary *transformism*.[2] This theory holds that single-celled amoeba-like organisms transformed through numerous intermediate stages to fish, then transformed somehow to reptiles, which gradually changed to mammals, leading eventually to man. An enormous amount of creative imagination is required to even envisage the evolutionary steps involved in many of these transformations. For example, transformists have to imagine how a hypothetical land mammal was converted into a whale. Transformism is not to be confused with adaptation within species, which is uncontroversial. Adaptation is sometimes called microevolution and transformism macroevolution.

Teilhard's conversion to transformism was largely due to his reading of Henri Bergson's *L'Evolution créatrice* (*Creative Evolution*)[3] and his gradual

---

[1]Teilhard de Chardin, *The Vision of the Past*, 246.

[2]The term *transformism* is often used as a synonym for the general theory of evolution—the theory that "all the living forms in the world have arisen from a single source which itself came from an inorganic form." See Gerald A. Kerkut, *Implications of Evolution* (Oxford: Pergamon, 1960) 157. The term *transformism* can also include the idea of a polyphyletic (multiple source) origin of life.

[3]On Teilhard and Bergson, see Barthélemy-Madaule, *Bergson et Teilhard de Chardin*

awareness of the central role played by the hypothesis of evolution in the sciences.[4] By 1950 he was arguing that to talk of an "evolutionary hypothesis" was "naive"; "taken sufficiently broadly, evolution is no longer a hypothesis—nor simply a method. It is in fact . . . a condition which all hypotheses must henceforth fulfil."[5] For Teilhard, evolution was a method of thinking that no scientist could any longer escape. In 1923 he wrote to Auguste Valensin S.J., "I don't know a *single* scientist who is not evolutionist."[6]

He venerated Bergson (1859–1941), professor of Philosophy at the College of France, "as a kind of saint,"[7] and through studying his work just prior to joining the military (1914), he made steps towards embracing fully the concept of "spiritual evolution."[8] He used the term *cosmogenesis* to refer to the global phenomenon of the evolution of the Universe involving its directed spiritualization. For Teilhard, the true name for spirit is *spiritualization*, a dynamic process linked to increasing interiorization, the growth of consciousness in its "systematic passage from the unconscious to the conscious, and from the conscious to the self-conscious. . . . [leading to] a 'cosmic change of state'."[9]

The term cosmogenesis emphasized the dynamic nature of the cosmos in contrast to static categories. It can be seen by man as involving four main movements; *Biogenesis* (the genesis of life), *Anthropogenesis* (the genesis of the human species), *Noogenesis* (genesis of spirit), and *Christogenesis* (genesis of the total Christ, of the Pleroma). Teilhard wrote: "To our clearer vision the universe is no longer a State but a Process. The cosmos has become a Cosmogenesis."[10]

For Teilhard the hypothesis of transformism became a necessary condition of all scientific thought.[11] He defined this hypothesis as "the fact of a *physical*

---

and her article of the same title in *Études bergsoniennes* (Presses Universitaires de France, 1960). Bergson also wrote *Two Sources of Morality and Religion, Time and Free Will*, and *Matter and Memory*. He was awarded the Nobel Prize in Literature in 1927.

[4]Raven, *Teilhard de Chardin, Scientist and Seer*, 164-65: "though his youthful dedication left no room for a conversion he did experience under the influence of his first contact with Bergson's *Creative Evolution* a revolutionary change in his cosmic philosophy. He had up till then accepted the traditional view of the fixity of species and apparently not realized the importance of Darwinism except as an interesting hypothesis. Bergson made him not only a convinced evolutionist but one who was not content with the *élan vital* or life force operating upon and striving to mold obdurate and preexisting matter."

[5]Teilhard de Chardin, *The Vision of the Past*, 246.

[6]Speaight, *Teilhard de Chardin: A Biography*, 116.

[7]Teilhard de Chardin, letter of 3 April 1930, in *Letters to Léontine Zanta*, 102: "I pray for that admirable man [Bergson] and venerate him as a kind of saint."

[8]Teilhard de Chardin, *Christianity and Evolution*, 104-108.

[9]Teilhard de Chardin, *Human Energy*, 96-97.

[10]Teilhard de Chardin, *The Future of Man*, 261.

[11]Cuénot, *Teilhard de Chardin*, 35.

*connection* between living beings. 'Living beings *hold together* biologically.' . . .
As a consequence of this observable connection between living forms we must
look for, and may find, a material basis, that is to say a scientific reason, for
their links with one another."[12]

The belief that the "successive growths of life may be the *substance of a
history*," was in Teilhard's view, "the sufficient and necessary 'faith' that makes
a transformist"[13]: "*transformism is, at bottom, no more than an admission that
we can plot the history of life* as we plot the history of human civilizations or of
matter."[14] He stressed that scientific transformism "imposes no philosophy"[15] but
may hint at one.

He recognized that what makes a transformist is not based on whether or not
someone "is a Darwinist or Lamarckian, a mechanist or vitalist, a mono- or poly-
phyletist," but rather it is an unshakable "faith" in the belief in a material explanation for the continuity of life's history.[16] John O'Manique notes that Teilhard
"attempted to present a scientific account of the mechanism of evolution which
would avoid the extremes of mechanism, blind chance and ectogenesis[17] on the
one hand, and of vitalism, determinism, and autogenesis on the other."[18] Whether
or not he succeeded is the subject of much debate among scholars.

Teilhard wrote that "By identifying transformism with its mechanistic or
materialist forms and more especially Darwinism many have misjudged it."[19]
While he acknowledged the importance of the Darwinian "mechanism" (natural
selection: "survival of the fittest") to evolution, he viewed it as an inadequate explanation.[20] He did not accept that "Darwinism" was a suitable synonym for

---

[12]Teilhard de Chardin, *The Vision of the Past*, 22. Italics in original.

[13]Ibid. Italics in original.

[14]Ibid., 152. Italics in original.

[15]Ibid., 23.

[16]Ibid., 21-22. Also see 98: "To be a transformist, as I have often said, is not to be
a Darwinian or a Lamarckian or the disciple of any particular school. It is quite simply
to admit that the appearance of living creatures on earth obeys an ascertainable law, whatever that law may be. Neither mutationism nor vitalism properly understood conflicts with
this attitude."

[17]Ectogenesis is an explanation of evolutionary change that relies heavily on factors
that are outside the developing being.

[18]John O'Manique, *Energy in Evolution* (London: Garnstone, 1969) 73.

[19]Teilhard de Chardin, *The Vision of the Past*, 136.

[20]Teilhard de Chardin, *Activation of Energy*, 301-302. He considered the phrase "survival of the fittest" "unfortunate and unsatisfactory" for two reasons: (1) "it is too vague
and lends itself to no precise standard of measurement," and (2) "because by expressing
a purely *relative* superiority among 'arrangements,' it does not bring out that factor in the
rise of life which, going beyond the effects of competition, gives unmistakable evidence
of an exuberant tendency to expand and of a sense of absolute advance." He suggested

"evolutionism,"[21] or evolution,[22] but rather held that the fundamental element behind evolution and "the zest for living," was psychic in both its nature and its dimensions.[23] For him, Christianity was not only fully compatible with transformism but was the only religion providing "an empirical view of things" in total harmony with it.[24] In an essay "The Transformist Question" (1921), he stated:

> For transformism to be dangerous to reason and faith, it would have to claim that the action of a Creator fills no purpose, to reduce the development of life to a process purely immanent in nature, to state that "the greater can automatically arise from the less." Too many evolutionists have, in fact, committed this serious mistake of taking their scientific explanation of life for a metaphysical solution of the world. Like the materialist biologist who thinks he is abolishing the soul when he analyses the physicochemical mechanisms of the living cell, zoologists have imagined that they have rendered the primal cause useless because they were discovering a little more clearly the general structure of its work. It is time definitely to shelve a theorem so badly stated. No, scientific transformism, strictly speaking, proves nothing for or against God. It simply notes the fact of a chain of connection in reality. It presents us with an anatomy of life, certainly not a final reason for it. It affirms that "something organized itself, something grew." But it is incapable of discerning the ultimate conditions of that growth. To decide whether the movement of evolution is intelligible in itself, or if it requires a progressive and continuous creation implemented by a prime mover, this is a question that depends on metaphysics.[25]

Teilhard's defence of the *neutrality* of transformism with respect to the question of God, relies on the a priori acceptance of the view that science only deals with secondary (or finite) causes, and that questions relating to primary causality (or First Causes) are restricted to the domain of theology and metaphysics. It was

---

that the phrase "most complex" be substituted for "survival of the fittest."

[21]Ibid., 256.

[22]Ibid., 272.

[23]Ibid., 234.

[24]Ibid., 23. As an example of this "compatibility" Teilhard wrote: " Christianity . . . is essentially founded on the double belief that man is an object specially pursued by the divine power throughout creation, and that Christ is the end supernaturally but physically marked out as the consummation of humanity. Could one ask for an empirical view of things in closer accordance with these statements of unity [found in 'Christianized' transformism] than this" (23).

[25]Teilhard de Chardin, *The Vision of the Past*, 22-23. Metaphysics is the philosophy of the nature of being. As Aristotle put it, it considers *being as being*.

because of his claim that transformism "imposes no philosophy" that Teilhard insisted in the introduction to his major work (*The Phenomenon of Man*), that it was a work involving no metaphysics. Teilhard believed that to understand anything material in science, one must restrict all explanations to material sequences:

> *Reduced to its essence*, transformism is not a hypothesis. It is the particular expression, applied to the case of life, of the law which conditions our whole knowledge of the sensible universe: the law that we can understand nothing, in the domain of matter, except as part of a sequence or collection. . . .
>
> Everything, in our experience is empirically introduced by something else: it "is born." This is what transformism affirms.
>
> Now, by virtue of what inner power and with a view to what "ontological" growth, does this birth take place? Pure science does not know, and it is philosophy's task to decide.[26]

The claim that transformism is a "law" cannot be sustained when applied to the question of the origin of biological life and primal matter, since it is beyond the domain of empirical science.[27] Rather it is a metaphysical belief adhered to by those committed to either (1) replacing the First Cause(s) of life's origins with secondary ones, or (2) replacing special creation with the view that God, the Primal Cause, can only create by making things make themselves, and that this was the method he employed.

For those in the first category, nonrationality, chance, and impersonality, are not only inevitably adopted, but *must* be adopted as being primary realities; with rationality, design and personality as secondary realities. First causes are erroneously interpreted as merely the by-product of impersonal, insentient forces. Transformism provides no physical explanation of how space/time is supplemented with complex coded information.

---

[26]Ibid., 25, 154. Italics in original.

[27]Empirical science is based on observation(s) or experiment(s), not on theory alone. It treats sense-data as valid information, deriving knowledge from experience. It is identified with the study of regularities making prediction the crucial test of scientific validity. It admits of only secondary (natural) causes and cannot deal with primary (intelligent) causes or supernatural causes, since these involve singularities excluding the possibility of reproducible observations and experimentation. The empirical method often involves an interplay between empirical observation(s) and theory/theories. There are many other definitions of the scientific method. However, the common denominator is Ziman's "logical inferences from empirical observations." See J. Ziman, "What Is Science?," in *Introductory Readings in the Philosophy of Science* ed. E. D. Klemke, Robert Hollinger, and David Kline (New York: Prometheus Books, 1980). Definitions of the scientific method based on positivist, materialist, and/or naturalistic presuppositions should be rejected.

Teilhard's attempt to construct a "Christian evolutionism" (the second category) is based on the dogma that all God's creative acts must conform to the *physical* laws of evolution. He stated:

Translated into creationist language, this law [transformism] is perfectly simple and orthodox. It means that when the primal cause operates, it does not insert itself among the elements of this world but acts directly on their natures, so that God, as one might say, does not so much "make" things as "make them make themselves." . . .

Even when we accept the transformist theory, the place remains open—indeed it yawns more widely than ever—for a primal creative power. And even better, a creation of evolutionary type (God *making things make themselves*) has for long seemed to some very great minds the most beautiful form imaginable in which God could act in the universe.[28]

Teilhard contrasted his position with what he called "ancient creationism," which he defined as a view "that represented creatures as appearing ready-made in surroundings which received them with indifference."[29] Teilhard claimed that Christian transformism was compatible with the concept of a First Cause:

[F]ar from being incompatible with the existence of a Primal Cause, [do not] transformist views, . . . present its influx in the noblest and most heartening manner possible? For the Christian transformist, God's creative action is no longer conceived as an intrusive thrusting of His works into the midst of preexistent beings, but as a *bringing to birth* of the successive stages of His work in the heart of things. It is no less essential, no less universal, no less intimate either on that account.[30]

Teilhard sought to merge two philosophical positions that are incompatible, by inserting a hidden "internal law" of evolutionary development into all matter and biology. Having insisted that only physical laws could be sought to explain life's origins, he introduced a "supraphysical" law to salvage his flawed synthesis:

Because life is a physical factor *of a higher order* than measurable forces, it is quite as possible to analyze its productions without meeting the thing itself as to explain a watch mechanically without thinking of the watchmaker: at every instant the universe, even if we assume it to possess psychic forces, takes the form of a closed circuit of determinisms which mutually induce one another. But on the other hand, because

---

[28]Teilhard de Chardin, *The Vision of the Past*, 25, 154. Italics in original.
[29]Ibid., 102.
[30]Ibid. Italics in original.

these psychic forces constitute the coordinating factor of various determined systems the totality of which forms the animate world, the successive transformations of this world cannot possibly be explained without recourse to some imponderable forces of synthesis.[31]

Having claimed that transformism is a belief as well as a "law," Teilhard goes on to claim that it forms the basis of all scientific explanations:

But is transformism fundamentally anything but the belief in a *natural* link between animal species? By the sole fact that you admit such a link in living nature you readmit the whole evolutionary point of view into your perspectives. And I recognize that you could not do otherwise. Broadly understood, as it should be, transformism is now a hypothesis no longer. It has become the form of thought without which no scientific explanation is possible.[32]

In 1951 he wrote that evolution could not be understood as simply "transformism" (or even simply Darwinism), but rather was "an expression of the structural law (both of "being" and of knowledge)," and had "nothing in common with a hypothesis."[33] Under the heading "The Moral Consequences of Transformism," Teilhard wrote: "Correctly understood, transformism is . . . a possible teacher of spiritual idealism and high morality."[34] He went on to consider how transformism could provide "a possible school of higher spirituality"[35] and "a possible school of high morality."[36]

The claim that transformism has major implications for morality and spirituality is hard to reconcile with Teilhard's claim that it "imposes no philosophy,"[37] offers no metaphysical solution, and "proves nothing for or against God."[38] So on what basis does it provide a higher spirituality and morality? Essentially his claim is that transformism highlights the limitations of the mind's ability to grasp the Absolute within a scientific framework:

Not only, one might say, does scientific evolution explain nothing, but it recalls and makes palpable to us this elementary truth: however far we extend our experience of the perceptible, we cannot but remain in the perceptible. If we were to meet somewhere, in time or space, an ob-

---

[31]Ibid., 96. Italics in original.
[32]Ibid., 87. Italics in original.
[33]Teilhard de Chardin, *Activation of Energy*, 272.
[34]Teilhard de Chardin, *The Vision of the Past*, 133.
[35]Ibid., 133-36.
[36]Ibid., 136-42.
[37]Ibid., 23.
[38]Ibid.

ject with no neighbor or an event without antecedent, we should find a
fissure through which to look beyond appearances. Now nothing seems
capable of piercing the veil of phenomena. When we begin to speak of
a universe in which the spatial and temporal series radiate without limit
around each element, many minds take fright and we begin to speak of
eternal matter. *The absence of all empirical beginnings, an essential
postulate of transformism and all history*, has a more modest and very
different meaning. It in no way entails the existence of a universe in-
vested with divine attributes. All that it means is that the world is so
constructed that our perceptions are the absolute prisoners of its immensity. The further our mind penetrates, the further its shores seem to re-
cede. Far from tending to discover a new god, science only goes on
showing us matter, which is the footstool of Divinity. One does not
draw near to the Absolute by travelling, but by ecstasy. Such is the intellectual lesson of transformism and its final moral and religious
teaching.[39]

Teilhard was well aware that the transformist theory suffered from a number
of criticisms and yet he found none of them compelling enough to abandon his
views. Roman Catholic scholar Louis Vialleton, professor of Anatomy at the
University of Montpellier, mounted a broadside attack on the "proofs" being
offered in support of transformism, in his famous book *L'Origine des Etres
Vivants*.[40] His attack was comprehensive and dealt with problems in embryology,
comparative anatomy, and systematics.

In the 1930s leading scientists like zoologist Douglas Dewar F.Z.S. (president of the Evolution Protest Movement in Britain for ten years; d. 1957) vigorously attacked the transformist doctrine.[41] Dewar collaborated in a number of publications with paleontologist L. Merson Davies, D.Sc., Ph.D., who was awarded
two doctorates for his research in geology. Such dissidents could not be disre-
garded, and at least one evolutionist book is understood to have been written as
a counterattack to Dewar. Dewar also took part in a written debate with Prof.

---

[39]Ibid., 131-32. Italics added.

[40]His best-known work is *L'Origine des Etres Vivants: L'Illusion Transformiste*
(Paris: Plon, 1929) which ran through fifteen editions by 1930. Also see L. Vialleton,
*Membres et ceintures des vertébrés tétrapodes: Critique morphologique du transformisme*
(Paris: Doin, 1924). He refuted the classical theories of Extreme Evolutionism and put
forward a theory of Moderate Evolutionism.

[41]Douglas Dewar, *Difficulties of the Evolution Theory* (1931); *Is Evolution Proved?:
A Debate* (London: Hollis, 1947); *More Difficulties of the Evolution Theory* (London:
Thynne, 1938); *The Transformist Illusion* (Murfreesboro TN: Dehoff, 1957). The latter
work was published posthumously and includes material from *More Difficulties* and
*Difficulties*.

J. B. S. Haldane, F.R.S., the debate being jointly sponsored by the Evolution Protest Movement and the Rationalist Press Association of London in 1947 under the title *Is Evolution a Myth?*[42] It seems that such debates were largely ignored as the belief in transformism became a central dogma of evolutionary biology during the last decade of Teilhard's life.

## 2.2 The Search for a Way Out of a Closed Universe

The Christian tradition has consistently maintained that creation is a nontemporal act of the divine will by which the whole temporal created order is maintained in existence, and that the creation and conservation of the universe is one timeless act. The whole eleventh book of the *Confessions* of St. Augustine is really an exposition and a development of the theme that the timeless and eternal God has posited the world not *in tempore* but *cum tempore*,[43] by bestowing upon it its whole being. God's existence is independent of time altogether.[44] God's concern with the world should not be conceived of as relating merely to His providing the world with its initial impulse into being, but as an incessant and intimate care for the beings to which He has given all that they have and all that they are.[45]

Teilhard portrays man as a prisoner of a closed universe and strictly a product of the phenomenal plane. Both views were derived from the doctrine of transformism. His idea that we cannot by using our mind go beyond the phenomenon is derived from the philosophy of Immanuel Kant (1724–1804).[46]

---

[42]Douglas Dewar, L. Merson Davies, and J. B. S. Haldane, *Is Evolution a Myth? A Debate* (London: C. A. Watts; Paternoster, 1949).

[43]The phrase is St. Augustine's: *Die Civitate Dei*, XI.vi.

[44]Mascall, *He Who Is*, 62, 100.

[45]Ibid., 101.

[46]To the question, What are the proper limits of human thought and knowledge?, Kant answered by making a distinction between *knowledge* which has to do with *phenomena* (everything that can be seen) and *faith* which has to do with *noumena* (truths beyond space and time). These are two completely different ways of knowing. Faith is concerned with things "in themselves," reality as it is, the truths of religion (e.g., the existence of God, free will, immortality, etc.). Knowledge, *phenomena*, is truth which can be perceived through science, truth about the external world of space and time. If these distinctions are accepted, we must accept the fact that we cannot know anything for certain beyond our direct experience of this world. Religious beliefs are seen to have their origin in the moral consciousness, but cannot be classed as knowledge. He argued that this limitation of knowledge ensures the possibility of religious faith, making it impervious to scientific criticism. The net result of the absorption of Kant's philosophy led to a tide of religious subjectivism. Christian apologetics moved from objective evidences for faith to emphasizing the moral grounds for faith or the beauties of faith itself. Kant said the external world

Teilhard espouses a veritable materialism when he speaks of "eternal matter," denies a temporal beginning to creation, and suggests that Divinity is somehow dependent upon matter.

For Teilhard, the emergence of Deity is tied to the subjugation of eternal matter, paralleling the emergence of a fully spiritual mankind from the infinitely diffuse matter. The heart of the anxiety that caused him disquiet was the problem of finding "a way out" of the closed universe so that the fruits of human endeavor could be saved. We find this theme in a solitary meditation he composed in the Flanders trenches in 1918: if man can see nothing beyond, then he can only turn away, or desperately attempt to turn away, "in horror from the terrifying cosmic machine in which he is caught up."[47]

In 1950 in his essay *The Heart of the Matter* Teilhard emphasized "the agony of feeling oneself imprisoned, not so much spatially as ontologically, in the cosmic bubble."[48] This is a constant theme in his writings, as illustrated in the following passages:

> In every direction we are, in a very true sense, enveloped as though in a veil with neither rent nor seam, and there is no point at which we can effect a direct breakthrough and emerge experientially from the phenomenon. Thus, for all its gigantic size, the universe is our prison; and holds us in such a way that it seems that we are never to escape alive from its curvature, both geometric and psychic.[49]

> I definitely perceive that if the universe before us were to show itself tomorrow, from a scientific point of view, so closed and stagnant that the whole psychic superstructure developed in it during thousands of years was destined one day to disintegrate, without trace—I clearly perceive, I say, that in a universe thus hermetically sealed I (and everyone with me) would feel myself physically asphyxiated.[50]

---

was an unknowable *noumena*, a position of agnosticism.

[47]"Réflections sur le bonheur," *Cahiers*, 70. Cited in De Lubac, *The Religion of Teilhard de Chardin*, 144.

[48]Ibid.

[49]Teilhard de Chardin, *Activation of Energy*, 187.

[50]Teilhard de Chardin, *The Appearance of Man* (London: Collins, 1965) 170. Cf. *Activation of Energy*, 236: "Imagine . . . man . . . caught in the trap of a blind universe, cold and hermetically sealed"; 403: "mankind would be possessed by a sort of panic claustrophobia simply at the idea that it might find itself hermetically sealed inside a closed universe"; *Science and Christ*, 212: "what would happen if one day we should see that the universe is so hermetically closed in upon itself that there is no possible way of our emerging from it."

[F]ears (differing symptoms of one and the same desire to survive and "transcend") rise in us and around us like a shadow. [They include the] fear of being *shut in*, imprisoned within an irremediably closed world, in which, even if it were not lost or arrested at present, humanity could not help striking tomorrow, when it reaches the peak of its trajectory, against an impassable barrier of reversibility which would force it to fall backwards. . . .

Fear of not being able to get out . . . *fear betraying at the heart of each thinking element in the Universe the same obstinate wish to be distinguished, completed, saved.*[51]

[D]isenchantment would be conceivable, and indeed inevitable, if as a result of growing reflection we came to believe that our end could only be collective death in an hermetically sealed world. Clearly in face of so appalling a discovery the psychic mechanism of evolution would come to a stop, undermined and shattered in its very substance, despite all the violent tuggings of the chain of planetary infolding.[52]

Out of necessity for an assurance of some future existence for mankind, and the accumulated fruit of millions of years of human effort, he postulated an opening as the end term of evolution—Omega Point—"the supreme focus point of evolution."[53] The term Omega was chosen to designate the last term in a series (Omega is the last letter in the Greek alphabet) and partly from the words of the Apocalypse.[54] Teilhard used the term, which is at once scientific and scriptural, as a symbol of the twofold character of the teaching summed up in it.

In *The Phenomenon of Man*, which is concerned with the process of anthropogenesis, his methodology is confusing since he uses the term "Omega," divorcing it from its scriptural meaning as designating the Risen Christ. However, he presupposes that the attainment of Omega will solve the problem of human death. This gives the impression that the cosmic process has an Omega point, a point of final convergence, which can be posited without reference to the Risen Christ. "The attributes of Omega" outlined in his book make it clear that "the Center of centers" is the creative presence of Absolute Self rather than the Risen Christ, who alone can raise the dead and draw all creation into its final liberated state (Rom. 8:19-23).

Teilhard described Omega "genetically speaking" as the center defined by the final concentration of the Noosphere—"a thinking layer which mankind con-

---

[51]Teilhard de Chardin, *The Appearance of Man*, 208-209.
[52]Teilhard de Chardin, *The Future of Man*, 296.
[53]Teilhard de Chardin, *Activation of Energy*, 111.
[54]Rev. 1:8; 21:6; 22:13.

stitutes on our planet"[55]—upon itself. "The temperature of the Noosphere" is constantly rising, he wrote: in other words there is "an intensification of consciousness" and everything is rising "towards an ultimate peak." He maintained that there were two primary stages in the formation of the noosphere: (1) socialization of expansion and (2) socialization of compression.[56]

Omega marked the maturity of a world that has become fully centered, having realized its unity, and undergone the completion of convergence, in the highest "complexity of consciousness." By "complexity" he did not mean a matter of simple multiplicity, but of organized multiplicity. The "line of escape" through Omega point he proposed, contrasted with the *individual* escape routes taught in the various creeds and in orthodox Christianity, for it was born of the concept of "cosmic totalization."[57]

He rejected the notion of individual "escape" because he felt it was based on a selfish refusal to accept one's cosmic duty. He considered that other "faiths" not built on Omega "did not explicitly . . . allow any room to a global and controlled transformation of the whole of life and thought in their entirety."[58] Orthodox Christianity, which he described as "a religion of individuals and of heaven," needed to be abandoned and replaced with a "religion of mankind and of the earth."[59] He concluded that his revised Christianity could play an "evolutionary role" in providing a "faith" in a "way out" for mankind:

> [W]hat happens when our minds awake first to a suspicion and then to clear evidence that the *Christ of Revelation* is one and the same as the *Omega of evolution*?
>
> Then in a flash, we both see and feel in our hearts that the experimental universe attains its fulfillment and is finally energized.
>
> On the one hand, we see above us the positive glimmer of an *opening* at the highest point in the future. In a world that quite certainly opens out at its peak into Christ Jesus, we no longer need fear to die, stifled in our prison.[60]

> [W]hat is most vitally necessary to the thinking earth is a faith—and a great faith—and ever more faith. To know that we are not prisoners. To know that there is a way out, that there is air, and light, and love, somewhere, beyond the reach of death. To know this, to know that it is neither an illusion nor a fairy story.—That, if we are not to perish

---

[55]Teilhard de Chardin, cited in Cuénot, *Teilhard de Chardin*, 120.

[56]Teilhard de Chardin, *Man's Place in Nature*, 71-100.

[57]Teilhard de Chardin, *Activation of Energy*, 240.

[58]Ibid.

[59]Ibid.

[60]Cuénot, *Teilhard de Chardin*, 372-73.

smothered in the very stuff of our being, is what we must at all costs secure. And it is there that we find what I may well be so bold as to call the *evolutionary role* of religions.[61]

Mankind's "escape" would be accomplished through a "paroxysm of transformation—that is to say, a critical transformation."[62] Teilhard wrote that "the play of the planetary forces of complexity/consciousness, *normally extended* summons us to and destines us for this peak of hominization (or . . . *point Omega*)."[63] He also referred to "Point Omega" as "the conjectured upper pole of human coreflexion" and the "summit of hominization," which possessed properties that were "indispensable to the functioning of evolution." These properties included its biological reality and its ability to preserve everything forever, that is ensuring the irreversibility of cosmic evolution (see §2.4, below).[64]

## 2.3 The Law of Complexity-Consciousness and Omega Point

Central to Teilhard's view of nature is the recognition that the whole is greater than the sum of its parts, and greater complexity is accompanied by greater consciousness or *interiorization*. Organic life exhibits many parallels to inorganic chemistry, in that separate and quite distinct elements can unite and produce a new compound which could not have been predicted by a study of the separate elements. New compounds can have a "unifying principle" which differs from that which operates within the constituent elements. Common table salt (sodium chloride), for example, has unique physical and chemical properties, which it does not share with either element in their pure state. Sodium (a metal) and chlorine (a gas) also differ from one another both in physical and chemical properties. The electron bonding arrangements within the sodium chloride molecule differ from both the arrangements found in the elements.

Teilhard believed that a unifying principle in biology gave direction to evolution leading towards the production of ever-increasing levels of complexity. Nature was conceived of as the product of the interplay of chance with a goal-directed process. He appears to have developed the ideas of the nineteenth-century French physiologist Claude Bernard who stated that living beings shared an interdependence "in the cosmic environment"[65] which was manifest "only in complex higher animals." "Living machines are therefore created and constructed

---

[61]Teilhard de Chardin, *Activation of Energy*, 238. Italics in original.

[62]Teilhard de Chardin, *The Appearance of Man*, 170.

[63]Ibid., 246. Italics in original.

[64]Ibid., 271.

[65]Claude Bernard, "Experimental Medicine," in *Interrelations: The Biological and Physical Sciences*, ed. Robert T. Blackburn (Chicago: Scott, Foresman, 1966) 23.

in such a way that, in perfecting themselves, they become freer and freer in the general cosmic environment."[66]

Bernard expresses his views here within a world view dominated by William Paley's machine analogy of nature, while Teilhard sought to free himself from this mechanistic metaphor system which had dominated biological thinking in the West. He defined a "Law of Complexity-Consciousness" to account for the recurring patterns of complexity-consciousness in nature. This law accounted for the increasing levels of "interiorization" or "psychical" development found in biology as one moved from the less complex to more complex. The following excerpts from his writings illustrate Teilhard's position:

> Left long enough to itself, under the prolonged and universal play of chance, matter manifests the property of arranging itself in more and more complex groupings, and at the same time in ever-deepening layers of consciousness; this double and combined movement of physical unfolding and psychic interiorization (or centration) once started, continuing, accelerating and growing to its utmost extent.[67]

> Spiritual perfection (or conscious "centreity") and material synthesis (or complexity) are but the two aspects or connected parts of one and the same phenomenon.[68]

> [A]s observation shows, it is the nature of Matter, when raised corpuscularly to a very high degree of complexity, to become centrated and interiorized—that is to say, to endow itself with Consciousness. This means that the degree of consciousness attained by living creatures (from the moment, naturally, when it becomes discernible) may be used as a parameter to estimate the direction and speed of Evolution . . . in terms of absolute values.[69]

This "law" constituted for Teilhard the privileged axis of cosmic development and humanity was positioned at its leading edge. The basis for Teilhard's selectivity is subjective, for he *assumes* that the segment of evolutionary development he has selected is of the highest significance and is determinative for all the rest.[70] He argued that Omega point becomes apparent to us "on the horizon as a center of purely immanent convergence,"[71] from the moment we accept that the

---

[66]Ibid., 32.

[67]Teilhard de Chardin, *The Appearance of Man*, 139.

[68]Teilhard de Chardin, *The Phenomenon of Man*, 60-61.

[69]Teilhard de Chardin, *The Future of Man*, 218.

[70]Hefner, *The Promise of Teilhard*, 35.

[71]Teilhard de Chardin, *Activation of Energy*, 145.

universe is "psychically convergent."[72] If this center is to hold together, he concluded, "it presupposes behind it, and deeper than it, a transcendent—a divine—nucleus."[73] He wrote:

> Unless it is to be powerless to form the keystone of the noosphere, "Omega" . . . can only be conceived as the *meeting point* between a universe that has reached the limit of centration, and another, even deeper, center—that being the self-subsistent center and absolutely final principle of irreversibility and personalization: the one and only true Omega.[74]

By observing the periodicity of evolutionary psychic advance (or "law of recurrence"[75] as he called it), from inanimate molecules to cells, and on up to man; he proposed that the emergence of Omega could be inferred. He took the "law of recurrence" to be "capable of extrapolation, in a suitable form, to the totality of space and time" and argued that Omega point belonged to the "physical" and not the "metaphysical" order.

In response to the observation of this "rising current of complexification accompanied by consciousness" he declared: "We must grasp this law of recurrence and try to follow it in all its implications. It is, I believe, the original thread which, through successive reinforcements, may well become the axis of a true and complete faith."[76]

The evolution of planetary consciousness (species one) was explained as emerging through "the specific effect of complexified matter." Just as life was explained as "a specific effect of corpuscular complexity"[77]: "life is, in scientific experience, no other than the a specific effect (*the* specific effect) of complexified matter: a property in itself coextensive with the whole stuff of the cosmos."[78] Once "species one" was extended beyond a certain critical value, he believed that it would converge on "species two," a "transcendent" Being which had already emerged. Therefore, beyond the limit of the axis of the synthesis and time to

---

[72]Ibid., 111.

[73]Ibid., 145.

[74]Teilhard de Chardin, *Man's Place in Nature*, 121. Italics in original.

[75]*Recurrence*: "A repetition that seems to reproduce an already manifested plan, and which combines a certain periodicity with, at the same time, something new." Teilhard de Chardin, *Let Me Explain*, 19. Teilhard referred to his theory of Creative Union (see later discussion) as the law of recurrence. Teilhard de Chardin, *Science and Christ*, 53.

[76]Teilhard de Chardin, *Activation of Energy*, 144.

[77]Teilhard de Chardin, *Science and Christ*, 210.

[78]Teilhard de Chardin, *Man's Place in Nature*, 24. Italics in original. Complexity was defined in terms of coded information.

which "species one" was tied, he proposed "a center, already emerged and actively moving of universal convergence," which he called Omega.

He maintained that each of the elements of human consciousness would be attracted to this center (Omega) as it acted, "not only on the complexity of their structure but directly on their center, independently of their structure."[79] Omega provided a "way out" for man beyond space and time. The whole question of human activation was bound up for Teilhard in the answer to the question, Is there a way out?:

> Like miners surprised by an explosion, who crouch dispiritedly where they are if they think that the gallery is blocked ahead of them, man (the more he is man) could not continue to go on ultracerebralizing at the behest of evolution without asking whether the universe, above his head, is open or closed; that is without putting the definite question to himself . . . [namely] whether—yes or no—the light towards which humanity is drifting by self-arrangement really denotes *a way out* into the open air, or if it is only caused by a momentary flash in the night; in which case there would be nothing left for us but to go on strike and, in spite of nature, come to a stop.[80]

> Imagine a party of miners, cut off when their roof collapses, and trying to regain the surface through a rescue tunnel. It is obvious that they will not continue to make their way towards the top unless they have reason to believe from some indication (a glimmer of light, a draught of air from above) that the passage is not blocked ahead of them. Similarly . . . man would have no heart, no reason, to exert himself in causing mankind to advance beyond itself through unification, if the only effect of this fine effort were one day to bring it up sharp, with added force and impetus, against an impassable wall.[81]

> The universe, again, causes us anguish . . . because of its impenetrability and opacity. Under its sealed vault, as among its echoless crowds, we feel that we are as isolated and lost as the miner in a narrow gallery, blocked perhaps, with the full weight of the rock threatening to fall on him. But supposing, in fact, the miner sees a ray of light high up above his head, supposing he feels a current of fresh air blowing on him from

---

[79]Teilhard de Chardin, *Activation of Energy*, 45-46. Cf. 113: "gathered up by Omega, these same centers enter into immortality from the very moment when they become eucentric (that is, personal) and so structurally capable of entering into contact center to center, with its supreme consistence."

[80]Teilhard de Chardin, *The Appearance of Man*, 264.

[81]Teilhard de Chardin, *Activation of Energy*, 173-74.

ahead—supposing, I mean, we ourselves, human beings busied in our work, can take hope again *because the world is converging* . . . then have we not, the miner and we human beings, good reason once again to rejoice?[82]

He believed that Omega point conformed to the law of complexity/consciousness and yet was "strictly speaking, outside the scientifically observable process to which it provides the conclusion."[83] How could such a point lie within the phenomenal plane and also outside it? To this question Teilhard supplied the following explanations:

[T]o attain Omega (by the very act, indeed, of attaining it) we step outside space and time. At the same time, this transcendence does not prevent it from appearing to our scientific thought as necessarily endowed with certain expressible properties.[84]

Teilhard claimed that the reality of Omega was not postulated for emotional reasons, nor to satisfy intellectual needs, but because human "psychological energetics" demand it if a solution is to be found to "the problem of action."[85] "Reflective action and the anticipation of total disappearance are *cosmically incompatible*."[86] He called for a formulation of an "energetics of man (a psycho-energetics), on the scale of, and for application by, a zoological group [man] which is in process of planetary totalization."[87]

## 2.4 The Demand for Irreversibility

According to Teilhard, the chief phenomenon of *noogenesis* (the genesis of spirit) is *hominization*—the critical point through which the evolution of cerebralization is alleged to have passed, associated with upright posture, to attain thinking man. He also wrote of the emergence within man "of an increased demand for irreversibility,"[88] (that is, immortality):

---

[82]Ibid., 193. Italics in original.

[83]Teilhard de Chardin, *Man's Place in Nature*, 116.

[84]Ibid.

[85]See Melvyn R. Thompson, "A Critical Analysis of the Problem of Action in the Writings of Teilhard de Chardin" (Ph.D. diss., King's College, University of London, 1979).

[86]Cited in De Lubac, *The Religion of Teilhard de Chardin*, 178.

[87]Teilhard de Chardin, *Activation of Energy*, 177-78.

[88]Ibid., 176. Cf. 144: "this apex ["of the cone of terrestrial evolution"] can be seen to bear within it a fundamental demand for irreversibility."

[F]rom the simple (but inflexible) point of view of energetics hominization cannot physically continue for very much longer without explicitly postulating the existence ahead of a *critical point of superreflexion*: something like an emergence of coreflexion from time and space into a definitely irreversibilized life.[89]

I attribute an essential place in the rise of this third reflection [superreflection] to what I call the demands (as a matter of energetics) of *irreversibility*.[90]

I am more and more convinced that, if it is to found a neo-humanism, evolution must not only be of a converging nature (as coreflection proves), but that it must converge in the direction of a *real* focus (i.e., not simply "virtual"). This, I repeat, is not for philosophical reasons, but on pure grounds of "psychological energetics." There must be, in the future, some integration on itself of the evolutive whole, under some superconscious form (an integration in which I may be, in some way, integrated myself). Otherwise, I feel, I lack the stimulus, I *would* lack the stimulus is what I mean to say—to go further.[91]

He insisted that the irreversibility of evolution was a biological expression of transcendence (a type of relationship in which one term constitutes the other, without being limited by it)[92]:

If biology is taken to its extreme limit in a certain direction, can it effect our emergence into the transcendent? To that question, I believe, we must answer that it can for the following reasons:

[B]y becoming reflective the evolutionary process *can continue only if it sees that it is irreversible, in other words transcendent*: since the complete irreversibility of a physical magnitude, in as much as it implies escape from the conditions productive of disintegration which are proper to time and space, is simply the biological expression of transcendence.[93]

As he became more deeply aware of the significance and "necessity of irreversibility," Teilhard's obsession with "the Ahead" (the future) became in-

---

[89]Teilhard de Chardin, *The Appearance of Man*, 264. Italics in original.

[90]Teilhard de Chardin, letter of 17 September, 1952. Cuénot, *Teilhard de Chardin*, 363.

[91]Teilhard de Chardin, letter of 31 January 1955. Ibid., 354. Italics in original.

[92]Teilhard de Chardin, *Let Me Explain*, 17.

[93]Teilhard de Chardin, *Science and Christ*, 212-13. Italics in original.

creasingly dominant.[94] The postulate of an "escape'" or a "way out" formed the second part of a dialectic built on the acceptance of the organic nature of human socialization. The postulate asserts "that the universe, by structural necessity, cannot disappoint the consciousness it produces,"[95] and he considered it contrary to reason to reject this position. It was born from "a sharp and concrete "realization" of the utter vanity of "human effort" unless there is both a natural and supernatural emergence of the universe towards some immortal consciousness."[96]

Teilhard maintained that the escape route offered rested on the existence of a Being who has both already emerged from cosmogenesis (involving the directed spiritualization of the universe) and is in process of emergence.[97] He argued that Christianity provided the unique current in which "the forward movement of our spirit can again be resumed,"[98] and without which no "emergence" is possible. He wrote:

[O]ur refusal to appreciate the organic value of the fact of society would (in the first stage of the dialectic) remove any reason for our believing in an ultrahuman continuation of evolution, so here again our refusal to recognize the fact of Christianity would mean our seeing the vault of the universe, which for a moment opened up overhead, once again hermetically sealed against us. . . .

Christianity, . . . more vigorously and realistically than any other spiritual current in sight, never ceases to persist—practically alone in the world—in preserving and sharpening its ardent vision of a universe that is not impersonal and closed, but opens out, beyond the future, upon a divine center.[99]

Teilhard destroyed the radical distinction between the Creator God and man the creature, by tying both to the same pole of Being. He treated any suggestion of a registrable temporal beginning to creation as "an illegitimate contamination of the phenomenal plane by the metaphysical."[100] However, he contradicted this

---

[94]De Lubac *The Religion of Teilhard de Chardin*, 104.

[95]"La Réflexion de l'énergie," *Revue des Questions Scientifues* (Louvain) (20 October 1952): 495.

[96]Letter to M. and S. Bégouen, 10 April 1934. Teilhard de Chardin, *Letters from a Traveller*, 202. This comment was made within the context of a reflection on the death of his colleague and close friend Davidson Black.

[97]A "Being who has emerged from cosmogenesis" is a pantheistic deity—quite different from the God of Jews and Christians.

[98]Teilhard de Chardin, *Activation of Energy*, 148.

[99]Ibid., 147-48; 179.

[100]Teilhard de Chardin, *The Vision of the Past*, 134.

principle when he postulated an intersection of the phenomenal and metaphysical realm at Omega Point.

## 2.5 The Religion of Evolution and the Gospel of Human Effort

Teilhard lived during a period that witnessed, as he put it, "the birth and establishment of a new faith: the religion of evolution."[101] He addressed himself to the rise of what he called "a God (*the* God) of evolution,"[102] and acknowledged that evolution had given a "new value" to "the whole domain of existence."[103]

He argued that the Christian should "learn to appreciate the value of *sacred evolution* as an instrument of beatification" and possessing mankind's "eternal hopes."[104] "The new temperatures and new tensions produced in the human mind by the appearance of the idea of evolution," he wrote, have provided "an optimum environment for development and communication" of Christianity.[105]

In fact it was these tensions that provoked his own attempts to reinterpret the Christian faith. In 1916 he wrote to a friend: "there are temperaments in which intuition is born from an excess of tension or vital ardor much more than from methodical effort: and probably it's to this type that I incline."[106]

Teilhard presented a version of the Christian gospel, which he defined as "a new faith: the 'religion of evolution',"[107] a 'religion of the future' (definable as a 'religion of evolution'),"[108] the "religion for the sake of research and effort,"[109] and "the Gospel of human Effort."[110] By the latter phrase he attempted to convey the idea that "Christianity is supremely futurist" and "the generator of a maximum human effort" (rather than being "passive and soporific").[111]

He claimed that "the Messiah whom we await, . . . is the universal Christ; . . . the Christ of evolution."[112] "By making plain the splendors of the universal

---

[101]Teilhard de Chardin, "How I Believe" (1934) in *Christianity and Evolution*, 123.

[102]Ibid., 237.

[103]Ibid., 238-39.

[104]Teilhard de Chardin, *Writings in Time of War*, 17.

[105]Teilhard de Chardin, *Christianity and Evolution*, 207.

[106]Teilhard de Chardin, letter of 29 June 1916. *The Making of a Mind*, 106.

[107]Teilhard de Chardin, *Christianity and Evolution*, 123.

[108]Ibid., 240.

[109]Teilhard de Chardin, *Science and Christ*, 111.

[110]Teilhard de Chardin, *The Heart of the Matter*, 214-17, 222. "The strictly Christian 'esoteric' phase of the Evangelization 'of human Effort' would consist (as I see it) in presenting Jesus Christ to men as the very Term, already vaguely apprehended by them, of universal development: men being able (by virtue of the supernaturalization of the World) to reach consummation only in his Unity" (215).

[111]Teilhard de Chardin, *Science and Christ*, 149-50.

[112]Teilhard de Chardin, *Christianity and Evolution*, 95.

Christ, Christianity . . . acquires a new value. . . . it is seen to be the form of
faith that is most fitted to modern needs: a religion for progress—the very religion of progress of the earth— . . . the very religion of evolution."[113]

Above all else, he wished to communicate the reconciliation of God and the
world, by bringing together the God of Christian faith and the God of mankind's
most ennobling labors. For Teilhard Evolution was synonymous with Divinity,[114]
and faith in God was identical to faith in Evolution. He wrote:

> A crisis of cosmic nature and magnitude, the social ferment which is to-
> day pervading human populations can only be dominated and guided by
> a clearer and more conscious faith in the supreme value of evolution.
> . . .
>
> There is, . . . only one method to keep the undisciplined crowd of
> human monads bound to the task of life: to make the passion for the
> whole prevail in them over elementary egoism, that is to say practically
> to increase their consciousness of the general evolution of which they
> are part.[115]

For Teilhard the Gospel consisted of the message that the whole World
sounded forth the immanent presence of the divine Christ. In June 1926 he wrote
to a friend stating:

> Believe me, when one has penetrated to this axis of the Christian atti-
> tude, the ritual, disciplinary and theological encrustations matter little
> more than musical or acoustical theories matter to the enjoyment of a
> beautiful piece of music. Truly, there is a Christian *note* which makes
> the whole World vibrate like an immense gong, in the divine Christ.
> This note is unique and universal and in it alone consists the Gospel.
> Only it is real (happily). And for this reason it is inevitable that, in try-
> ing to fix hold of its reality, men analyze it out of sight . . . there is
> only one road that can lead to God, and this is fidelity to remain
> constantly true to yourself, to what you feel is highest in you. Do not
> worry about the rest. The road will open before you as you go.[116]

Teilhard tried to advance a strictly naturalistic explanation of the General
Theory of Evolution (i.e., molecules-to-man *transformism*), yet he maintained a

---

[113]Ibid., 124.

[114]Teilhard de Chardin, *Writings in Time of War*, 78: "It is, indeed, the mysterious
Divinity that 'possesses' and stirs up nations at the turning points of history; *it is* once
again *that same Divinity, it is Evolution.*" Italics in original.

[115]Teilhard de Chardin, *The Vision of the Past*, 76-77.

[116]Teilhard de Chardin, letter of 11 June 1926, in *Letters to Two Friends*, 30-31.

"supernatural" element. He imbued matter with "spirit," a term he tried unsuccessfully to limit strictly to the phenomenal realm. As noted, he argued for the concept or "law" of "complexification," a pivotal argument in his theory: subatomic particles spontaneously gained increasingly elaborate organization during the course of "cosmogenesis," evolving upwards eventually to produce humans and civilized societies.[117]

Complexity was for Teilhard a third dimension of knowledge to add to what he called "Pascal's two abysses,"[118] or "infinities of dispersion"; namely "the infinitesimal and the immense." The third, "cerebralization of beings" (mental complexity) was seen to be "the true index of their vitalization."[119] The "abyss of synthesis," was now added to "the lower abyss of fragmentation" and that at the other extreme—the abyss of agglomeration.[120] Teilhard sought to dispose of what he called the Pascalian obsession of the "two abysses," to teach us the "gesture," as he put it, to enable us to "overcome the illusion of quantity."[121]

N. M. Wildiers notes that "Christianity became for Teilhard the religion of progress, the religion of evolution. . . . [and] teaches us about 'superevolution'."[122] Indeed, Teilhard maintained that the doctrines of the Trinity, the divinity of the historic Christ, Revelation, Miracles, Original Sin, and Redemption (as he interpreted them.) all took a "natural, functional place in the setting of a Christian 'superevolution'."[123]

He wrote that "the ascending force of Christianity is directly geared to the propulsive mechanism of human superevolution,"[124] or "superevolution of Man."[125] "The fundamental question really at issue is whether or not official authority [of the Roman Catholic Church] is willing to accept (and to integrate into the Christian faith) 'faith' in a future (i.e., a superevolution) of Humanity on earth."[126]

---

[117]H. James Birx, *Pièrre Teilhard de Chardin's Philosophy of Evolution* (Springfield IL: Charles C. Thomas, 1972) 102-103.

[118]Teilhard de Chardin, *Man's Place in Nature*, 23. He also referred to "Pascal's two abysses" as "the abyss of number, a terrifying flood tide all around us of bodies and particles; and the abyss of time, an endless axis around which are carried out the coilings and uncoilings of space. . . . " See Teilhard de Chardin, *Activation of Energy*, 186; Pascal's "second infinite" in *Science and Christ*, 24; and "Pascal's twin infinities" in *Writings in Time of War*, 19.

[119]Teilhard de Chardin, *Man's Place in Nature*, 49.

[120]Teilhard de Chardin, *Activation of Energy*, 28.

[121]Teilhard de Chardin, *Christianity and Evolution*, 106n.1.

[122]N. M. Wildiers, foreword to *Toward the Future* (London: Collins, 1975) 11.

[123]Teilhard de Chardin, *Christianity and Evolution*, 157.

[124]Teilhard de Chardin, *The Future of Man*, 224.

[125]Ibid., 176.

[126]Teilhard de Chardin, letter of 13 August 1948, in *Letters to Two Friends*, 106.

Many of Teilhard's basic metaphysical emphases[127] resemble those of the process philosopher Alfred North Whitehead[128] (1861–1947), whose work Teilhard appears not to have read.[129] Whitehead, who did not accept the concept of a transcendent God, produced the first systematic presentation of dipolar panentheism.[130] Both scholars believed that concrete matter has no precise beginning, but emerges from a state of infinite plurality and dissociation, representing the lower or "negative pole of being,"[131] towards a higher state of being. Both contributed to science-orientated process philosophy/theology.

Teilhard's dogma was that "God cannot create except evolutively."[132] However, he did not consider his work to be metaphysical[133] but rather a philosophi-

---

[127]Teilhard claimed that he dissociated himself from metaphysics, since it represented for him a purely abstract and a priori science of being, a "geometrical deduction of conclusions from premises." See Rideau, *Teilhard de Chardin: A Guide to His Thought*, 42; and Duggan, *Teilhardism and the Faith*, 25. Duggan notes that Teilhard *does* expound metaphysics if the term is defined in the traditional sense—"as a rational explanation of the whole of reality in terms of its ultimate causes."

[128]Barbour, "Five Ways of Reading Teilhard," 3-20. See Alfred N. Whitehead, *Science and the Modern World: The Lowell Lectures* (New York: MacMillan, 1925); *Process and Reality: An Essay in Cosmology (Gifford Lectures, 1927–1928)* (London: Cambridge University Press, 1929); *Adventures of Ideas* (New York: MacMillan, 1933); *Modes of Thought* (New York: MacMillan, 1938). For Whitehead, God and the world are ontologically interrelated through a reciprocal relationship of everlasting creativity seeking a perfected unity. See Birx, *Pierre Teilhard de Chardin's Philosophy of Evolution*, 147. Whitehead's doctrine of God is a doctrine of immanence. God is not needed by Whitehead as the self-existent infinite Being upon whose love and power the world depends for all that it is and has.

[129]Charles E. Raven, "Orthodoxy and Science," in *Teilhard de Chardin: Pilgrim of the Future*, ed. Braybrooke, 56. See Ian G. Barbour, "Whitehead and Teilhard de Chardin," in *Process Theology: Basic Writings*, ed. Ewert H. Cousins (New York: Newman Press, 1977).

[130]Panentheism (lit: all in God) may degenerate into a form which is often referred to as *dipolar* or *bipolar theism*. In contrast to traditional monopolar theism, the latter holds that there are two poles to God: an actual temporal pole and potential eternal pole. Nowadays, the major form of this position is represented by "Process theology," which holds that the finite dipolar God is in a continual process of change.

[131]Teilhard de Chardin, *Science and Christ*, 78: "However far back we look into the past, we see the waves of the Multiple breaking into foam as though they emerged from a negative pole of being. The fringes of our universe . . . are lost in material and unconscious plurality."

[132]Teilhard de Chardin, *Christianity and Evolution*, 179.

[133]In the preface to *The Phenomenon of Man* Teilhard wrote: "If this book is to be properly understood, it must be read not as a work of metaphysics, still less as a sort of theological essay, but purely and simply as a scientific treatise" (29). In the foreword he

cal phenomenology.[134] The basic principle of his phenomenology is, that the coming into being of anything must be understood in terms of its culmination. He believed that the purpose he saw operating at the core of the cosmos was intrinsic in character and essentially immanent, immanent in the sense that it could be legitimately studied by the methods of natural science.[135]

## 2.6 Teilhard's Conception of Evolution

While never a declared Darwinist, Teilhard's vision of evolution was Darwinist to a high degree[136] in its emphasis on progress and he seemed to have a deep

---

wrote: "do not expect a final explanation of things here, nor a metaphysical system." In a letter dated 9 May 1940 he stated: "my book [*The Phenomenon of Man*] has an excellent chance of being finished before July. . . . I rather wonder what effect it will have if it ever gets published—as I hope it will. I shall have the pure scientists against me as well as the experts in pure metaphysics; but as I shall say in my conclusion, I do not see what else you could say if once you try to work out to its conclusion a coherent place for man in this universe of ours." *Letters From a Traveller*, 263. Also see letter of 21 August 1919 in *Making of a Mind*, 302: "I'm less concerned than they [my friends] are with the metaphysical side of things, with what might have been or might not have been, with the abstract conditions of existence: all that seems to me inevitably misleading or shaky." In his essay "Man's Place in the Universe: Reflexions on Complexity" (1942) Teilhard provides the reader with a warning which includes the statement: "Being concerned with the links and order of succession revealed by these phenomena, I shall not deal with their deep causality. Perhaps I shall risk an 'ultraphysical' excursus. But look for no metaphysics here." *The Vision of the Past*, 217. N.B.: You cannot dispense with metaphysics unless you have a metaphysics of your own.

[134]The word "phenomenology" is used by Teilhard as a synonym for "generalized physics," an expression best understood as indicating not only a kinship with classical physics, but a science of matter or cosmology, Rideau, *Teilhard de Chardin: A Guide to His Thought*, 332. Such a phenomenology of the cosmic has been defined as "a science which seeks to describe the universe as an observable phenomenon in its totality and its intrinsic cohesion, and to discover the meaning concealed in that totality," N. M. Wildiers, *An Introduction to Teilhard de Chardin* (London: Collins, Fontana, 1968) 48. Cuénot notes that Teilhard's phenomenology had practically nothing in common with that of Edmund Husserl (1859–1938) and still less with that of Hegel. Cuénot, *Teilhard de Chardin*, 376. Hegel's phenomenology sought to construct a total logic of reality, a rational dialectical development of history and the categories of the mind. Teilhard's phenomenology also differs from that of Merleau-Ponty. Teilhard explicitly stated: "My phenomenology is not the phenomenology of Husserl and Merleau-Ponty."

[135]Bernard Towers, "Jung and Teilhard," in *Teilhard de Chardin: Pilgrim of the Future*, ed. Braybrooke, 81-82.

[136]Teilhard resorted to Lamarckian explanations, as did Darwin in later versions of his theory. In a footnote to *The Phenomenon of Man* (149n.1) Teilhard wrote: "In various

emotional need to be assured of the reality of progress. He described how "what was at first a happy accident or means of survival, is promptly transformed and used as an instrument of progress or conquest."[137]

He was a supporter of the concept of orthogenesis[138] (directed evolution) and referred to an "*internal* law which governs the development of life,"[139] "the secret

---

quarters I shall be accused of showing too Lamarckian a bent in the explanations which follow, of giving an exaggerated influence to the *Within* in the organic arrangement of bodies . . . Properly understood, the 'anti-chance' of the Neo-Lamarckian is not the mere negation of Darwinian chance. On the contrary it appears as its utilization." See Marie-Rose Carriere, *L'evolution biologique et psychique selon Charles Darwin et Pierre Teilhard de Chardin* (Ottawa: Bibliotheque nationale du Canada, 1994). (Two microfiches: Canadian theses, MA thesis, University of Ottawa, 1993.)

[137]Teilhard de Chardin, *The Phenomenon of Man*, 104.

[138]"Orthogenesis" is a term that was first used in 1893 by the biologist Wilhelm Haacke. Later, Gustav Eimer gave it a definition as "the general law according to which evolutionary development takes place in a noticeable direction, above all in specialized groups." Many biologists, such as George Gaylord Simpson, object to the term since it includes, as Simpson put it, "an element of mysticism." Teilhard saw orthogenesis as the only complete form of heredity—evolution along straight and predetermined lines. He viewed orthogenesis as playing an indispensable part in the ascent of evolution. He wrote: "the normal development of living forms before the coming of man. It can be character-ized [as] Phyletic . . . : every species (or group of species) formed a sort of shoot (or phylum) which is obliged to evolve 'orthogenetically' along certain prescribed lines (re-duction or adaptation of limbs, . . .)."

In a note he wrote: "The word 'orthogenesis' is here used in its widest sense: 'A pre-scribed orientation offsetting the effect of chance in the play of heredity'." See Teilhard de Chardin, *The Future of Man*, 158n. In a letter of 16 March 1952, Teilhard recognized that biologists have problems with this term "because it seems to represent an intrusion into science by philosophy (e.g., the notion of Finality, especially a Finality directed by some Creative Idea). But these prejudices simply don't hold up." See *Letters from my Friend Teilhard*, 123.

Both orthogenesis and Lamarckian views gain little support among modern biolo-gists. Both the Jesuit philosopher Joseph F. Donceel and evolutionary biologist Prof. Maynard Smith, maintain that orthogenesis is implicit in Teilhard's idea of evolution, and he has been severely criticized for supporting such ideas. Donceel has dealt at length with the apparent disagreement between Teilhard's ideas of orthogenesis and those of many paleontologists. See "Teilhard de Chardin: Scientist or Philosopher," *International Philo-sophical Quarterly* 5/2 (1965): 248-66. Also see P. G. Fothergill, "Teilhard and the Question of Orthogenesis," in *Evolution, Marxism, and Christianity: Studies in the Teil-hardian Synthesis* (contributors: Claude Cuénot et al.) (London: Garnstone, 1967) 30-46. Cuénot maintained that Teilhard was a supporter of orthogenesis. Also see Edward O. Dodson, *The Teilhardian Synthesis, Lamarckism, and Orthogenesis* (Chambersburg PA: Anima Books, 1993).

[139]Teilhard de Chardin, *The Vision of the Past*, 18. Italics in original. Also see 17: "Taken as a single mass, the whole group of mammals manifestly obeys an *internal* law of development and irradiation."

law of development,"[140] and "certain internal forces of preference."[141] He considered the term "orthogenesis" "essential and indispensable for singling out and affirming the manifest property of living matter to form a system in which 'terms *succeed each other* experimentally, following the constantly increasing values of centrocomplexity'."[142] In his view, "life is, in scientific experience, no other than a specific effect of complexified matter."[143]

According to Canon Charles Raven, Teilhard never accepted the idea of an *élan vital* acting upon and subjugating matter.[144] Rather, he rejected the Bergsonian idea of a vital impulse having no finality. Teilhard was most definitely a vitalist—or, more precisely, an advocate of orthogenesis, but did acknowledge the role of mechanisms in the evolution of complex life forms.[145]

His "law of complexity/consciousness," involving "two levels of operation,"[146] the "within" (or "internal aspect") and "without" (or "exterior aspect") of things, would indeed indicate that he applies the term "orthogenesis" in a sense that includes the concept of a vital principle. Such a principle is generally rejected by modern biologists.[147]

Teilhard felt that Bergson's "élan vital" was only valid as an explanation for the formation of the "reflective zones of the Noosphere"[148] since it expressed "no

---

[140]Ibid., 21.

[141]Ibid., 254.

[142]Teilhard de Chardin, *The Phenomenon of Man*, 108n. Italics in original.

[143]Teilhard de Chardin, *Man's Place in Nature*, 24.

[144]Charles E. Raven, "Orthodoxy and Science," *Teilhard de Chardin: Pilgrim of the Future,* ed. Braybrooke, 56.

[145]Cuénot, *Teilhard de Chardin*, 35.

[146]Teilhard de Chardin, *The Appearance of Man*, 265.

[147]O'Manique, *Energy in Evolution*, 69: "The Darwinian explanation of evolution relies heavily on chance and on the influence of factors which are outside of the developing being—in other words, on ectogenesis, and hence it would conflict with any concept of a determined and autogenetic evolution" as is found in Teilhard's use of the term "orthogenesis."

[148]Teilhard's first reference to the Noosphere was in an article on Man written about 1927. The term, modelled on geologist Edouard Suess's "Biosphere," was applied to the Earth's "thinking envelope." See Teilhard de Chardin, *The Heart of the Matter*, 30-31, 78n.9. This "thinking layer" which has developed since the first appearance of true man, involves conscious rationality, inventiveness, and union between souls. From the Greek *nous*, meaning mind. Teilhard stated: "Compared with the magnitude of the stars, the noosphere is an almost insignificant film. In reality this thin surface is nothing less than the most progressive form under which it has been given to us to apprehend and contemplate the energy of the universe. This tenuous envelope holds the secret essence of the vastness that it fringes: the highest note reached by the vibration of the worlds." Teilhard de Chardin, *Human Energy*, 121. Also see Teilhard de Chardin, "The Formation of the Noo-

more than the dynamic rigor of the situation."[149] Teilhard wrote: "of all the living we know none is more really, more intensely, living than the noosphere."[150]

Teilhard also adopted Bergson's notion of *duration* as the characteristic mark of consciousness,[151] in an attempt to inject new life into the old theory of matter and form. Bergson contrasted time, which in physical science has been "spatialized" (that is, broken up into a series of discreet points or instants), with the duration we immediately apprehend in consciousness, which is a continuous indivisible becoming.[152]

"Duration" is a name for the general insight that everything is related to everything else. All of space-time constitutes a *cosmos*, a seamless fabric, an infinite continuum and anything, anywhere in space and time, is connected in its very being to everything else in space and time. This is essentially what Teilhard meant when he said that every individual atom is coextensive with the whole universe, that the dimensions of every atom are the length and breadth of the universe.

Teilhard coined the term "evolutionary pressure," which he considered "the ultimate mainspring of all vital movement" and wrote of its "progressively more marked emergence throughout the ages."[153] In man, he believed this "evolutionary pressure" was replaced by an "inner nature [that was] decisively 'psychized'," referring to this factor as "the zest for living."[154]

He considered that the observation of a constant increase in *psyche* throughout time, conformed to a "great law" of "universal evolution," referring to this

---

sphere," (1947), *The Future of Man*, 155-84. Teilhard notes that as far as he could tell the word "noosphere" was his invention, but he credits his colleague and friend Edouard le Roy for launching the term in lectures at the Collège de France. Cuénot, *Teilhard de Chardin*, 59. Also see "The Formation of the Noosphere," chap. 4 in *Man's Place in Nature* (79-121).

[149]Teilhard de Chardin, *The Appearance of Man*, 261.

[150]Teilhard de Chardin, *Activation of Energy*, 288.

[151]For an early reference to Bergson's concept see Teilhard de Chardin, letter of 19 June 1916, in *The Making of a Mind*, 103.

[152]John Macquarrie, *Twentieth Century Religious Thought: The Frontiers of Philosophy and Theology, 1900–1970* (London: SCM Press, 1973), 170-71. The time of physical science has been, as Bergson expresses it—"spatialized"—meaning that time as apprehended by the intellect, has become represented as a rapid series of static pictures (cf. cinematography), and this in turn leads to a deterministic view of reality. In contrast, the time of duration, grasped by the intuition of our consciousness, has genuine unbroken movement, and since this implies an element of novelty and creativity, it allows for the possibility of free will and spontaneity.

[153]Teilhard de Chardin, *Christianity and Evolution*, 204.

[154]Ibid.

as "an evolution with a basis of spirit."[155] He proposed that the mechanism of evolutionary change was the appetite or desire of the basic "stuff of the universe" for greater Being. He propounded a theory of groping, which revolves around his concept of directed chance, as his explanation of the mechanism of evolution:

> [O]n the plane of animate particles, we find the fundamental technique of *groping* . . . [which] strangely combines the blind fantasy of large numbers with the precise orientation of a specific target. It would be a mistake to see it as mere chance. Groping is *directed chance*. It means pervading everything so as to try everything, and trying everything so as to find everything. . . .[156]

> At the outset the phylum corresponds to the "discovery," by groping, of a new type of organism that is both viable and advantageous. But this new type will not attain its most economical or efficient form all at once. For a certain period of time it devotes all its strength, so to speak, to groping about within itself. . . . Then at last perfection comes within sight, and from that moment the rhythm of change slows down. The new invention, having reached the limit of its potentialities, enters into its phase of conquest. . . . "[157]

> It is only really through strokes of chance that life proceeds, but strokes of chance which are recognized and grasped—i.e., psychically selected. . . .[158] If life has been able to advance, it is because, by ceaseless groping, it has successively found the points of least resistance at which reality yielded to its thrust.[159]

> The world, seen by experience at our level, is an immense groping, an immense search, an immense attack; its progress can take place only at the expense of many failures, of many wounds.[160]

Bernard Towers, a former vice president of the Teilhard Center, considers Teilhard's coining of the word "groping"[161] as "a stroke of genius," since groping

---

[155]Ibid., 107.

[156]Teilhard de Chardin, *The Phenomenon of Man*, 110.

[157]Ibid., 116.

[158]Ibid., 149n.

[159]Ibid., 281. Italics in original. On 118 he refers to "the idea or symbol of *groping*." Also see pp. 223-34, 242, 250, 308, 312.

[160]Teilhard de Chardin, *Human Energy*, 50.

[161]Groping is a phenomenon he saw occurring at the microlevel of evolution where natural selection and mutations can be seen to act directly. It is the random nature of these processes, the uncertainties of mutation and the "luck" of selection, operating on large numbers of organisms, which cause the groping. Groping is thus a manifestation of

movements may *appear* random in isolation, but have a degree of directionality. Towers considers this process the essence of evolutionary change.[162] Thomas Berry, a historian of religion and former president of the American Teilhard Association for the Future of Man, also defends the term: "Groping itself implies a disquiet, an incompleteness; it also has the excitement of discovery, ecstatic transformation, and the advance toward new levels of integration."[163]

A third Teilhardian to defend the term was Theodosius Dobzhansky (1900–1975), a world-famous evolutionist. Concerning the term "groping," he wrote: "This is a more poetic and impressionistic than a rigorously scientific characterization, and yet it is remarkably apposite."[164] Dobzhansky goes on to explain why "groping" is indeed a very good way of describing how natural selection operates, and concludes that Teilhard's "general conception of the nature of evolution harmonizes with the fundamentals of biological theory far better (than orthogenesis)."[165]

---

mutation combined with selection, but it is evident only when one observes their combined action from outside, in statistically significant quantities. Teilhard also applied the term "groping" to the evolution of inventions and ideas. See *The Appearance of Man*, 243: "By what mysterious labor of groping and selection is it formed, this *additive* and *irreversible* kernel of institutions and viewpoints to which we adjust ourselves at birth and which we each contribute to enlarge, more or less consciously and infinitesimally, throughout our lives? What is it that makes one invention or idea among millions of others 'take on'?" Italics in original.

Also see Teilhard de Chardin, *The Activation of Energy*, 123-24: "we can see life developing plurality and ramifying— . . . it is no more than the manifestation also of a method of *groping* in which there is a happy combination of the play of chance (which is physical) and that of finality (which is psychic)"; 233: "So it is that by dint of and under the impact of tentative gropings, by the operation of chances that are seized and added one to another, life automatically functions and increases around us."

[162]Towers, *Concerning Teilhard*, 51-55, 109; "Toward an Evolutionary Ethic," *Teilhard Review* 12/3 (October 1977): 81. "The struggle within the evolutionary process at the biological level is always one of 'groping.' At close range it appears random. Groping movements are often—usually in fact—fruitless. But when a 'solution' or set of solutions is arrived at, it or they are immediately grasped, provided only that the biological group concerned is 'aware' enough to recognize it then, and not yet hidebound enough to fail so to do."

[163]Thomas Berry, "The Cosmology of Peace," in *Humanity's Quest For Unity*, ed. Zonneveld, 57.

[164]Theodosius Dobzhansky, *The Biology of Ultimate Concern* (New York: New American Library, 1967) 121.

[165]Ibid.

Sir John Eccles, Nobel prize winner and authority on the human brain, refers to Teilhard's concept of "blind groping" as expressing precisely the biological process of evolution. He states:

> Teilhard de Chardin (1959) has likened the evolutionary process to a "blind groping." The randomness of the mutational changes gives essentially a blind trial of an enormous number of possible changes, while natural selection is responsible for the survival of all "favorable" mutations. Hence from an initial process of pure chance there can be wrought by natural selection all the marvelous structural and functional features of living organisms with their amazing adaptiveness and inventiveness. . . . This theory stemming from DARWIN must rank as one of the grandest conceptual achievements of man.[166]

Teilhard's use of the concept of chance arises from his acceptance of the Darwinian theory as the explanation of the mechanism of evolutionary change. The autogenetic element in his theory is his reliance on "psychic selection," by which he meant that organisms "recognize" and "select" those traits that are useful. Selection here is Darwinian selection which incorporates a psychic aspect.

## 2.7 Teilhard: Apostle of a "Superior" Gospel?

Teilhard viewed "cosmogenesis" as Christocentric and progressing towards "Omega Point" a "deduced and conjectural" Entity rather than one entered into and experienced"[167] (compare with the Parousia[168]). He thereby grafted biblical eschatology on to Darwinism. He recognized that "Darwinism afforded a scientific justification of faith in progress,"[169] and that "until the coming of Man it was natural selection that set the course of morphogenesis and cerebration."[170]

---

[166]John C. Eccles, *Facing Reality: Philosophical adventures by a brain scientist* (New York; Heidelberg-Berlin: Springer Verlag, 1970) 87.

[167]Teilhard de Chardin, *The Heart of Matter*, 40. Cf. 91: "Nevertheless, however strongly convinced we may be of the existence of this Omega Pole, we can never in the end reach it except by extrapolation: it remains by nature conjectural, it remains a postulate."

[168]Teilhard stated: "The parousia (or Christ's return in glory at the end of all time) occupies a central position in the firmament of the Christian world. . . . —It is in this unique and supreme event, in which (so faith tells us) the historic is to be fused in the transcendent, that the mystery of the Incarnation culminates: and this asserts itself with all the realism of a physical explanation of the universe." See Teilhard de Chardin, *Toward the Future*, 153.

[169]Teilhard de Chardin, *The Future of Man*, 299.

[170]Ibid., 293.

He referred to the "superiority" of his "vision" compared with what had been taught to him by the Roman Catholic Church,[171] and in support of his "'eschatological' vision,"[172] as he called it, he drew selected passages from the writings of St Paul and St John to support his theories.[173] Prof. R. J. Berry, a leading theistic evolutionist, argues that he "sought to graft Christianity on to secular evolutionism."[174] Martin Lings is scathing in criticisms of Teilhard's "synthesis" of Christianity and evolutionism:

> An eminent prisoner within this [self-imposed] framework of mental paralysis [the modern pseudoreligion] is Teilhard de Chardin, who also blocks the main and obvious channels of thought in his desperate attempts to combine religion with evolutionism. His appeal lies in his providing certain ingeniously devised side channels which relieve the paralytic by keeping up an illusion of normal mental activity. In other words, with an extraordinary capacity for turning a blind eye and a deaf ear to this and that, he creates a kind of mental hubbub in order to drown the voice of reason . . . God and evolutionism . . . [are] two incompatibles . . . [by attempting to reconcile the two] you will be left with a deity who is not the Lord of All Mystery but a subhuman monster of incompetence, which is precisely what Teilhardism implies of God. But outside the very special climate of this pseudomystical fantasy, one only needs to be able to put two and two together to see that either evolutionism or God must go.[175]

---

[171]Teilhard de Chardin, *The Heart of the Matter*, 101: "there is the evidence contained in the *superiority* of my vision compared with that I had been taught—even though there is at the same time an *identity* with it."

[172]Teilhard de Chardin, *The Future of Man*, 268.

[173]The chief texts he relied on are the following: Rom. 8:22; 1 Cor. 15:28; Eph. 1:10, 19-22, 2:20-22, 3:18, 4:13, 16; Phil. 3:20-21, 4:8; Col. 1:15-20, 2:3; John 1:3-10; and Rev. 1:8. Teilhard draws from the account of the Transfiguration in the vision he describes in "Christ in the World of Matter," in Teilhard de Chardin *Hymn of the Universe* (London: Collins/Fount, 1981) 39-51. The few symbols he retained from Old Testament passages include Elijah's ascent to heaven in the fiery chariot (2 Kgs. 2:11-14); Jacob's battle during the night with God (Gen. 32: 23-33); and the Burning Bush scene (Ex. 3:1-5). He introduced the figure of Job in his discussion of evil (*Le Milieu Divin*, 60,66). See Richard W. Kropf, *Teilhard, Scripture, and Revelation: A Study of Teilhard de Chardin's Reinterpretation of Pauline Themes* (Rutherford, Madison, Teaneck: Fairleigh Dickinson University Press, 1980).

[174]R. J. Berry, *God and Evolution* (London: Hodder & Stoughton, 1988) 154.

[175]Martin Lings, *The Eleventh Hour: The Spiritual Crisis of the Modern World in the Light of Tradition and Prophecy* (Cambridge: Quinta Essentia, 1987) 31-32.

Some who knew Teilhard well became convinced that he was "trying to start a religion of his own."[176] One of Teilhard's critics, André Billy, even announced on 5 July 1950, in the Paris press, that this remarkable philosopher might even have sown the seeds for a "religion of the future."[177] There seems no doubt that Teilhard considered himself the apostle of a new gospel, for he wrote:

> I should wish, Lord, in my very humble way, to be the apostle and, if I may ask so much, the evangelist of your *Christ in the Universe*. I should wish . . . to bring Christ, by virtue of strictly organic connections, into the heart of realities that are considered the most fraught with danger, the least supernatural, the most pagan—such is my gospel and such my mission. . . . I should like to reveal the life of our Lord Jesus permeating all things, *a veritable world soul*.[178]

The notion of God being "a veritable world soul" finds no support whatsoever in scripture, but rather can be traced to the pagan philosophies of Stoic pantheism. As Mascall notes, "the logical outcome of a purely immanentist theology is pantheism, the doctrine that God and the world are simply identical."[179] The concept of a "world soul" is in full harmony with Teilhard's pantheistic and monistic orientation, and was integral to his "mysticism." However, true mysticism is at the antipodes of pantheism and monism, for as Nicolas Berdyaev, the Russian Orthodox mystic, notes: "there can be no greater error than to interpret mystical experience in terms of monistic metaphysics . . . mystical experience is free from monism or pantheism."[180]

Teilhard promoted a *pseudo*mystical interpretation of a universe, irreversibly advancing by convergent evolution towards a spiritualized cosmos (or "matter") and towards a unification with a personal God. So radically personal was God in his view, that Teilhard personalized the entire universe through Man, whom he considered to be "the center of perspective, [and] the *center of construction of the universe*."[181]

He argued that "the mysterious *Compound* formed by Christ and the universe—(by a universe centered on Christ) must have a specific and unique

---

[176]Comment made by Mrs Swan, Teilhard's close confidant. Cited in Mary Lukas and Ellen Lukas, *Teilhard: A Biography* (London: Collins, 1977) 111.

[177]Ibid., 268. André Billy of the Académie Goncourt, 5 July 1950, *Figaro Littéraire*. Review of *Milieu Divin*, the *Espirit de la Terre*, and the *Comment Je Crois*.

[178]Teilhard de Chardin, Le Prête (1918), cited in Cuénot, *Teilhard de Chardin*, 40.

[179]Mascall, *He Who Is*, 132.

[180]Nicolas Berdyaev, *Spirit and Reality* (London: Geoffrey Bles, 1939) 133-34.

[181]Teilhard de Chardin, *The Phenomenon of Man*, 33. Italics in original.

value."[182] As Speaight notes, for Teilhard "everything was God and God was everything, and Jesus was 'God and everything combined'."[183] God and the world are not to be separated, Teilhard stressed, but neither are they to be confused. Both are distinct foci on which man's love is directed and should be seen as invoking one another in mutual complementarity.

Just as the rays of man's love converge on his fellowman enabling him to see something of the "image of God"[184]; so man's love converging on all creation enables him to understand something of the invisible attributes of God—"His eternal power and Godhead" (Rom. 1:19-20). God must be loved through the world and through man, argued Teilhard, for He is the "heart" of all. God must also be loved through a world of convergent evolution whose focus lies in the future (Teilhard's "Omega Point").

This focus coincides with another focal point, the full manifestation of the Incarnate God in Glory. God works through the world to reach man, and the world depends "upon God to escape its contingency."[185] If all could disappear then He would remain, His "rays . . . drawn back into their source."[186]

We can conclude that Teilhard was not an apostle of a *superior* Gospel. Rather, he sought to propagate an erroneous religiophilosophical worldview. He held to the erroneous modernist assumption that the "doctrine" of transformism, as expounded by evolutionary biologists, can be equally applied to the doctrines of the Church. This view suggests that the doctrines of Christianity should be accommodated to the light of modern knowledge and are subject to the Darwinian selection principle—"survival of the fittest." His is essentially an immanentist theology grounded in evolutionary transformism, pantheism, and monism, some of the hallmarks of New Age thinking.

In the next chapter we examine closely Teilhard's relationship to the modernist movement. New Age thought draws heavily on the "theology" of modernism, a marketing strategy that allows it to infiltrate within the Church, widening its appeal, and consequently drawing into its orbit many churchgoers with an inadequate or faulty understanding of Christian teaching.

---

[182]Teilhard de Chardin, *Science and Christ*, 17. Italics in original.

[183]Speaight, *Teilhard de Chardin: A Biography*, 81-82.

[184]Gen.1:27. The "image of God," however, has been marred by the Fall of Man, Gen. 3; Rom. 8:20-22.

[185]Teilhard de Chardin, "Mon Univers" (1918). Cited in Mooney, *Teilhard and the Mystery of Christ*, 23-24.

[186]Teilhard de Chardin, *Hymn of the Universe*.

# Teilhard de Chardin: "Patron Saint" of "New Age" Catholicism?

> The modernism or neomodernism within Christianity, and especially within the Roman Catholic Church . . . is above all characterized by a turning away from the supernatural and an exclusive predilection for the world. . . . Teilhard's ideology was a precondition for this . . . *he . . . fused God and the supernatural with the process of universal evolutionism*, and proclaimed religion to be an active participation in a progressive development ending in Point Omega, the basis was given for a humanistic cult of the secular.[1]
> —*Albert Drexel*

> Teilhard's affinity lies with the modernizers and progressives of other religions, not with the traditionalists.[2]
> —*Ursula King*

> What we now have to do without delay is to modify the position occupied by the central core of Christianity.[3]
> —*Teilhard de Chardin*

## 3.1 Teilhard's Transformation of Christian Doctrines

Teilhard considered that "Christianity represented the highest point attained by the consciousness of Mankind in its striving to humanize itself."[4] Since it was only an element within the evolutive process, he argued that its doctrines must

---

[1] Albert Drexel, *Ein Neuer Prophet* (Stein am Rhein: Christiana, 1971) 115. Cited in Wolfgang Smith, *Teilhardism and the New Religion* (Rockford IL: Tan, 1989) 211.

[2] King, "Science and Mysticism: Teilhard de Chardin in Religious Thought Today," 10.

[3] Teilhard de Chardin, *Christianity and Evolution*, 77.

[4] Teilhard de Chardin, *The Future of Man*, 93. Teilhard adds: "But does it still hold this position, or at the best can it continue to hold it for long?"

evolve like any other biological organism: "the comparative value of religious creeds may be measured by their respective power of evolutive activation."[5] In answer to his own question concerning the most "suitable Religion of tomorrow" for mankind, he declared one month before he died, that there was one indisputable fact:

[T]he sort of Faith that is needed, in terms of energy, for the correct functioning of a totalized human world has not yet been satisfactorily formulated in any quarter at all—neither among the *religions of the Ahead* (Marxist and other Humanisms) nor among the *religions of the Above* (the various theisms and pantheisms).[6]

By the term "religions of the *Ahead*," he meant those focused on a future hope *exclusively* rooted in man's destiny in this world, rather than in one which transcends this one (that is, Heaven *Above*). In his effort to produce a more effective apologetic, he felt a responsibility to "modernize" Christianity, in order, as he put it, that he might make it "get off to a completely new start."[7] He believed his writings contained the seeds for a reformulation of what he termed "classical" Christianity, giving rise to a New Religion of Evolution which amalgamated the best features of the religions of "Above" and "Ahead" (the *En Haut* and the *En Avant*). "My life's whole effort," he wrote in 1955, can be summed up as a search for "the synthesis of the Above with the Ahead."[8]

He referred to this synthesis in 1951 as "a single religious thought (a Christology), adjusted to the new size of the universe."[9] He argued that the synthesis of the Above and the still-to-come (Ahead) operates, *essentially*, at the moment of the Incarnation, continues through the Eucharist, and will be consummated at the Parousia. He sought to incorporate into Christian faith, a faith in human progress and a faith in Man. In 1947 he wrote to a friend:

As I have been repeating constantly for the past year, the great event of modern times is the discovery that for Man, imprisoned within himself, there is a way out *ahead* (by self-development of something beyond Man), whereas previously the only way out we saw was *above* (by escape into God). It is the dawn of this "faith in Man" that appears about to eclipse the traditional faith in God. Under these conditions, my conviction is that if "ahead" (carried to the limit) cannot be understood

[5]Teilhard de Chardin, "The Christic," (1955), *The Heart of Matter*, 97.
[6]Ibid. Italics in original.
[7]Teilhard de Chardin, "Introduction to the Christian life" (1944), *Christianity and Evolution*, 160n.4.
[8]Teilhard de Chardin, *The Heart of Matter*, 44.
[9]Ibid., 108.

without "above," conversely "above" is even less understandable without "ahead," which means that the Christian faith can recover and survive only by incorporating faith in human progress.[10]

Here we see his advocacy of the old religion of progress. A year later he expressed his synthesis in terms of a complementarity between the upward (God of Above) and the forward (God of Ahead):

> [T]he conflict is not between Christianity and atheism, but between the old and traditional faith in a celestial escape *upward* and another new faith, in an evolutionary escape *forward*; and the capital thing to see is that between *upward* and *forward* there is no contradiction but essential complementarity. This is the very "core" of my message to Rome.[11]

He confined his criticisms of the religions of the Above to what he termed "false pantheism" and "classical" Christianity. He repudiated the latter for (1) failing to treat advances in knowledge and technology as the *primary* accompanying condition of human spiritualization, (2) overemphasis on the sanctifying value of suffering and failure, to the detriment of human progress and success, (3) emphasis on the Cross as a reminder of mankind's original sin and need of a Savior, and (4) the emphasis of coming catastrophe associated with the parousia at the expense of the message of the earth's fulfillment.[12]

He believed the Church was guilty of exaggerating the effects of the Fall on the world, of allowing the notions of sin and individual salvation to become "hypertrophied," and promoting a too-negative image of the Cross.[13] He regarded his "religion of Evolution" as an attempt to formulate a "Christianized" Humanism. As formulated, his religion is totally incompatible with all forms of true theism including Biblical Christianity.

Orthodox theologians have severely criticized Teilhard's writings. In five volumes expressing his anger, the French Carmelite Philip of the Trinity has shown definitively that Teilhard was not a Thomist. Jacques Maritain (1882–1973),[14] a leading and influential Thomist, referred to his work as "theological-

---

[10]Teilhard de Chardin, 16 October 1947, in *Letters to Two Friends*, 102. Italics in original.

[11]Teilhard de Chardin, letter 18 September 1948, in ibid., 186.

[12]Teilhard de Chardin, "The Christic" (1955), in *The Heart of Matter*, 98.

[13]Teilhard de Chardin, *Science and Christ*, 116.

[14]Maritain was professor at Paris 1913–1940 and at Toronto 1940–1944, and then French ambassador to the Vatican 1945–1948. For an insight into Teilhard's opinion on Maritain's theology see his letter of 16 April 1953, in *Letters From My Friend Teilhard*, 165: "Maritain . . . [is] incapable of thinking in terms of the dimensions of Cosmogenesis. He can only imagine 'changing' Man morally, of course; and he doesn't even seem to suspect that since the time of Aristotle and St. Thomas, Man has changed radically."

fiction" and accused him of "a sin against the intellect." He considered Teilhard's mishmash of science, faith, mysticism, theology, and philosophy as "inextricably mingled and confounded." He wrote that: Teilhard had "turned Christianity upside down, so that no longer [was it] rooted in the Trinity and Redemption but in the evolving Cosmos. No theologian, mystic, or meditative scholar, no matter how hard he tries, is equal to that—nor even a wonder-worker."[15]

The Roman Catholic scholar Dietrich von Hildebrand, who attended one of Teilhard's lectures in 1951, also referred to his work as "theology fiction." In his book *The Trojan Horse in the City of God*, he wrote:

> It was only after reading several of Teilhard's works, however, that I fully realized the catastrophic implications of his philosophical ideas and the absolute incompatibility of his *theology fiction* (as Etienne Gilson calls it) with Christian revelation and the doctrine of the Church. . . . writing on Teilhard is no easy matter. I do not know of another thinker who artfully jumps from one position to another contradictory one, without being disturbed by the jump or even noticing it.[16]

In a later book, *The Devastated Vineyard*, von Hildebrand documented the devastation wrought in the Roman Catholic Church by Teilhard's "theories" which he described as "absolutely incompatible . . . with the teaching of the holy Church."[17] He referred to "the faithful who are fighting the devastation of the vineyard of the Lord which is raging under the influence of Teilhardism."[18]

Etienne Henry Gilson (1884–1978) was a French Thomist thinker and historian of medieval philosophy. His comment on Teilhardism is well known: "We feel as though we were before an empty tomb: they have taken away Our Lord, and we don't know where they have laid him." Even the extreme radical (a)theologian Thomas J. J. Altizer (1927–), of the "Death of God" school,[19] has pointed out Teilhard's theological unorthodoxy:

---

[15]Jacques Maritain, "Teilhard de Chardin and Teilhardism," *U.S. Catholic* 33 (1967): 9-10. Father François Biot was indignant that Maritain dared to criticize Teilhard's work. See *Témoignage Chretien* (15 December 1966).

[16]Dietrich von Hildebrand, *The Trojan Horse in the City of God* (Chicago: Franciscan Herald Press, 1967) 228-29.

[17]Dietrich von Hildebrand, *The Devastated Vineyard*, trans. John Crosby and Fred Teichert (Chicago: Franciscan Herald, 1973) 254n.80.

[18]Ibid., 103.

[19]For Altizer the question of God is not a peripheral one but a very existential one. He claims we must deny God in order to be liberated as human beings. In Altizer's quasi-Hegelian metaphysics, God completely incarnates himself in the world and by the act of dying liberates man from an alien transcendent power. See T. J. J. Altizer and William Hamilton, *Radical Theology and the Death of God* (Indianapolis: Bobbs-Merrill, 1966).

It is true that Teilhard occasionally and inconsistently introduces traditional Christian language into the pages of *The Phenomenon of Man*, but this fact scarcely obviates the truth that virtually the whole body of Christian belief either disappears or is transformed in Teilhard's evolutionary vision of the cosmos.[20]

Some reviewers of Teilhard's work described him as "a Catholic deviationist." Many within his church have tried to refute this charge. Among them was the late C. C. Martindale SJ, who some believe refuted the charge once and for all in a letter he wrote about his friend to *The Times Literary Supplement.*

From my many talks with him [Teilhard], I am entitled to say that *he never meant to assert, or even think, that there was any "break" with, or even "discrepancy from," Catholic orthodoxy* in his view of human existence, though he knew that what he said (including his annoying neologisms)[21] would be surely misunderstood. . . . *He was quite sure (as I am) that he never meant to deviate from any of the great Catholic dogmas in which he wholeheartedly believed.*[22]

However, Teilhard himself made it clear that his intention was to transform orthodox Christian doctrine and bring about the appearance of the "trans-Christian" God.[23] In trying to bring Christianity into line with the dogma of evolution, he abandoned what he referred to as the "immobilist" and "extrinsicist" God of a prescientific humanity. He sought to replace this form of Christianity with "a Christianity reincarnated for the second time . . . in the spiritual energies of Matter. It is precisely the "ultra-Christianity" we need here and now to meet the ever more urgent demands of the "ultrahuman" (Superman-kind).[24] He wrote elsewhere:

What we now have to do without delay is to modify the position occupied by the central core of Christianity—and this precisely in order that it may not lose its illuminative value.

---

[20]Altizer, cited in Colin Chapman, *The Case for Christianity* (Herts UK: Lion Publishing, 1981) 132.

[21]Philip Hefner has noted: "Of course, he [Teilhard] was not the first thinker who felt obliged to exasperate his readers by writing his own dictionary of terms, but few have given birth to more verbal offspring than he." See Hefner, *The Promise of Teilhard*, 29.

[22]C. C. Martindale SJ, letter in the *Times Literary Supplement*, cited in *Teilhard de Chardin: Pilgrim of the Future*, ed. Braybrooke, 12. Italics mine.

[23]Lukas and Lukas, *Teilhard: A Biography*, 322.

[24]Teilhard de Chardin, *The Heart of Matter*, 96.

If we ask in what exactly this correction in *relationship* consists, the answer must be in bringing Christology and evolution into line with one another.

> . . . *nothing can any longer find place in our constructions which does not first satisfy the conditions* of a universe in process of transformation. A Christ whose features do not adapt themselves to the requirements of a world that is evolutive in structure will tend more and more to be eliminated out of hand—just as in learned societies today articles on perpetual motion or squaring the circle are consigned to the wastepaper basket, unread. And correspondingly, if a Christ is to be completely acceptable as an object of worship, he must be presented as a savior of the idea and reality of evolution.[25]

In his effort to resolve the conflict between what he called "the 'supernatural' Sense of the Divine" which he gained from his mother, and his "'natural' Sense of Plenitude", Teilhard allowed the "supernatural" to be assimilated by the "natural." The only way this assimilation could be effected, he wrote, was "by an interior adjustment of the Divine to the Evolutive."[26] An example from his writings of such an adjustment or transformation of Christian doctrine is the following:

> If we may slightly alter a hallowed expression, we could say that the great mystery of Christianity is not exactly the appearance, but the transparence, of God in the universe. *Yes, Lord, not only the ray that strikes the surface, but the ray that penetrates, not only Your Epiphany, Jesus, but Your diaphany.*[27]

To apply the word "transparence" to God involves a fundamental shift in outlook, from the traditional transcendence-language (God "above") and immanental-perspective (God "in" the world), to a third dimension in Christology.[28]

---

[25]Teilhard de Chardin, *Christianity and Evolution*, 77-78. Italics in original.

[26]Teilhard de Chardin, *The Heart of Matter*, 42. Teilhard added: "this is to say, of being unable to worship anything except from a starting point in the Tangible and Resistant."

[27]Teilhard de Chardin, *Le Divine Milieu*, 121. Italics in original.

[28]Anthony O. Dyson, "Marxism, Evolution and the Person of Christ," in *Evolution, Marxism and Christianity*, 81. See excursus entitled "The Transparence of God" in Thorleif Boman, *Hebrew Thought Compared with Greek* (Philadelphia: Westminster, 1960) 190-92. Boman points out that God's overall relation to the world is designated neither clearly nor exhaustively by the two concepts transcendence and immanence.

> What has been lacking up until now in the doctrine of God's relation to the world is a third term or relationship or a third dimension in the relation. God is not only above the world and in the world, but he is also *through* the world. . . . God's being

Rather than the universe demonstrating God's character and invisible attributes as taught in Scripture,[29] it now exhibits God's character for what it actually is. This approach ignores the impact of the Fall upon the natural world (Rom. 8:22) which means that unlike the written revelation of God, it fails to mirror a perfect image of God's character (Jas. 1:23-25).

If by the concept of "transparence" Teilhard meant that God was revealed *through* the world, then his statement is perfectly orthodox (see Eph. 4:6: "Who is Lord of all, works *through all* and is in all"). However, he meant something quite different. He was so enamored by the concept of Christ incarnated in the physical immensity of the cosmos that he wrote:

> If I firmly believe that everything around me is the body and blood of the Word [Christ], then for me . . . is brought about that marvelous "diaphany" which causes the luminous warmth of a single life to be objectively discernible in and to shine forth from the depths of every event, [and] every element.[30]

The depersonalizing of the blood and body of Christ in this fashion is a perversion of Christian doctrine.[31] Teilhard quite literally adored the Mass, believing that in the Transubstantiation[32] we see the beginning of the transfiguration of matter into God, a process he believed the entire cosmos would participate in at the end of evolution. In his famous essay "The Mass on the World" the transposition of bread and wine is mystically linked with the transubstantiation of the entire Universe in the Eucharist.

---

*through* the world is a separate category which expresses what is most characteristic of God's relation to the world in Greek as well as in Israelite terms. . . .

. . . God's transparence thus asserts that God is known through the world as the one who really is. . . .

We have found therefore, that the overall relationship between God and the world is three-sided, or perhaps better, it is triadic, which is precisely what we should have expected in a trinitarian religion. Perhaps this throws some light on the doctrine of the Trinity and particularly on Christology, for as the First Person of the Trinity corresponds to the transcendence and the Third Person to the immanence, so the Second Person of the Trinity corresponds to the transparence.

[29]E.g., Ps. 19:1-4; Rom. 1:19-20.

[30]Teilhard de Chardin, *The Heart of Matter*, 127.

[31]The biblical view, as Francis A. Schaeffer notes, is that "all of God's external creation is not an extension of His essence, but the thought of the Trinity preceded it and it reveals God." Schaeffer, *True Spirituality* (London: Hodder & Stoughton, 1972) 141.

[32]The Roman Catholic doctrine of Transubstantiation: "The changing of bread and wine into the Body and Blood of our Lord; the changing of one substance into another substance while retaining the accidents of the former things." *Concise Catholic Dictionary*, comp. Robert C. Broderick, 335-36.

In view of Teilhard's emphasis, it is understandable that he saw his duty as priest to "Christify" evolution:[33] "To Christify Matter: that sums up the whole venture of my innermost being . . . a grand and glorious venture."[34] He called the "Christification" of evolution *cosmogenesis*.[35] He sought to establish a new religion pursuing his mission with a zeal that few could match:

> What increasingly dominates my interest and my inner preoccupations, . . . is the effort to establish within myself, and to diffuse around me, a new religion (let's call it an improved Christianity, if you like) whose personal God is no longer the great "neolithic" landowner[36] of times gone by, but the Soul of the world—as demanded by the cultural and religious stage we have now reached. . . . it is a matter not of super-imposing Christ on the world, but of "panchristizing" the universe. . . . if you follow this path, you are led not only to widening your views, but to turning your perspectives upside down; evil (no longer punish-ment for a fault, but "sign and effect" of progress) and matter (no longer a guilty and lower element, but "the stuff of the Spirit") assume a meaning diametrically opposed to the meaning *customarily* viewed as Christian. Christ emerges from the transformation incredibly enlarged. . . . But is this really the Christ of the gospel? And if not, on what henceforward do we base what we are trying to build?[37]

Here are all the essentials of modernism, that is, the belief that Christian doctrine should be accommodated to the light of modern knowledge. Modernists believe that all doctrinal construction is relative, that the locus of revelation is experi-ence, and that doctrine develops in evolutionary jumps rather than as a gradual unfolding, as in the older image.[38]

More disturbing is the hint that Teilhard accepted that his "transformation" of Christian doctrine may drive one far from the Christ of the Gospels. He saw

---

[33]Cuénot, *Teilhard de Chardin*, 395.

[34]Teilhard de Chardin, *The Heart of Matter*, 47.

[35]Letter of 1 February 1954, cited in Cuénot, *Teilhard de Chardin*, 368.

[36]Henri de Lubac SJ agreed with Teilhard's perception of the problem when he wrote: "And if we have to take more care than in the past not to represent the divinity in the guise of a 'great "neolithic" landowner,' this in no way means suppressing or toning down God's personal characteristics—the very opposite. Nothing was nearer his [Teilhard's] heart than establishing and promoting faith in a personal God." See Henri de Lubac in Teilhard de Chardin, *Letters to Léontine Zanta*, 43.

[37]Ibid., 114. Italics in original.

[38]Anne Roche Muggeridge, *The Desolate City: The Catholic Church in Ruins* (Toronto: McClelland and Stewart, 1986) 38.

Christ as not only the "higher Soul [of] creation,"[39] "the true soul of the world,"[40] the "organizing soul of the Pleroma,"[41] but also the "'soul' of evolution." In the person of Christ, he saw "the cosmic aspect and function which make him organically the prime mover and controller, the 'soul' of evolution."[42] In his view, Christ acts on the evolutionary movement as a kind of "soul," organizing, constructing, guiding, and directing it, by drawing it into His final and perfect Unity at Point Omega.

He argued that his "Gospel of Human Effort" should first be promoted by the Church, with Jesus Christ presented to men "as the very Term, already vaguely apprehended by them, of universal development."[43] Men would be instructed that the World could only reach consummation through the Unity found in Christ.

Christian revelation, he wrote, can only be introduced into a Mankind "that has thus been sensitized and unified by the religious expectation of some *soul of the World*."[44] One may well wonder why Teilhard described his gospel as one of "Human Effort." This is answered in part in a letter he wrote to his cousin in 1915: "One of the surest marks of the truth of religion, in itself and in an individual soul, is to note to what extent it brings into action, that is, causes to rise up from sources deep within each one of us, a certain maximum of energy and effort."[45]

Another example of Teilhard's transposition of Christian doctrine is the following:

> To worship was formerly to prefer God to things, relating them to him and sacrificing them for him. To worship is now becoming to devote oneself body and soul to the creative act, associating oneself with that act in order to fulfil the world by hard work and intellectual exploration.[46]

In Teilhard's writings we find a complete reversal of the Christian hierarchy of values. For him cosmic processes rank higher than the individual soul.

---

[39]Teilhard de Chardin, *The Heart of Matter*, 124: "but do you, Lord Jesus . . . show yourself to those who love you as the higher Soul and the physical center of your creation?"

[40]Teilhard de Chardin, *Writings in Time of War*, 220.

[41]Teilhard de Chardin, *Le Milieu Divin*, 111.

[42]Teilhard de Chardin, *Christianity and Evolution*, 180.

[43]Teilhard de Chardin, *The Heart of Matter*, 215.

[44]Ibid.

[45]Teilhard de Chardin, letter of 4 July 1915. *The Making of a Mind*, 58.

[46]Teilhard de Chardin, *Christianity and Evolution*, 92.

Research and work rank higher than moral values.[47] He wrote that "research is the highest human function, embracing the spirit of war and bright with the splendor of religion. . . . [Research is] the supreme faith in Being, and therefore the highest form of adoration."[48] Teilhard "justified" his "transposition of concepts"—the immemorial metaphysical doctrines—because he considered that it was necessary at this present stage of human evolution, "necessary to justify the ambitions newly emerging in the heart of man."[49] In his earlier correspondence he admitted his qualms over his scientization of Christian belief:

> Sometimes I am a bit frightened to think of the transposition to which I have to subject the *vulgar* notions of creation, inspiration, miracle, original sin, resurrection, and so forth, in order to be able to accept them.[50]

The fact that Teilhard applies the term "vulgar," even if not in the pejorative sense, to the doctrines of sacred Scripture, should, as Hildebrand notes, "suffice to disclose the gnostic and esoteric character of his thought."[51] In Gnosticism, the creator god is not the ultimate reality, but rather a degeneration of the unknown and unknowable fullness of Being. The escape of the divine spark from its incarceration in the material, can be understood as the salvation of the deity itself.[52]

So should we classify Teilhard as a deviationist from Christian orthodoxy? To those who accused him of being an innovator and by implication a deviationist, he replied that his religion "in no way represents a compromise between Christianity and the modern world."[53] This answer could not have been further from the truth. In 1922 Teilhard confided in a friend his thoughts on his radical "reformulation of historical views on [the doctrine of] original sin."[54] A certain smugness is detectable in his comments:

> I don't think that in the history of the [Roman Catholic] Church anyone has "pulled off" such an adjustment (in the way of representation) of dogma as that of which we're speaking—though similar attempts have

---

[47]Hildebrand, *The Trojan Horse in the City of God*, 241.

[48]Teilhard de Chardin, *Building the Earth* (Wilkes-Barre PA: Dimension, 1965) 56.

[49]Teilhard de Chardin, *Science and Christ*, 181.

[50]Letter dated 17 December 1922, cited in Philippe de la Trinité, *Rome et Teilhard de Chardin* (Paris: Arthème, Fayard, 1964) 47.

[51]Hildebrand, *The Trojan Horse in the City of God*, 239.

[52]Douglas Groothuis, *Revealing the New Age Jesus* (Leicester UK: InterVarsity Press, 1990) 79.

[53]Teilhard de Chardin, "Some Reflections on the Conversion of the World" (1936), *Science and Christ*, 123.

[54]This doctrine is dealt with in detail in my second book.

been made and carried halfway, for example when geocentrism was abandoned.[55]

## 3.2 Teilhard and the "New Catholicism"

Teilhard's thought has been central to the change in Catholic spirituality over the last four decades. Even within the leadership of the conservative wing of the Catholic church, there are those who treat Teilhard as a "saint." Bishop Fulton J. Sheen, for example, described Teilhard as "faithful to his priesthood and his faith" and strongly urged that Teilhard should be canonized:

> As one looks at the various trends in our day, one sees that Teilhard's conception of spirituality is in the forefront. He knew that he had to pass through many hazards, but his was directed principally to the cosmic world. Others have been directed to the human world. This does not mean to say that Teilhard limited himself to anthropology and physics. His fundamental orientation was "to attain heaven through the fulfillment of earth. Christify matter."
>
> It is very likely that within fifty years when all the trivial, verbal disputes about the meaning of Teilhard's "unfortunate" vocabulary will have died away or have taken a secondary place, Teilhard will appear like John of the Cross and St. Teresa of Avila, as the spiritual genius of the twentieth century.[56]

Today, within the Roman Catholic Church in most parts of Europe and America, Teilhardism is the dominant trend. Teilhard is referred to with adulation by many of the "progressives" within that Church. In her book *The Desolate City: The Catholic Church in Ruins*, Anne Roche Muggeridge backgrounds the ready acceptance of Teilhard's ideas by modernists:

> A radical theory of theological evolution was essential to modernism if revolutionary doctrines were to be presented as legitimate developments of scriptural revelation. . . . Modernists . . . attached themselves to the charismatic figure of the Jesuit paleontologist Pierre Teilhard de Chardin, whose parascientific theory of cosmic evolution became the vehicle for their ideas about radical development in the structures and dogmas of the Church. . . . from before the First Word War through the

---

[55]Teilhard de Chardin, letter of 14 May 1944, cited in Rideau, *Teilhard: A Guide to His Thought*, 539. Teilhard also noted his abandonment of the idea of a worldwide flood as documented in Scripture (Gen. 6–8; 1 Pet. 1:20; 2 Pet. 2:5; 3:6).

[56]Fulton J. Sheen, *Footprints in a Darkened Forest* (New York: Meredith, 1967) 73.

Second Vatican Council, he was the single most important figure for modernist survival. If he had not existed, modernists would have had to invent him, which, in large measure, is what they did, glossing over embarrassing defects in his personality and scholarship while using his celebrity status and his theory of the cosmos evolving towards divinity to transport their own process theology.[57]

Teilhard has even been hailed by some theologians as a "prophet" of the "New Catholicism," because the emphasis on relativism in their "new theology" finds its roots largely in Teilhardism.[58] "Dogmatic relativism" was rejected by Pope Pius XII in the Encyclical *Humani Generis*. Malachi Martin notes:

> As Teilhard had filled the gap of "scientific" underpinnings for the new [liberal] theology of George Tyrrell S.J., so Liberation Theology— championed largely by Latin American Jesuits—provided a tangible objective for the new theories of Pierre Teilhard de Chardin S.J.: the liquidation of capitalist and transnational (i.e., American) economic imperialism.[59]

In Latin America a number of theologians, like Juan Luis Segundo, have developed links between the themes of liberation theology and evolution. In his book *An Evolutionary Approach to Jesus of Nazareth*,[60] Segundo interprets the "limited options" we find in the life of Jesus, and in Christian political practice today. He does this in terms of the constraints imposed by biology (as shown in the study of the evolutionary histories of organisms), and in terms of the concept of entropy (used in the physical sciences). His five-volume work includes many extended expositions of Teilhard, including the value of human work, guilt, the church in dialogue, and humanity taking charge of its destiny.

The general spirit of Teilhard can be identified in the many forms of political or liberation theology.[61] One its leading theologians, Leonardo Boff OFM, a Franciscan working in Brazil, was sentenced to a year of "devoted silence" by Rome in 1985 for his controversial theology. He resigned in April

---

[57]Muggeridge, *The Desolate City*, 38-40.

[58]W. Hurvey Woodson, "The New Roman Catholicism," in *The Banner of Truth* 58/9 (1968): 41.

[59]Malachi Martin, *The Jesuits: The Society of Jesus and The Betrayal of the Catholic Church* (New York: Simon and Schuster, 1987) 302.

[60]Juan Luis Segundo, *An Evolutionary Approach to the Study of Jesus of Nazareth* (Maryknoll NY: Orbis Press, 1988).

[61]See Eulalio R. Baltazar, "Liberation Theology and Teilhard de Chardin" (the 8th annual Teilhard Lecture), *Teilhard Review* 22/3 (August 1987): 71-86.

1992 and in his letter of resignation pointed to the friction with the Vatican, with its alleged "boxing-in of intelligent theology," as the reason for his resignation.

In a major work *Jesus Christ Liberator: A Critical Christology for our Times*[62] Boff presents a multidimensional interpretation of the Kingdom of God, set in a framework of Teilhardian salvation-history. A leading scholar of liberation theology in Britain, Gilbert Markus OP, has expressed regret at the retirement of Boff, describing the movement as "a Christian response to difficult political and economic problems, and to violence."[63] Albert Drexel, a Catholic ecclesiastic, has explained the Teilhardian connection underlying Liberation Theology:

> The modernism or neomodernism within Christianity, and especially within the Roman Catholic Church after the Second Vatican Council, is above all characterized by a turning away from the supernatural and an exclusive predilection for the world . . . *Teilhard's ideology was a precondition for this.* Inasmuch as he turned his back to the past, *fused God and the supernatural with the process of universal evolutionism,* and proclaimed religion to be an active participation in a progressive development ending in Point Omega, the basis was given for a humanistic cult of the secular ("ein humanistischer Diesseitskult").[64]

In her book *The Gates of Hell: The Struggle for the Catholic Church*, Anne Roche Muggeridge maintains that the "new Catholic left" including those in South America, are "committed to the transformation of society by revolution."

> The Marxist view [she adds], of the irresistible evolutionary process of humanity has been opportunely bolstered for the Catholic left by Teilhard de Chardin's "evolutionary Cosmos" process theology. Neither Marxism nor Teilhardianism has room for the concept of original sin and the fall of man, therefore no need for a belief in individual redemption. Both are deterministic and progressive, both hold that change is always for the better and man and society perfectible. To this

---

[62]Leonardo Boff, *Jesus Christ Liberator: A Critical Christology for our Times* (ET: London: SPCK, 1979; orig. 1972). Also see his work *Church, Charism, and Power: Liberation Theology and the Institutional Church* (ET: Petropolis RJ, Brazil: Vozes Editora, 1988).

[63]*The New Zealand Tablet* (5 August 1992): 9. Statements quoted from the *Catholic Herald.*

[64]*Ein Neuer Prophet?* (Stein am Rhein: Christiana, 1971) 115, cited in Smith, *Teilhardism and the New Religion,* 211.

worldview, the traditional Christian like [C. S.] Lewis or any conservative Catholic, is in total opposition.[65]

The Catholic Modernist movement which began in 1890 and crested prior to a papal condemnation in 1907, was an attempt at a theological response to the explosion of knowledge and criticism that confronted the believer as a result of nineteenth century intellectual and scientific developments. It was contracted from rationalist German Protestant biblical scholarship, and like process theology, which was developed out of the Enlightenment philosophy of Descartes, Hegel, Spinoza, and Kant, it rejected the historical truth of Sacred Scripture. The concepts of Divine "revelation" imparted to Man and God's intervention in human history, were abandoned and redefined as products or expressions of human religious psychology.

A number of outstanding Catholic theologians in England and continental Europe were attracted to "Modernist" theology derived from liberal Protestantism, including Alfred Firmin Loisy SJ (1857–1940),[66] George Tyrrell SJ (1861–1909), the Oratorian Lucien Laberthonière (1860–1932), Henri Bremond SJ, and layman Baron Friedrich von Hügel. The only woman among its major English figures, Maude Dominica Petre (1863–1942), outlived the movement by three decades to become its first historian and sympathetic critic. All felt that unless the traditional concept of faith was revamped, the Church had no chance of survival in an age of scientific criticism. All believed that once "historically conditioned" elements of Christianity were understood and set aside, the doctrines of the Church could then be adapted to the exigencies of contemporary thought. Religion and theology must stress both change and evolution, unhampered by frayed doctrines and mythologies. Modernist theology was popularized to such an extent that a growing "crisis in faith" developed within the Roman Catholic Church.

It is noteworthy that Alec Vidler, historian of Modernism and a thoughtful observer of the modern theological scene, wrote: "[Maude Petre] considered Teilhard de Chardin was attempting to do what the Roman Catholic Modernists would have done if they had been permitted to do their work."[67] However, Teilhard would certainly have resented being linked with the names of

---

[65]Anne Roche Muggeridge, *The Gates of Hell: The Struggle for the Catholic Church* (Toronto: McClelland & Stewart, 1975) 227.

[66]See M. D. Petre, Alfred Loisy: *His Religious Significance* (London: Cambridge University Press, 1944). For a brief summary of Loisy's deviations from orthodox Catholic belief, see George A. Kelly, *The Battle for the American Church* (Garden City NY: Doubleday, Image Books, 1981) 41-43. Loisy was excommunicated by name on 7 March 1908. He then not only left his Catholicism but Christianity as well.

[67]Clyde F. Crews, *English Catholic Modernism: Maude Petre's Way of Faith* (Notre Dame IN: University of Notre Dame Press; Turnbridge Wells, Kent UK: Burns & Oates, 1984) 93.

modernists like Loisy and Tyrrell. He had done his theological studies at the time of the modernist crisis and had read Tyrrell, Loisy, and many other writers of the period. Teilhard's supporters such as Henri de Lubac argue that he always remained "completely a stranger to modernism."[68] In his biography on Teilhard, Robert Speaight makes the same point:

> It would be a serious mistake, however, to suppose that [Teilhard's] tutors and contemporaries, or that Teilhard himself, were tinged with Modernism. The tendency of Modernism is to diminish the transcendent stature of Christ: Teilhard's concern was to enlarge it to cosmic proportions. So far from inventing a Christ to fit his own ideas, Teilhard had already found him in St. Paul. It was "He in whom all things consist"; "He who fills all things"; "the Christ who is all in all"; and "has ascended high above all the heavens to fill all things with his presence." It was the Christus Pantocrator of Byzantium, and more particularly the Christ of the Sacred Heart, freed from its popular iconography. Where the Modernist tends to imprison Christ in history at the same time as he questions the historicity of the Gospels which give him to us, Teilhard adores him when he is transfigured on the mountain, rises from the tomb, or is lost in the clouds above the heads of the Apostles. Whatever certain neomodernists may pretend to the contrary, the opposition could not be more clear.[69]

Unlike modernists, adds Speaight, Teilhard had no thought of "deducing Christian dogma from a mere inspection of those qualities which, according to the light of reason, characterize the structure of the world."[70] Teilhard claimed that his position was at the "antipodes of Modernism" when he wrote to his friend Pierre Lamare, who was well acquainted with the Moslem world and was attracted to it:

> Instinctively I share your preference for a Christ who would be "simply the Word." But a Christ, without historical personification, would not be capable (either in fact or reason) of emerging from metaphysical abstractions or hypotheses. The "success" of the Christ of Christianity is due to the association of his birth (which gives him the value of a *fact* or concrete *element* in the world) and his resurrection (which lets us grant him superhuman, and as it were, cosmic attributes). . . . The Modernists wanted to reduce Christ to a Mahomet, and this would mean

---

[68]Georges Crespy, *La Pensée théologique de Teilhard de Chardin* (Switzerland: Editions universitaires, 1961) 168. Cited in De Lubac, *The Eternal Feminine*, 165.

[69]Speaight, *Teilhard de Chardin*, 37-38.

[70]Ibid., 112.

the collapse of the whole physical edifice of the universe in Christ. Personally I feel myself at the antipodes of Modernism. . . . Christ must be endowed with certain physical properties—"theandric" as theology puts it—radically different from those of a simple prophet—who is a vehicle of truth without being in the least a center which organizes the universe. Christ must always be far greater than our greatest conceptions of the world, but for two or three centuries we have allowed him to appear hardly equal to them, or even smaller. That is why Christianity is so anemic at the present moment.[71]

Although Teilhard, as he insisted, may not have been a modernist in the classical sense, his approach differed little to that of the modernists, in that he allowed the language of dogma to be retained, while at the same time emptying it of its traditional intellectual content.[72] In its most extreme formulation, the theological "new paradigm," which emerged from the Modernist premises outlined, maintained that the Church has no special access to the truth about God (via revelation). God is present, or can be known, only within the world. His will is revealed by a directly inspiring "spirit" (which may or may not be the Holy Spirit) through existential experience. Man cannot have a "soul" distinct from the body, so therefore "salvation" is redefined in terms of a utopian "Kingdom of God" built on earth. Humans are all seen as potential incarnations of God.[73] Donna Steichen has admirably expressed the fallacy underlying the "postmodern paradigm":

If God is not a transcendent and incomparably superior Person but, as neomodernism maintains, simply the depersonalized "spirit" of mankind yearning for meaning, there can be no divine moral law, because there is no One "out there" whose nature it expresses. Man is adrift in an existential sea—with no hope of finding the right way home, because there is no right, and no home. Process thought sees his yearning as evidence of his collective divinity, creating the future. Man "perfects" God by cooperating in the prescribed revolution and establishing the utopian Kingdom.[74]

The concept as promulgated by Vatican II (11 October 1962 to 8 December 1965) that "the tradition of the church is a tradition of progress in understanding the truth,"[75] has been interpreted by modernists in the Darwinian sense, in

---

[71]Letters to Pierre Lamare, 23 April and 26 December 1929, in ibid., 162.

[72]Muggeridge, *The Desolate City*, 41.

[73]Donna Steichen, *Ungodly Rage: The Hidden Face of Catholic Feminism* (San Francisco: Ignatius Press, 1991) 256-58.

[74]Ibid., 281.

[75]Vatican II was called by Pope John XXIII in 1962 and was continued under Pope

keeping with Teilhard's "theology." Rama Coomaraswamy has responded to such claims as follows:

> But doctrine and the tradition that is its vehicle, cannot *develop* or *evolve* in some Darwinian manner any more than can that Truth which was given us by Christ and the Apostles. . . . Dogma may become clearer to us; it may be more tightly defined by the teaching magisterium (as part of its function of preserving what was revealed . . . ), but *it does not and cannot change.* . . . It should be clear that either Truth is important, and doesn't change, or it changes and then is of no importance. After all, the truth as a whole is eternal, incapable as such of any improvement or advancement.[76]

The Vatican II documents teach:

> Let them (the faithful) blend modern science and its theories and the understanding of the most recent discoveries with Christian morality and doctrine. Thus their religious practice and morality can keep pace with their scientific knowledge and with an ever advancing technology.[77]

The "spirit of Vatican II" is a spirit that accepts almost all the modernist concepts—"progress," "dynamic evolution," and "universalism." In fact, the concept of evolution underpins the Vatican II statements in the "Pastoral Constitution on the Church in the Modern World." Donald Campion SJ, a translator of this document, has said that: "Here as elsewhere, it is easy to recognize the compatibility of insights developed by thinkers such as Teilhard de Chardin in his *Divine Milieu* with the fundamental outlook of the [Vatican] Council."[78]

Pertinent to our analysis is the centrality of evolutionary dogma to the reformulations of Christian doctrine. The Pastoral Constitution, a document Pope Paul VI considered one of the most important and one in which he personally played an important role, states: "Thus the human race has passed from a rather static concept of reality to a more dynamic evolutionary one. In consequence there has arisen a new series of problems, a series as important as can be, calling for new efforts of analysis and synthesis."[79]

---

Paul VI until 1965. For a good introduction to the theology of Vatican II, see Christopher Butler, *The Theology of Vatican II*, rev. and enl. ed. (London: Longman & Todd, 1981; orig. 1967).

[76]Rama P. Coomaraswamy, *The Destruction of the Christian Tradition* (London: Perennial Books, 1981) 65-66.

[77]Ibid., 128.

[78]Walter M. Abbott SJ, ed., *The Documents of Vatican II* (New York: Guild, 1968) cited in Coomaraswamy, *The Destruction of the Christian Tradition*, 118.

[79]*Gaudium et spes*, par. 5, in *The Documents of Vatican II*.

This may well be true, but it does not follow that the timeless truths of Christian doctrine warrant reformulation just because the Darwinian delusion, or "cosmogenetic myth,"[80] as molecular biologist Michael Denton calls it, has been absorbed into our cultural milieu as a supposed fact. A number of scholars would dispute the view that the pre-Darwinian cultures of antiquity including the Hebrews held to a "static concept of reality," as Teilhard puts it.[81]

It is the idea of progress that underlies the modernist's compulsion to "adapt" the "faith once delivered to the saints" (Jude 3) to the modern world. Pope Pius XII warned that it was "these false evolutionary notions with their denial of all that is fixed or abiding in human experience, that have paved the way for a new philosophy of error." Despite these warnings the Pontifical Academy of Sciences issued a statement in 1982:

> We freely acknowledge that there is room for differences of opinion on such problems as species formation and the mechanisms of evolutionary change; nonetheless, *we are convinced that masses of evidence render the application of the concept of evolution to man and other primates beyond serious dispute.*

Robert Faricy SJ, who teaches at the Gregorian University in Rome, believes that: "Behind the Christocentric teleology of *Gaudium et spes* [Vatican II's Pastoral Document] lies the theology of Pierre Teilhard de Chardin, clearly the most important influence, even a dominating one."[82] Henri de Lubac considers that in the document the Council expresses "precisely what Père Teilhard sought to do."[83] Gregory Baum, a Canadian liberation theologian and a leading Teilhardian in the years just before and during Vatican II, is another who believes

---

[80]Michael Denton, *Evolution: A Theory in Crisis* (Bethesda MD: Adler & Adler, 1985) 358. Denton states: "Ultimately the Darwinian theory of evolution is no more nor less than the great cosmogenetic myth of the twentieth century."

[81]Edward M. Blaiklock, *Layman's Answer: An Examination of the New Theology* (London: Hodder & Stoughton, 1968) 16-25 (chap. 1, "No New World"). Blaiklock was professor of Classics at Auckland University, N.Z. He was a recognized authority in the spheres of N.T. studies and Greek classical drama.

[82]Faricy, "Teleology, Prophecy, and Apocalyptic in Teilhard's Eschatology," 3.

[83]De Lubac, *The Eternal Feminine*, 136:

> In its Constitution *Gaudium et Spes* the Council, it is true urges us to follow this course [outlined by Teilhard, namely, that our future hope lies in the Construction of the World] and so construct the world, but it would not have us lose our way. It points out to us, in the first principles of our faith, the only permanent foundation, the only permanent conditions, the only ultimate Term to be envisaged in such construction; and it shows us the only spirit in which it is rightly to be undertaken. This, again, is precisely what Père Teilhard sought to do.

that *Gaudium spes* embodied Teilhard's thought, though without explicit reference to him.[84]

In the foreword to his biography on Teilhard, Robert Speaight wrote that "much that he [Teilhard] had clamored for was implied or incorporated in [the Second Vatican Council's] decrees."[85] Michael Negus considers that a measure of the success of Teilhard's works, "can be seen by the influence of evolutionary thought on the Second Vatican Council, both in some of the Council's documents and the liturgical changes which followed."[86] Such claims have been disputed by some conservative scholars. Jacques Maritain, for example, would tell Teilhardians that if they went through the Council documents with a magnifying glass they would not find "the shadow of a shadow of encouragement" for their doctrine.[87]

Rama Coomaraswamy is quite correct when he states:

> These concepts of "progress" and "evolution" are the most pernicious pseudodogmas and pseudomyths that the world has ever produced. This is not to state that they do not exist, but their existence is partial and of quite limited applicability, and never without their antithesis in degradation and degeneration. The Truth, being timeless and immutable, is clearly immune from such "forces of change."[88]

### 3.3 Teilhard's Ecumenical Legacy

On 2 March 1978 about 400 people met at Caxton Hall in London to hear Professor William Johnston, an Irish Jesuit, give a talk on "Jung, Zen, and Yoga in the West." The meeting was organized jointly by the Guild of Pastoral Psychology and the Teilhard Center (London). Johnston, who is a former vice president of the Teilhard Center is famous as an interpreter of Zen and other forms of Buddhism and is active in Christian-Zen dialogue. He is director of the Institute of Oriental Religions, Sophia University, Tokyo. He spoke about the increasing communication between the world's religions, and made reference to his own experiences with students of Zen at Sophia University, in Japan.

---

[84]Teilhardian language is constantly resorted to by *Gaudium et Spes*: "an evolution towards unity, a process of wholesome socialization"; "a new age of human history"; "things in their mutable and evolutionary aspects"; "the human race is involved in a new stage of history."

[85]Speaight, *Teilhard de Chardin: A Biography*, 14.

[86]Michael Negus, "Reactions to the Theory of Evolution," *Studies in Comparative Religion* (Summer/Autumn 1978): 188.

[87]King, "The Milieux Teilhard left Behind," 91.

[88]Coomaraswamy, *The Destruction of the Christian Tradition*, 129-30.

In his book *The Still Point: Reflections on Zen and Christian Mysticism*, Johnston stated:

Not only Zen but all forms of Buddhism are going to make an enormous impact on the Christianity of the coming century. . . . There is every likelihood that the future will see the rise of an Oriental Christianity in which the role of Buddhism will be incalculably profound. Indeed this process has already begun.[89]

In another book, *The Inner Eye of Love*, Johnston deals with the convergent aspects of Christianity and Buddhism. He argues that "while the great religions differ in their beliefs, their members can be deeply united in faith."[90]

In a report entitled "Reawakening Christian Mysticism" in the *Teilhard Review*,[91] Johnston is quoted as stating: "It is as though one Spirit, filling and animating the universe, is driving us towards a point of convergence, a common point of intersection, where Buddhist and Christian, Hindu and Jew will meet." According to the report, he argued that "this one spirit in each religious tradition comes through the intuitive and mystical insight and experience, the knowing of the timeless and spaceless oneness of all." He accused the Christian Church of discouraging direct experience, with the result that "Christian mystics like Mother Julian and Teilhard are songbirds who have sung alone, to the silence, and are almost unknown to most people."[92]

Johnston believes the Christian culture needs to return to the Christian mystical traditions. In his book *Silent Music*, he refers to the mystic as "the builder of the future because he loves." With obvious Teilhardian emphasis he adds:

It is love that builds the earth and carries forward the thrust of evolution. It is love that brings together the great traditions in a union which cross-fertilizes even when it differentiates. It is love that leads them on towards Omega, the point of convergence, which is also the mountains, the solitary wooded valleys, strange islands. . . . silent music.[93]

Omega, the supposed point of intersection of all religious traditions, is defined here in terms consistent with monism and pantheism. Teilhard mapped out this path of evolutionary convergence involving all the major world traditions, arguing that a merger of mysticism and science would be the common factor

---

[89]Cited in Anthony de Mello, *Sadhana: A Way to God, Christian Exercises in Eastern Forms* (St Louis: The Institute of Jesuit Sources, 1978) x.

[90]William Johnston, *The Inner Eye of Love* (London: Collins, 1978) 69.

[91]Guy Dauncey, *The Teilhard Review* 13/2 (Summer 1978): 104.

[92]Ibid.

[93]William Johnston, *Silent Music: The Science of Meditation* (London: Collins, 1974) 173.

drawing them together. In 1941 he presented an address entitled "On the possible bases of a universal human creed" to the Congress of Science and Religion in New York.

Wolfgang Smith has noted that a number of Protestant and interdenominational institutions such as the World Council of Churches have "begun to turn in the direction mapped out by Teilhard de Chardin."[94] The following *Statement of Faith*, consisting of a blending of readings from Teilhard, included material from *The Phenomenon of Man* and *The Divine Milieu*, and was recited by 1,000 ministers and delegates in a liturgy at a convention of the National Council of Churches (USA):

| *Leaders Reading* | *People Reading* |
| --- | --- |
| Some thousands of millions of years ago, a fragment of matter composed of particularly stable atoms was detached from the surface of the sun. | WE BELIEVE IN GOD<br><br>WHO CALLS THE WORLDS |
| This fragment began to condense, to roll itself up, to take shape. | INTO BEING, |
| The curve doubles back, the surface contracts, the solid disintegrates, the liquid boils, the germ cell divides, intuition suddenly bursts. | CREATES US AND SETS BEFORE US |
| We are responsible for the quality of our future. We are *evolving* into an interdependent whole of which every person is called upon to become a vital part. | THE WAYS OF LIFE |
| Every organization insensitive to our need for personal involvement in the well-being of our fellow humans is disintegrating. | AND DEATH |
| Shock troopers of *evolutionary change* are now attacking all separatist structures. | WHO JUDGES PEOPLE AND NATIONS; TO BE CHRIST'S SERVANTS IN THE SERVICE OF HUMANKIND |

---

[94]Smith, *Teilhardism and the New Religion*, 211.

Whoever has discovered . . . the
secret of serving the *evolving Universe* and identifying with it . . .
BLESSING AND HONOR, GLORY AND POWER BE UNTO HIM. AMEN.[95]

The representatives of the five great historic religions who attended the
conference "One Is the Human Spirit" held in New York City 19-23 October
1975 on the occasion of the thirtieth anniversary of the United Nations, affirmed
the following statement:

> [T]he crises of our time are challenging the world religions to release
> a new spiritual force transcending religious, cultural, and national
> boundaries into a new consciousness of the oneness of the human
> community and so putting into effect a spiritual dynamic toward the
> solutions of the world's problems. This quickening spirit seen, for
> instance, in ecumenical events, such as Vatican Council II and the
> World Fellowship of Buddhists, is rising in our midst as a powerful
> operation of Spirit in history. We affirm a new spirituality divested of
> insularity and directed toward planetary consciousness. . . . It is crucial
> at this time to listen to those traditions that possess a deep bond and
> communion with nature and that foster a sacred and harmonious relation
> between man and earth.[96]

The forming of a "planetary consciousness" via "planetization" was
envisaged by Teilhard as coming about through the operation of the "law of
complexity-consciousness." In his writings the term "socialization" becomes
synonymous with terms such as "planetization of Mankind" or even the
"totalization" of humankind. In a postscript to *The Phenomenon of Man*, written
ten years after its completion, he described the social phase of human evolution
as "the ascent towards a collective threshold of reflection," a second stage of
hominization. He believed that during the phase of "ultrahominization," mankind,
under the pressure of external and internal forces, would create in itself a
"common Soul" aroused by the "Spirit of the Earth."

In his view, faith in the human being was the uniting basis for a humanity
seeking the spirit at its summit, and he saw the pull as coming from a point of
universal convergence in the future. True convergence implied an overall direc-

---

[95]NCC (USA), *A Statement of Faith* (program of Convention); cited in W. R. Bird,
*The Origin of Species Revisited: The Theories of Evolution and Abrupt Appearance*, 2
vols. (New York: Philosophical Library, 1989) 2:291-92.

[96]UN Declaration, *Houston Chronicle*, 3 November 1975, G-12. Cited in Marilyn Ferguson, *The Aquarian Conspiracy: Personal and Social Transformation in the 1980's* (Los
Angeles: J. P. Tarcher, 1980) 369.

tion and orientation as well as a common vision as to the nature of the summit to which the various currents were converging. He frequently referred to the energy driving the convergence as "amorization," the energy of love or attraction. It is based on a belief that everything that rises beyond itself through the love of something greater will, in fact, converge towards a summit. It is this Teilhardian vision of unity-in-diversity that is at the heart of the ecumenical movement within the United Nations and the drive towards establishing the Parliament of World Religions.

Teilhard was one of the early supporters of the World Congress of Faiths (WCF) which was founded in England in 1936 at the initiative of Sir Francis Younghusband. He wholeheartedly encouraged its promotion of what we call today "interreligious encounter and dialogue," an activity it is still engaged in. He once referred to the Congress as a "summit movement," thereby emphasizing its importance as a vehicle for directing the world religions towards a common focal point, a summit for diverse religious aspirations.[97]

After his return from China in May 1946, Teilhard was associated with the activities of The Congress's French branch (founded in 1947) for which he wrote several talks and lectures. Between 1947 and 1950 he wrote five direct contributions, one of which was written as an inaugural address to the branch, but was read by René Grousset, director of the Oriental museum in Paris. It was his writing that led Teilhard to a closer study of comparative mysticism.[98] Cuénot believes that "talking with Grousset helped Teilhard to see more clearly the implications of the religious currents he had become familiar with in the East."[99]

The theme of the inaugural address which Teilhard was invited to present, was that all peoples of different backgrounds and convictions can come together and cooperate through their common "faith in man." This faith is defined as "the more or less active and fervent conviction that Mankind as an organic and organized whole possesses a future," a future which is not defined as mere survival, but one that involves some form of higher life.[100] Fifteen years after the address was given, Louis Massignon, the well-known scholar of Islamic studies, in reflecting on the development of the French branch of the World Congress of Faiths, called the address "an outstanding text" which from the start provided a direction for the World Congress of Faiths.[101]

As stated in its journal *World Faiths*, the Congress aims "to break down the barrier of exclusivism and to build bridges between faiths." The orientalist Jacques Bacot speaks of Teilhard as a "guest and adviser who contributed all his

---

[97]King, *The Spirit of One Earth*, 119.
[98]Ibid., 135-37.
[99]Cuénot, *Teilhard de Chardin*, 298.
[100]Teilhard de Chardin, *The Future of Man*, 185.
[101]*Le Congrès Universel des Croyants—Historique—1946–1962*, 2.

ardor"[102] to the work of the association, and one of the general secretaries confirmed that Teilhard attended many of the committee meetings.[103] He consistently called for an awakening of faith in life, for without it he believed the forces of collectivity would break. This *gout de vivre*—the will to live and love life, was the title of his last contribution to the work of the Congress, an essay written on 9 December 1950. He argued that "The Zest for Living" was indispensable for the continuity of life and its dynamic was needed for the development of a higher life.[104]

He saw as one of the aims of the Congress to help work out a faith which allows people to become one with others. To achieve such a rapprochement people must be given opportunities for meeting and getting to know each other. If the human community was to attain a common Soul it must recognize the evolutionary role of religions and harness the untapped energies contained therein. An "ecumenism at the base" needs to be pursued, "a religion of mankind and the earth." For the "total terrestrial religious consciousness" to emerge, it would be necessary for the diversity and complementarity of all the "active currents of faiths," which today we call the "living religious traditions," to be recognized.

None could be seen as containing the whole truth, for it is only the sum total of these many visions and experiences that constitute the full religious heritage of humanity. A higher synthesis needs to be sought so that the many fragments of truth can express a supreme Ineffable. Mankind needs to be "sustained and guided by the tradition of the great human mysticisms," according to Teilhard, and "succeed, through contemplation and prayer, in entering directly into receptive communication with the very source of all inner drive (élan)."[105] He envisaged a coming together of East and West into a new unity linked to the sense of one earth and intimately related to what he called the development of a "terrestrial religious consciousness," or what New Agers and Teilhardians call today a "global spirituality." He referred to the process many time as the emergence of a new mysticism of action and convergence.

The spiritual crisis facing mankind "at the very peak of its power" he observed, was due to the fact that "it has not defined its spiritual pole. It lacks religion."[106] However, the nature of the religion it seeks cannot be found among the traditional ones of the past, for these he argued are tied to static categories. What is urgently needed is a new dynamic religion—"the religion of Evolu-

---

[102]J. Bacot, "Quelques Evocations," 146. Cited in King, *The Spirit of One Earth*, 136.
[103]Ibid.
[104]See Teilhard de Chardin, *Activation of Energy*, 229-43.
[105]Ibid., 242.
[106]Teilhard de Chardin, *Science and Christ*, 102.

tion"—one that could make good use of the "free energy" of the earth to build humankind into greater unity.

For Teilhard, all religions throughout time serve the human being's basic need for some Absolute. They give us, he stated, "a dominating principle or order, and an axis of movement . . . something of supreme value, to create, to hold in awe, or to love."[107] It is the biological function of religion to give form to the spiritual energies released in the cosmos with the emergence of man. Because of the advent of *noogenesis*—the thrust forward of life towards consciousness and self-reflective thought—an "ocean of free energy"[108] is created, an energy as real and as cosmic as the energy of matter. Since man was advancing through self-evolution, religion, too, must grow and redefine itself.[109]

The great gathering of the Assembly of World Religions in New Jersey in 1985 and others which have followed, are evidence of the growing interest in interreligious encounter and dialogue.[110] It is noteworthy that Ewert Cousins, general editor of the *Encyclopedia of World Spirituality*, says in his preface to the series: "it may well be that the meeting of spiritual paths—the assimilation not only of one's own spiritual heritage but that of the human community as a whole—is the distinctive spiritual journey of our time."[111] The American theologian Robley Edward Whitson, who has studied the implications of contemporary cultural and religious convergence in his stimulating book *The Coming Convergence of World Religions*, has questioned the ability of any religious tradition to remain separate and survive. He believes that a new "unity out of their diversity"[112] will emerge if dialogue-in-depth is more widely practiced.

Ursula King has noted: "Contemporary religiosity is characterized by a great search for interiority and a new inwardness, a longing to explore our 'inner space,' . . . accompanied and matched by a search for a greater outward unification and unity at all levels."[113] She also notes that many of today's "consciousness-raising" groups which seek to create "social transformation grounded in personal transformation," many of which have links to the New Age Movement, pursue goals in keeping with Teilhard's vision:

---

[107]Ibid., 99.

[108]Ibid.

[109]King, *The Spirit of One Earth*, 104.

[110]See M.D. Bryant, J. Maniatis, and T. Hendricks, eds., *Assembly of World Religions 1985. Spiritual Unity and the Future of the Earth* (New York: Paragon House, 1986).

[111]Ewert Cousins ed. *Encyclopedia of World Spirituality* (New York: Crossroad, 1985; London: Routledge & Kegan Paul, 1986).

[112]R.E. Whitson, *The Coming Convergence of World Religions* (New York: Newman Press, 1971) 52.

[113]King, *The Spirit of One Earth*, 16.

Such personal and social transformations are coming together in many contemporary liberation movements which are explicitly connected with the experience of consciousness raising, whether in political freedom movements or in the women's liberation movement. Such an actively initiated process of changing consciousness, of making individuals and groups more intensely and critically aware, is directly linked with the rise of consciousness in humankind of which Teilhard speaks.[114]

King fully endorses the pathway mapped out by Teilhard for the emergence of a "terrestrial religious consciousness." "For the spirit of one earth to emerge," she wrote, "we have to foster planetary consciousness and a global outlook. Our need for human transformation and spiritual evolution is great and urgent. . . . Through blending the insights of science, rationality, love, and mysticism, Teilhard de Chardin has much to give to our time where these aspects are still kept apart to our peril."[115] The integration of these aspects of Teilhard's thought have been highlighted in a number of publications which marked the centenary of his death. Sister Margaret McGurn's work entitled *Global Spirituality: Planetary Consciousness in the Thought of Teilhard de Chardin and Robert Muller*[116] is of particular interest. Muller, as noted, is a self-confessed active participant in the Aquarian conspiracy.

Muller, as a "true Teilhardian," considers the further development of spirituality as the next step necessary in the work of the United Nations in order to bring about the unification of the world rather than its disintegration. Although Teilhard was sensitive to other religious worldviews, he saw the further evolution of religion itself on a pattern of convergence, through the unification of the aims of the different faiths. Muller has expressed the ecumenical goals which need to be pursued by world religious bodies such as the World Congress of Faiths and it is not surprising to find that they are fully in tune with Teilhard's vision:

> While continuing to learn more about our planet and its proper management, we must now pass from the national to the planetary age and from the rational to the moral and spiritual age. We must reinsert ourselves into the total visions of the great religions and prophets. . . . The world's major religions must speed up dramatically their ecumenical movement and recognize the unity of their objectives in the diversity of their cults. Religions must actively cooperate to bring to unprecedent-

---

[114]Ibid.

[115]Ibid., 183.

[116]Sister Margaret McGurn, I.H.M., *Global Spirituality: Planetary Consciousness in the Thought of Teilhard de Chardin and Robert Muller* (Ardsley-on-Hudson NY: World Happiness and Cooperation, 1981). Also see Perlinski, ed., *The Spirit of the Earth.*

ed heights a better understanding of the mysteries of life and of our place in the universe. "My religion, right or wrong," and "My nation, right or wrong" must be abandoned forever in the planetary age.[117]

Muller closes his book *New Genesis* with a rewrite of the Genesis account of creation incorporating his Teilhardian vision for humanity. He envisages all nations of the earth, and all of the creeds, "sending their emissaries to a tall glass house [the United Nations] on the shores of the River of the Rising Sun, on the Island of Manhattan to study together, to think together and to care together for the world and all its people." He describes how "God" declared the activities of this group "good." On the seventh day he writes: "And God saw humans restore God and the human person as the alpha and omega, reducing institutions, beliefs, politics, governments, and all man-made entities to mere servants of God." The story ends with God declaring mankind mature, for having succeeded in bringing "heaven down to earth" and finding its proper place in the universe. God declares: "I now pronounce you Planet of God . . . Enjoy your divine lives." God then departs for another part of the universe to "turn [His] sight to other troubled and unfinished celestial bodies," leaving man alone to revel in "divine" ecstasy and bliss.[118]

Here we have a parody of the true Christian eschatological hope, namely Christ's coming again in Glory to reign and establish an everlasting Kingdom. The New Age/Teilhardian parody relies on the "deification" of Man and his works and the syncretistic gropings of mankind in a "trial and error" process towards a common unity based on a "new spirituality." Under the heading "A Moral and Spiritual Dimension," Muller wrote:

> After so many years of trial and error, the pattern of the prodigious human march toward greater fulfillment and consciousness is now becoming clear: For the first time in evolution, mankind is emerging as a true global entity, with a bloodstream, a nervous system, a heart, a brain, and a sense of common destiny . . . humanity is now being forged into a unit above and beyond all separate partial units. . . . mankind's vision is becoming all-inclusive in time. Our view is reaching from the Creation to the Apocalypse. . . . This revolution in thinking, this new time dimension of the human mind, this birth of futurology is just another major aspect of the gigantic and rapid march of man toward total consciousness.[119]

---

[117]Muller, *New Genesis*, 183.
[118]Ibid., 190-91.
[119]Muller, *Most of All They Taught Me Happiness*, 190-91.

The New Age vision of a syncretistic "unity-in-diversity" is a parody of the Christian eschatological hope in which unity is based on love of the truth, sound doctrine, joint participation in the Divine life through the "new birth" (see John 3:1-16), and membership of the Body of Christ. The New Age parody ignores the sober warnings of Scripture that the end of the Age will involve a cataclysmic destruction, an escalation in immorality and lawlessness, and mankind's deliberate turning away from the truth of revelation. These are the explicit teachings of Christ and His Apostles.[120] Christian eschatology rests on revealed truth, not wishful thinking. It is realistic rather than pessimistic. It calls for an action-oriented spirituality—one that can nourish all of human endeavor, a sober evaluation of the true nature of man, and an investment in those things that will last for eternity.

> But the day of the Lord will come like a thief, in which the heavens will pass away with a roar and the elements will be destroyed with intense heat, and the earth and its works will be burned up. Since all these things are to be destroyed in this way, what sort of people ought you to be in holy conduct and godliness, looking for and hastening the coming of the day of God, on account of which the heavens will be destroyed by burning, and the elements will melt with intense heat! But according to His promise we are looking for new heavens and a new earth, in which righteousness dwells.                                    —2 Peter 3:10-13

---

[120]E.g., Matt. 24 and 2 Peter 3:9-13.

# The "Conspiracy"

Teilhard was really a pioneer of what is today called "new age think-ing," one of the early observers of our planet Earth who clearly saw its need for a profound transformation, for an entirely new culture which cannot come about without a new spirituality. . . . The general principle of his spirituality is the emphasis on *creative transformation*.[1]

—*Ursula King*

*[W]e have reached a decisive point in human evolution*, at which the only way forward is in the direction of a common passion, a "conspira-tion."[2]

—*Teilhard de Chardin*

Planetary events are, in a sense, *conspiring to inspire us* to recognize our oneness and interdependence.[3]

—*Mark Satin*

For the spirit of one earth to emerge we have to foster planetary con-sciousness and a global outlook. Our need for human transformation and spiritual evolution is great and urgent. . . . Through blending the in-sights of science, rationality, love, and mysticism, Teilhard de Chardin has much to give our time where these aspects are still kept apart to our peril.[4]

—*Ursula King*

The open conspiracy must begin as a movement of explanation and propaganda.[5]

—*H. G. Wells*

---

[1]Ursula King, "Science and Mysticism: Teilhard de Chardin in Religious Thought To-day," *Teilhard Review* 19/1 (Spring 1984): 8, 11.

[2]Teilhard de Chardin, *Human Energy*, 153. Italics in original.

[3]Mark Satin, *New Age Politics: Healing Self and Society* (New York: Dell, 1979) 149.

[4]King, *The Spirit of One Earth*, 183.

[5]H.G. Wells, *The Open Conspiracy: Blueprints for a World Revolution*, rev. ed. (London: Leonard and Virginia Wolf, 1930).

## 4.1 The New Age Movement

The first comprehensive analysis of the goals, direction, and composition, of what has come to be called the "New Age" Movement, was provided by Marilyn Ferguson in her best-seller *The Aquarian Conspiracy: Personal and Social Transformations in the 1980s*,[6] first published in 1980. Aquarius the Water Bearer is the zodiac sign under whose influence New Agers believe man will discover his infinite potential, through a fundamental shift in people's consciousnesses and their relationships to the rest of the planet. Astrologers argue that for the last 2,100 years or so the spring equinox (approximately 21 March in the Northern Hemisphere) has been in Pisces, but is now shifting into Aquarius. Astrologers usually take the spring equinox as the beginning of the astrological year, and the position of this equinox in the zodiac determines the characteristic age.

Ferguson, a New Age advocate and consciousness researcher, is well known for her other book *The Brain Revolution*[7] and as editor of a bimonthly research report, the *Brain/Mind Bulletin*. She refers to the "pervasive dream in our popular culture," that with the closing of a dark, violent age, the Piscean, there will be the dawning of the Age of Aquarius.[8] It is believed that this millennium of love and light and global spirituality/consciousness will quench mankind's innermost longings.[9] Many New Agers believe we are about to enter this period, while some believe that we have recently entered it. The general consensus among those in the latter group is that this transition occurred around the late 1960s, with a focusing of votes around 1967.[10]

In a review of *The Aquarian Conspiracy* published in *The Teilhard Review*, Austin Wise stated: "Dr. Ferguson comes very near to Teilhard's idea of the nature of reality."[11] In the course of research for her book, Ferguson interviewed 185 New Age Movement leaders and asked them: "Which modern thinker/writer has had the most influence on your work?" The name most frequently mentioned was that of Teilhard de Chardin.[12] As yet, no detailed analysis has been made of

---

[6]Marilyn Ferguson, *The Aquarian Conspiracy: Personal and Social Transformations in the 1980s* (Los Angeles: J. P. Tarcher, 1980).

[7]Marilyn Ferguson, *The Brain Revolution* (New York: Taplinger, 1973).

[8]See V. W. Reid, *Toward Aquarius* (New York: Arc Books, 1971) 95, 97-98, 108-109.

[9]Ferguson, *The Aquarian Conspiracy*, 19.

[10]Peter Russell, *The Global Brain: Speculations on the Evolutionary Leap to Planetary Consciousness* (Los Angeles: J. P. Tarcher, 1983) 175.

[11]Austin Wise, review of *The Aquarian Conspiracy*, *Teilhard Review* 19/2 (Summer 1984): 62-63.

[12]Ferguson, *The Aquarian Conspiracy*, 50, 420. She received responses from 185 lead-

the link between Teilhard's thinking and New Age thought. The present work seeks to establish this link and the sequel will provide a more comprehensive analysis of Teilhard's thought.

The Aquarian Conspiracy is defined by Ferguson as a transnational network of "segmented polycentric integrated networks" (SPINs). Such a network has the characteristic of looseness: it is evolutive, and its centre is everywhere. It is a tool for change, for the next step forward in human evolution (cf. Teilhard's concept of the socialization of man). The Aquarian Conspiracy (the New Age network and its activities) is considered to constitute a Radical Centre, facilitating the emergence and development of the individual, within the "holistic universe" as a centre of power, a centre which is helped to function by personal and group applications. While Ferguson and others have denied that the Movement has leaders and structure, their statements are belied by the abundance of network data, statements of purpose, organizational charts, and directories—all indicating a high level of leadership and structure. The SPINs are in collusion and the "conspirators" are actively seeking a radical transformation of humankind in order to issue in a higher centre of consciousness at the apogee of Evolution. They are all, to use Teilhard's term, "servants of Evolution."

The New Age Movement has been identified by Eileen Barker,[13] a sociologist of religion from the London School of Economics, as involving a number of seemingly disparate groups including the Human Potential Movement[14] (or transpersonal psychology),[15] occultism, neopaganism, witchcraft, shamanism, and

---

ers of whom 131 were male and 54 female. Other leading influences included psychologists C. G. Jung (1875–1961), Abraham Maslow (1908–1970), Carl Rogers, British author Aldous Huxley (cofounder of the human potential movement), Roberto Assagioli, and J. Krishnamurti.

[13]Eileen Barker, *New Religious Movements: A Practical Introduction* (London: Her Majesty's Stationary Office, 1989).

[14]Ibid., 180-82. The Human Potential Movement, founded by Aldous Huxley, refers to a wide variety of activities, all resting on the belief that there is more to most of us than meets the eye, that we have much unrealized potential. It further rests on the assumption that individual change can be brought about through self-help. Primarily, one merely needs to be open to the possibilities of change, to be educated about some of these possibilities, to experiment with them, and to be determined to have them make a difference. Practically any activity or interest can be entered under the aegis of the human potential belief, including nutrition, astrology, graphology, meditation, mysticism, and psychotherapy. See Stephen Appelbaum, *Out in Inner Space: A Psychoanalyst explores the New Therapies* (New York: Doubleday/Anchor, 1979).

[15]Transpersonal psychology (TP) has been defined by Walsh and Vaughan as "the study of optimal psychological health and well-being. It recognizes the potential for experiencing a broad range of states of consciousness, in some of which identity may extend beyond the usual limits of the ego and personality." See Roger N. Walsh and Frances E.

satanism. Barker believes it is a very complex sociological phenomenon and its significant influence on cultural developments in the West has not as yet received much exposure by the media. When journalists do try to expose some of the more extreme components of the movement, they are often amazed to discover what a mishmash of beliefs have been accepted by gullible, yet sincere, disciples of New Age thought.

A case and point is a recent "60 Minutes" documentary on a New Age cult based in Sydney, Australia, which screened on Television One in New Zealand on 21 January 1996. While the cult was not identified as New Age as such, it clearly exhibited all the hallmarks of New Age thought. The cult leader believed himself to be a reincarnation of Tutankhamen, Jesus Christ, and Buddha, and regularly made vocal communications from the Sydney Coast to whales from whom he received direct messages. He called his group of devoted followers "the pod" and claimed to have miraculous powers as "evidenced" by the testimonies of those within the cult who had been healed by him. He claimed to have "all truth" and impart "fuller being" to his followers. He taught them how to gain "enlightenment" through the experience of "cosmic consciousness" and unfolding their inner potential. The interviewer was aghast at the practices and beliefs of cult members, who through regular tithing, supported the opulent lifestyle of their leader.

Some scholars who have recognized the existence of the New Age Movement genuinely believe it is limited to a few visionaries whose impact on society will be very minimal at most. Stanford history professor Paul Robinson has gone as far as to suggest that the New Age Movement may in fact exist "largely in Marilyn Ferguson's head." He has criticized her *Aquarian Conspiracy* as "an exercise in mindlessness" that obliterates "most of what our civilization has achieved" in its "thoughtless pages." He accuses her of an analysis that "is wholly uncritical, an abdication of the power of the mind." If the movement does

---

Vaughan, "Beyond the Ego: Toward Transpersonal Models of the Person and Psychotherapy," *Journal of Humanistic Psychology* 20/1 (1980): 9. TP encourages input from the experiences of people in altered states of consciousness, whether chemically induced or brought about by any number of consciousness disciplines (e.g., yoga, meditation, etc.), since these states result in the TP experiences that produce the sense of unity with the universe. Ibid., 9, 10. The TP model is defined in terms of four dimensions: consciousness, conditioning, personality, and identity. TP explains consciousness in terms of four levels, with reality appearing differently at each level of consciousness. Thus reality is relative, and a full description of reality must take into account the findings at all levels. TP is concerned with going beyond (trans)personal awareness to the state of unconditioned pure awareness where a person is one with everything. Absolute transcendence is the ultimate concern of TP. See George B. Leonard, *The Transformation: A Guide to the Inevitable Changes in Humankind* (New York: Dell, 1972).

exist, he condemns it and describes those who might be part of it as displaying "a psychological immaturity and a contempt for the mind that are truly chilling."[16]

Leaders of the New Age Movement claim that thousands of followers are involved belonging to a wide variety of societies and networks, ranging from health-food chains and meditation groups to political parties like the (American) Human Ecology Party and such lobby groups as Planetary Citizens and World Goodwill.[17] There are groups pursuing the development of "paranormal" abilities such as aura reading, telepathy, and past-life experiences, and various forms of divination from astrology and tarot to geomancy and radionics.

There are magazines entitled *New Age*, *New Directions*, *New Humanity*, *New Equinox*, *New Times*, *New Roots*, and *New Realities*. There are also mass gatherings—celebrations of consciousness, awakening festivals, Aquarian festivals, festivals of mind-body-spirit, world symposiums of humanity, and omniversal symposiums.[18] While not a cult in the strict sense, the New Age Movement includes groups like the Movement of Spiritual Awareness (MSIA) and the Sufi Order in the West which are *less* exclusive than most cults, as well as a few true cults (for example, Transcendental Meditation).[19]

Barker considers that the New Age Movement is "not so much *a* 'movement' as a number of groups and individuals that have a number of beliefs and orientations" that share a "family resemblance."[20] This useful phrase, as she points out, was coined by philosopher Ludwig Wittgenstein. It is based on the fact that two family members may bear almost no resemblance to each other, although they both resemble a third member. The borderlines between member groups often appear fuzzy and ill-defined.

Donna Steichen has come to similar conclusions. The New Age Movement "is not a centrally directed cult like the Unification Church. It is an esoteric socioreligious worldview shared by many loosely affiliated autonomous groups on different intellectual and cultural levels, *which at first glance seem to bear little resemblance to each other*."[21]

Barker links the "radical change" in consciousness promoted by New Agers to their belief in Man's progressive evolution and spiritual change. "One belief

---

[16]Paul Robinson, "The Coming Unenlightenment," *Psychology Today* (February 1980): 108-14.

[17]Most of the important groups are listed in E. Campbell and J. H. Brennan, *The Aquarian Guide to the New Age* (Wellingborough, 1990) 339-52.

[18]Russell, *The Global Brain*, 174.

[19]Elliot Miller, *A Crash Course on the New Age Movement* (Grand Rapids MI: Baker Book House, 1982) 16.

[20]Barker, *New Religious Movements: A Practical Introduction*, 189.

[21]Steichen, *Ungodly Rage*, 211.

commonly found among New Agers," she states, "is that humanity is entering the dawn of a new form of consciousness: humanity is currently undergoing radical spiritual change; it has reached the Aquarian frontier. . . . Evolution is important, but it is spiritual rather than material or technological evolution that is celebrated."[22]

Ferguson states that "the paradigm of the Aquarian Conspiracy sees humankind embedded in nature. . . . Heirs to evolutionary riches, we are capable of imagination, invention, and experiences we have only glimpsed. Human nature is neither good nor bad but open to continuous transformation and transcendence. It has only to discover itself."[23] This "vision" of "spiritual evolution" is elaborated in New Age Movement literature such as *Unfinished Animal: The Aquarian Frontier and the Evolution of Consciousness* by Theodore Roszak.[24]

It is Teilhard's "vision" of a new progressive stage in Man's spiritual evolution issuing in a New Age of Enlightenment that has provided some of the philosophical underpinnings for the New Age Movement. Its leaders see the potential for change and transformation as lying within the natural resources of the mind. As Ferguson states, "Only through a new mind can humanity remake itself, and the potential for such a new mind is *natural*."[25] "The proven plasticity of the human brain and human awareness offers the possibility that *individual evolution* may lead to *collective evolution*."[26]

At the 1976 *Habitat: United Nations Conference on Human Settlements* held in Vancouver, Pierre Trudeau, the then prime minister of Canada, concluded his opening address after specifically referring to Teilhard:

> It is clear that in order to survive, we will be forced to socialize ourselves more and more. What is actually meant by "socializing?" From a human viewpoint, it means loving one another. We will have not only to tolerate one another, but also love one another in a way which will require of us an unprecedented desire to change ourselves. Such a change will be more drastic than a major mutation of our species.
>
> The only type of love which would be effective in the tightly packed world we already live in would be a passionate love. The fact that such a statement sounds slightly absurd is a measure of the extent of the change we must make if we are to save ourselves.

---

[22]Barker, *New Religious Movements*, 190.

[23]Ferguson, *The Aquarian Conspiracy*, 29.

[24]Theodore Roszak, *Unfinished Animal: The Aquarian Frontier and the Evolution of Consciousness* (New York: Harper & Row, 1975). In this book Roszak states that the goal of NAM is "to awaken to the god who sleeps at the root of the human being" (225).

[25]Ferguson, *The Aquarian Conspiracy*, 45.

[26]Ibid., 70.

"Love one another, or you will perish," writes Teilhard in "L'Energie Humaine," adding that we have reached a critical point in human
evolution in which the only path open to us is to move toward a
common passion, a *"conspiracy" of love.*

*The conspiracy of men with men and the conspiracy of the universe*
with an even more just humanity: In this lies the salvation of human
settlements.[27]

What exactly is this "conspiracy" of love which will be effected by a change in
mankind "more drastic than a major mutation of our species" and lead to our
salvation? In what sense will this "major *mutation* of our species" take place?

To answer these questions we need to examine the writings of Teilhard de
Chardin, of whom Claude Cuénot (1911–1992) his major biographer wrote: "by
himself [he] personifies in a certain way, on the spiritual plane, a *mutation* of
homo sapiens."[28] We also need to examine the concept of a "conspiracy" of love
in material written by New Age Movement leaders and those promoting
Teilhardianism.

Ursula King has stated:

Like most of his contemporaries, Teilhard takes it for granted that a
basic mutation has already taken place in modern post-Darwinian, post-
Marxian, and post-Freudian consciousness, but he postulates yet another
necessary mutation: a greater awareness of humanity's necessary
collectivity and the emergence of a higher collective consciousness,
composed of innumerable individuals, just as the individual brain is
formed of innumerable cells.[29]

In Teilhardian language a "mutation" is a jump to a higher plane of consciousness through "enlightenment," a new state of self-transcendence, or a new way
of "seeing" with the spiritual intellect.

New Age Movement leader Fritjof Capra (professor of theoretical physics,
University of California, Berkeley) has documented the objectives and thinking
behind the movement in his book *The Turning Point: Science, Society and the
Rising Culture*,[30] first published in 1982. He has noted that the various components of the movement, advocate a "shift to the value system" and are "supported

---

[27]Opening address from UN conference quoted by Bernard Towers, "Toward an Evolutionary Ethic," *Teilhard Review* 12/3 (October 1977): 84.

[28]Claude Cuénot, *Teilhard de Chardin* (Ed. Il Saggiatore) 67. Cited in Zonneveld, ed.,
*Humanity's Quest for Unity*, 113.

[29]King, *The Spirit of the One Earth*, 39.

[30]Fritjof Capra, *The Turning Point: Science, Society and the Rising Culture* (New
York: Simon and Schuster, 1982; repr. New York: Bantam, 1983).

by a number of spiritual movements that reemphasize the quest for meaning and the spiritual dimensions of life." He sees components of the New Age Movement such as the holistic health movement, the human potential movement, and the ecology movement, as involved in this "cultural transformation."[31]

Another New Age Movement leader, Robert Muller, whom as we have noted above in §1.1 is ex-general secretary of the United Nations, chancellor of the University for Peace, and a former vice president of the Teilhard Center (London), has stated:

> If Christ came back to Earth one of his first visits would be to the United Nations to see if his dream of human oneness and brotherhood had become true. He would be happy to see representatives of all nations, North and South, East and West, rich and poor, believers and nonbelievers, young and old, Philistines and Samaritans, try[ing] to find answers to the perennial questions of human destiny and fulfillment.[32]

It is significant that all three New Age leaders (Muller, Ferguson, and Capra) were drawn together as official conference speakers at a United Nations sponsored conference "Spirit of Peace," held in Malta in early March 1985. This intercultural gathering was organized by the United Nations-approved University for Peace to celebrate forty years of the United Nations. In the same year, the University published the colloquium papers delivered in honor of Teilhard de Chardin at the United Nations in 1983. This publication, discussed above in §1.1, was the first in a series called "Great Visionaries of World Peace."

The promotional literature for the event in Malta referred to the need for a global "mass consciousness." In order to achieve this objective, the brochure stated: "a number of renowned speakers from different cultures [and] different spiritual traditions," have been invited, including "scientists of various disciplines." "Together they represent a wide variety of cultural backgrounds, religious persuasions. . . . It is precisely this variety and richness which, we believe, will reveal the 'spirit of peace' as being an absolute constant in all systems of ethics. Taking a stand on common ground we will address our invocation to this spirit."

The list of conference speakers also included Cornela Durant (international director of Greenpeace), His Holiness Tenzin Gyatso (the XIV Dalai Lama of Tibet), Zentatsu Richard Baker-Roshi (Zen Buddhist proponent), Rai Zalman Schacter Shalomi (professor of religion in Jewish Mysticism and Psychology of

---

[31]Ibid., 415.

[32]Robert Muller, "Establishing Right Human Relations," *Teilhard Review* 16/3 (Winter 1981): 27. Talk given in New York to the New Group of World Servers. Article originally appeared in *World Goodwill Occasional Papers* (1978).

Religion at Temple University), two Nobel peace prizewinners—Bishop Desmond Tutu and Mother Teresa, Phillip Deere (a medicine man and spiritual advisor to the American Indians), and others.

In an article on science and mysticism published in *The Teilhard Review* in 1984, Ursula King stated:

> Teilhard was really a pioneer of what is today called "new age think-ing," one of the early observers of our planet Earth who clearly saw its need for a profound transformation, for an entirely new culture which cannot come about without a new spirituality. . . . The general principle of his spirituality is the emphasis on *creative transformation.*[33]

King points out that in the late thirties Teilhard reflected on the role of spirituality and pleaded for technicians and engineers of spiritual energy resources who can help to develop the sense of one world, of one human family. He saw their urgent task was "to develop, by awakening and convergence, the individual riches of the earth."[34] He was concerned that humanity would lose its zest and love for life, the will to work for a better life, for building up one world together in the spirit of love and unification rather than hatred and division. He emphasized the need for the religions themselves to change in order to meet the new needs of the modern world; and to develop a new morality and ethics to deal with our global problems.[35]

In the introduction to her book *The Spirit of One Earth: Reflections on Teil-hard de Chardin and global spirituality* (1989), King notes: "Although he did not use the recently coined term 'global spirituality,' [Teilhard] nonetheless possessed the vision to which this expression points."[36] The expression is central to Aquarian ("New Age") thought and aspirations.[37]

## 4.2 Teilhard and the "Conspiracy" of Love

Teilhard rejoiced unreservedly at the creation of the United Nations in 1945 and the development of the prototypes of the "noospheric" structures he envisioned. No doubt he would have been delighted in the initiatives shown by the United Nations to foster peace through such a gathering as the one held in Malta in 1985. He believed that "Mankind is not only capable of living in peace but by

---

[33]King, "Science and Mysticism: Teilhard de Chardin in Religious Thought Today," 8, 11.

[34]Teilhard de Chardin, *Human Energy*, 106.

[35]King, "Science and Mysticism," 8.

[36]King, *The Spirit of One Earth*, 1-2.

[37]See McGurn, *Global Spirituality*.

its very structure *cannot fail eventually to achieve peace*."[38] The process of peace fitted into his theory of creative union: unity-in-diversity; where union/peace is the growth and development towards fuller being. Peace would be the inevitable fruit of "planetary convergence" or "planetary consciousness," and the product of "psychic evolution."

His faith in the future of man was inspired by his understanding of the past evolution of man involving the mysterious crossing of a "critical point" from "animal psychism" to "reflection." He believed that this "critical point" foreshadowed "*a decisive point in human evolution*, at which the only way forward is in the direction of a common passion, a 'conspiration'."[39]

> All that matters at this crucial moment is that the massing together of individualities should not take the form of a functional and enforced mechanization of human energies (the totalitarian principle), but of a "conspiracy" informed by love.[40]

Teilhard believed that "animal psychism" could not continue to unify indefinitely without finding itself compelled to change its nature by "some deep creative force." He did not concern himself with the metaphysical conditions of this force's existence, but rather, focused on the "curve of phenomena" of psychic development.[41] He believed that once the hominid brain reached a specific point of evolutionary development in terms of self-awareness, it crossed into "reflectivity."

"Reflection," according to Teilhard, "is the faculty possessed by every human consciousness of turning in on itself in order to recognize the conditions and mechanism of its activity."[42] From this "psychic" factor, "has arisen the discovery of the artificial instrument and, consequently, the invasion of the world by the human species."[43] Through man's inventions he believed "psychic energies [were] invading the domain of transformation from within."[44] In 1954, under the heading "Critical point of reflection," he wrote:

> As a result of some "hominizing" cerebral mutation, which appears among the anthropoids [ape-like creatures] towards the end of the Tertiary period, psychic reflection—not simply "knowing" but "knowing that

---

[38]Teilhard de Chardin, "Faith in Peace" (1947), *The Future of Man*, 151-52. Italics in original.

[39]Teilhard de Chardin, *Human Energy*, 153.

[40]Teilhard de Chardin, *The Future of Man*, 54.

[41]Teilhard de Chardin, "Hominization" (1923), *The Vision of the Past*, 73n.1.

[42]Ibid., 60.

[43]Ibid.

[44]Ibid., 71.

one knows"—burst upon the world and opens up an entirely new domain for evolution.[45]

With the triumphant emergence of a uniquely human quality, namely, the tendency of man to identify consciously with the others of his species and cooperate in common work, evolution could progress to even higher levels. Teilhard suggested that "by the direct converging of its members," mankind will be able, "as though by resonance, to release psychic powers whose existence is still unsuspected."[46]

He argued that the end of Man involved passing through "a *critical point of speciation* . . . not disintegration and death, but a new breakthrough and a rebirth, this time outside Time and Space, through the very excess of unification and co-reflection."[47] He believed that this psychic energy had been accumulating since the birth of true man in the form of a developing Noosphere, or thinking envelope around the earth.

Teilhard's friend Edouard Le Roy (1870–1954), a French professor of philosophy, coined the word "conspiration" to describe man's unique quality of conscious cooperation.[48] Teilhard applied this favorite expression of his friend to refer to "the noospherical phenomena of *sympathy*."[49] From "conspiration," wrote Teilhard, "is born the entirely new form of connection that distinguishes the human layer from all other departments of earthly life." It is "the aptitude of different consciousnesses, taken in a group, to unite (by language and countless other, more obscure links) so as to constitute a single All, in which, by way of reflexion, each element is conscious of its aggregation to all the rest."[50]

He believed that there was no healthier or more realistic foundation for the modern world, than the quest for human "conspiration."[51] He predicted "at a finite distance in the future, a critical point or peak of common [human] encounter," which he defined as an "ultimate centre of coreflection or, more completely, as a focus point of 'conspiration' of the thinking monads."[52]

---

[45]Teilhard de Chardin, "A Summary of My 'Phenomenological View' of the World" (1954), *Toward the Future*, 213.

[46]Teilhard de Chardin, "The Formation of the Noosphere" (1947), *The Future of Man*, 177.

[47]Ibid., 302. Italics in original.

[48]Teilhard acknowledges Le Roy's use of the expression in a number of places. See Teilhard de Chardin, *The Vision of the Past*, 60; *Activation of Energy*, 345. Teilhard also borrowed from Le Roy the idea of an invention as an example of "the awakening and translation into an organism of a desire and a potentiality." *The Vision of the Past*, 97.

[49]Teilhard de Chardin, *The Appearance of Man*, 255. Italics in original.

[50]Teilhard de Chardin, *The Vision of the Past*, 60.

[51]Teilhard de Chardin, *Activation of Energy*, 17.

[52]Ibid., 345.

This focus was "necessarily determin[ed]," in his view, by the existence of a "psychic trend in the universe—a trend that draws the human mass under pressure (and *because* it is under pressure) towards ever-more-reflective states of consciousness."[53] The development of a "worldwide human organization" seemed to be demanded, according to Teilhard "by the generally disseminated evidence of [man's] phyletic convergence to some yet unsuspected form of 'sense of species'."[54]

"In the midst of such an atmosphere of 'conspiration'," Teilhard wrote, "certain operations of a universal character may be envisaged as realizable, which would be out of the question in the state of psychic disaggregation."[55] He believed that our inventory of the known properties of humanity, all emanate from the two "essentially human properties" or "special psychic factors," namely, reflexion and "conspiration." Furthermore, these factors were "observable scientifically as any other measurable energy."[56] It was the intensification of *conspiration* (the "conspiracy") leading to Omega point that so enthralled Teilhard. He wrote:

> Something is afoot in the universe, a result is working out which can best be compared to a gestation and birth: the birth of a spiritual reality formed by souls and the matter they draw after them. Laboriously, by way of human activity and thanks to it, the new earth is gathering, isolating and purifying itself.[57]

He believed that under Omega's influence, "each separate soul becomes capable of breathing itself out in a single act [conspiring] into which the incalculable plurality of its perceptions and activities, its sufferings and desires, pass without confusion." He observed that "the sum of elementary energies constituting the global mass of human energy" seemed "to be moving towards an analogous metamorphosis of a far higher order."[58]

In Teilhard's view:

> All that matters at this crucial moment [in history] is that the massing together of individualities should not take the form of a functional and enforced mechanization of human energies (the totalitarian principle), but of a "conspiracy" informed with love.

He added:

[53]Ibid.
[54]Teilhard de Chardin, *The Appearance of Man*, 258.
[55]Ibid.
[56]Teilhard de Chardin, *The Vision of the Past*, 60.
[57]Teilhard de Chardin, *Human Energy*, 49.
[58]Ibid., 154.

Having been initially the fundamental choice of the individual, the Grand Option, that which decides in favor of a convergent Universe, is destined sooner or later to become the *common choice* of the mass of Mankind. Thus a particular and generalized state of consciousness is presaged for our species in the future: a 'conspiracy' in terms of perspective and intention.[59]

In a lyrical essay called "The Spirit of the Earth," written as a sequel to *The Phenomenon of Man*,[60] Teilhard examined the "conspiracy" of individuals from every class and background, which he believed was engaged in the great task of lifting mankind to a new, higher stage of evolution. He declared his famous dictum: "The age of nations has passed. Now, unless we wish to perish we must shake off our old prejudices and build the earth."[61]

In a lecture he gave in 1951, he stated: "Economically and spiritually speaking, the age of *civilizations* has ended, and that of *one civilization* is beginning."[62] This dictum was the basis of the theme for the Twelfth International Teilhard Conference held in April 1992: "World Without Frontiers." The participants met under the twelve gold stars, symbolizing European unity-in-diversity. The opening speaker introduced "a sense of urgency as he related the Conference to current events in Europe, where an effort is being made to reconcile ancient enemies within a new and greater common union."[63]

Teilhard believed that humanity was evolving into a single organism with a single heart and nervous system. The formation of the Noosphere (a thinking envelope around the earth) was considered "a possible element in a sort of higher organism which might form itself, one from all, *by conspiration*."[64]

He wrote of "'the *conspiration*' of activities from which the collective [world] soul proceeds" as originating in "the common *aspiration* exerted by hope."[65] "Now this soul, if it exists, can only be the 'conspiration' of individuals, associating to *raise* the edifice of life *to a new stage*."[66] For "*we have reached*

[59]Teilhard de Chardin, *The Future of Man*, 54, 57.

[60]Teilhard de Chardin, *Letters From a Traveller*, 172.

[61]Teilhard de Chardin, "The Spirit of the Earth," *Human Energy*, 37.

[62]Teilhard de Chardin, *The Appearance of Man*, 158. Italics in original.

[63]Conference Report: "World without Frontiers," *Teilhard Review* 27/3 (Winter 1992): 85. Held at All Saints Pastoral Center.

[64]Teilhard de Chardin, *The Vision of the Past*, 73. Italics in original.

[65]Teilhard de Chardin, *Human Energy*, 138-39. Italics in original.

[66]Ibid., 37. Italics in original. Cf. Teilhard de Chardin *Building the Earth*, 54: "But this soul can only be a "conspiracy" of individuals who associate themselves to raise to a new stage the edifice of life."

*a decisive point in human evolution*, at which the only way forward is in the direction of a common passion, a 'conspiration'."[67]

It was Teilhard's philosophical insights into the nature and driving force of this *conspiracy*, that has made him a kind of "patron saint" of the New Age Movement. For Teilhardians, his message is the Holy Grail that humanity has been searching for. In an essay entitled "Love's Conspirators: Builders of Earth-House-Hold," published in *The Spirit of the Earth*, Francis Tiso expressed it well:

> We are led to look for these fragile accumulations of energy, form, and freedom, in the hope of glimpsing the Grail, the Philosopher's Stone, the presence of realistic hope in this present moment of ordinary reality. *Teilhard takes us to the Grail Castle and lets us find our way toward that love which is the activation of energy and the goal of evolving*, and which moves us with the same unmistakable touch as it moves the sun and other stars.[68]

## 4.3 The New Age "Conspiracy" of Love

The popular appeal of New Age books like Ferguson's *Aquarian Conspiracy*, derives from the sense of hope and possibility for the future inspired by the new transformative insights described. Ferguson's focus is not on New Age ideology but on awakening the human spirit to a "new paradigm," a new evolutionary path for Mankind. Like Teilhard, she sees her task in terms of being a "technician of the Spirit." Teilhard stated:

> The great point to which the *technician of the Spirit* should direct his attention in dealing with human beings is to leave them the possibility of discovering themselves, in the transformation which he is seeking to bring about in them, and the freedom to differentiate themselves ever more and more.[69]

The role of the "technician of the Spirit," as Teilhard saw it, was to apply the appropriate stimulus to awaken mankind to its evolutionary destiny:

> If . . . we step down into ourselves, we shall be horrified to find there, *beneath the man of surface relationships and reflection*, an unknown—a man as yet hardly emerged from unconsciousness, still, for lack of the

---

[67]Teilhard de Chardin, *Human Energy*, 153.

[68]Francis Tiso, "Love's Conspirators: Builders of Earth-House-Hold," in *The Spirit of the Earth*, ed. Perlinski, 92.

[69]Teilhard de Chardin, *Building the Earth*, 77.

appropriate stimulus, no more than half-awake: one whose features, seen in the half-shadow, seem to be merging into the countenance of the world.

No brutal shock, no, nor gentle caress can compare with the vehemence and possessive force of the contact between ourselves as individuals and the universe, when suddenly, *beneath the ordinariness of our most familiar experiences*, we realize, with religious horror, that what is *emerging in us is the great cosmos.*[70]

In many ways *The Aquarian Conspiracy* is reminiscent of novelist-historian H. G. Wells' prophetic book *The Open Conspiracy: Blueprints for a World Revolution*. This work, published in 1928, is like Ferguson's, charged with optimism, and proposed that the world was on the threshold of momentous change for the better.

Wells predicted the spontaneous independent emergence of groups worldwide, as a result of the rapid increase of knowledge, who would seek to implement a global vision. He preached the gospel of one-world government with religious fervor and influenced an entire generation to think in global terms. He wrote: "The open conspiracy must begin as a movement of explanation and propaganda."[71] Ferguson draws on the same themes emphasized by Wells' work, quoting him as stating:

And a day will come, one day in the *unending* succession of days, when beings who are now latent in our loins shall stand upon this earth as one stands upon a footstool and shall touch the stars.[72]

Such a picture of a world without end and Man's destiny based in his discovery of God-like powers appeals to all New Agers, for it fits in with their ideology. It appears to parody the message of Scripture. For example, Isaiah declares: "Thus says the Lord, 'Heaven is My throne, and the earth is My footstool'" (Isa. 66:1).

Fritjof Capra, a leading exponent of New Age thought, states that the mechanistic worldview inherited from Descartes and Newton needs to be abandoned, since it effected a dualism between body and mind.[73] He rejects the distinction Descartes made between the impermanent human body and the indestructible soul,[74] and argues that a paradigm shift is needed in the perception of reality. His

---

[70]Teilhard de Chardin, "Cosmic Life" (1916), *Writings in Time of War*, 27.
[71]Wells, *The Open Conspiracy*.
[72]Wells cited in Ferguson, *The Aquarian Conspiracy*, 49.
[73]Capra, *The Turning Point*, 40, 53-74.
[74]Ibid., 164.

book *The Tao of Physics* (1975)[75] and other New Age books like Ken Wilber's *Up from Eden: A Transpersonal View of Human Evolution* (1983)[76] are attempts to weld Eastern mysticism to recent developments in science. In a review of Wilber's book, Ursula King notes: "the hidden premise of the book, frequently alluded to rather than made explicit, is a modern popularized version of the basic tenets of the Indian Advaita Vedanta philosophy mixed with a considerable amount of Buddhist Mahayana terminology (rather than Mahayana thought)."[77]

Wilber judges the current "New Age" movements as "the strangest mixture of a handful of truly transpersonal souls and masses of prepersonal addicts."[78] He looks forward to the emergence of a true Wisdom culture. In his book *The Atman Project*[79] the theme is basically simple: development is evolution, evolution is transcendence, and transcendence has as its final goal Atman, or ultimate Unity Consciousness. Peter Russell, a Teilhardian, has described the book as "probably the most comprehensive investigation of inner evolution in print."[80]

In a much-quoted statement, Ferguson described the New Age Movement in the following terms:

> A leaderless but powerful network is working to bring about radical change in the United States. Its members have broken with certain key elements of Western thought, and may have broken continuity with history.
>
>     This network is the *Aquarian Conspiracy.* . . . Broader than reform, deeper than revolution, this benign conspiracy for a new human agenda has triggered the most rapid cultural realignment in history. The great shuddering, irrevocable shift overtaking us is not a new political, religious, or philosophical system. It is a new mind—the ascendance of a startling worldview that gathers into its framework breakthrough science and insights from earliest recorded thought.[81]

She pointed out that the word "conspire," in its literal sense, means "to breathe together" and involves an intimate joining. To emphasize what she described as

---

[75]Fritjof Capra, *The Tao of Physics: An Exploration of the Parallels Between Modern Physics and Eastern Mysticism* (Boulder CO: Shambala, 1975). The principal characteristic of the Tao is the cyclical nature of its ceaseless motion.

[76]Ken Wilber, *Up From Eden* (London: Routledge and Kegan Paul, 1983). Also see his other work *The Spectrum of Consciousness* (Wheaton IL: Theosophical Publ. House, 1977).

[77]Ursula King, *Teilhard Review* 18/3 (1983): 93.

[78]Wilber, *Up From Eden*, 323.

[79]Ken Wilber, *The Atman Project* (Wheaton IL: Theosophical Publ. House, 1980).

[80]Russell, *The Global Brain*, 246.

[81]Ferguson, *The Aquarian Conspiracy*, 23.

"the benevolent nature of this joining," Ferguson chose the word *Aquarian* to describe the "conspiracy." In the third Annual Teilhard Lecture, Bernard Towers, ex-president of the Teilhard Center for the Future of Man (London), explained the term "conspiracy" used by Teilhard and Ferguson:

> I too am a "coconspirator" with Teilhard and the rest [Carl Jung, Abraham Maslow, Carl Rogers, and Aldous Huxley—all listed by Ferguson]. The word ["conspire"] has no sinister implications. It doesn't mean that we conspirators think alike or feel alike. It means, literally, that we "breathe together," even though we don't know each other very much to speak of. The air we breathe is that of *respect* for the phenomenon of man and for the cosmogenesis that produced the complex creatures that we are.[82]

In the foreword to Robert Muller's book *Most of All They Taught Me Happiness*, Norman Cousins wrote:

> The oncoming generations . . . will need living examples of the conspiracy of love that Teilhard de Chardin has said will be essential to man's salvation. Robert Muller is involved in such a conspiracy.[83]

Scientist Arthur C. Clarke, author of the best-selling novel *2001: A Space Odyssey* and many others, is a dedicated New Ager. He predicts that consciousness expansion, leading to superintelligence and human immortality, will have been achieved by the year 2001. He forecasts a glorious future for mankind and argues not only that mankind's destiny is godhood, but that it will be achieved.[84] New Agers, like Mark Satin, maintain that: "Planetary events are, in a sense, *conspiring to inspire us* to recognize our oneness and interdependence.[85]

The New Age Movement is a worldwide loosely structured network of organizations and individuals who find a sense of common vision based on Aquarian aspirations. They may share common beliefs often rooted in evolutionism, syncretism, monism, pantheism, and gnosticism. "New Age" thought also often emphasizes the "spiritual evolution" of Man towards "Divinity"—Man discovering his innate Godhood through "mysticism" and other means.

C. S. Lewis's prophetic novel *That Hideous Strength*[86] illustrates the danger of this merger. A postmodern agnostic science synthesizes with the occult, pro-

---

[82]Bernard Towers, "On the Practice of Teilhardian Principles: The Role of Empathy in Transdisciplinary Studies," *Teilhard Review* 17/1 (Spring 1982): 11.

[83]Muller, *Most of All They Taught Me Happiness*, 10-11.

[84]Arthur C. Clarke, *Profiles of the Future* (New York: Holt, Rinehart, Winston, 1984).

[85]Satin, *New Age Politics*, 149.

[86]C. S. Lewis, *That Hideous Strength*, 1st USA ed. (New York: MacMillan, 1946).

ducing a strange amalgam. In the process, former enemies of Christianity are seen as "allies." The irony is that philosophy has come full circle. True theology has been destroyed and replaced with the reality of nothingness or regressed into occultism.

A number of professing Christian leaders express their support for the aspirations of the Aquarian Conspiracy. In his book *God and the Aquarian Age: The New Era of the Kingdom*,[87] Catholic priest Adrian B. Smith states: "There is no contradiction between the new Age of Aquarius and the New Age of Christ." Smith is an acknowledged Teilhardian and believes that Transcendental Meditation should be used as an aid to Christian growth.[88] Here we see the promotion of a merger between Eastern religion and Christianity so typical of the New Age message.

Canon Peter Spink, founder of *The Omega Order*, published a book recently entitled *A Christian in the New Age*.[89] In it he acknowledges his great debt to Teilhard and espouses a vision in full harmony with Teilhardism. He notes that in the United Kingdom there now exist 200 "Open Centers" (like the famous New Age Findhorn Community)[90] promoting New Age philosophies. The Omega Order has "a distinctly New Age character" according to a report in *The Teilhard Review*. The late Claude Curling, formerly a subdean of Science at Kings College (London), and John Newson, ex-editor of *The Teilhard Review*, contribute to courses organized by the Omega Order.[91]

Some New Age leaders, like British aristocrat Sir George Trevelyan, interpret the apocalyptic images in the Bible (for example, those in Revelation), as referring to the "passage from the Piscean to the Aquarian Age."[92] In his book *From Nation to Emancipation*, mystically inclined cultural historian William Irwin Thompson considers the New Age Movement to be central to the development of a new world order. "Whether the movement from one world system to another will involve stumbling or total collapse," he writes, "may very

---

[87]Adrian B. Smith, *God and the Aquarian Age: The New Era of the Kingdom* (McCrimmons, 1990).

[88]Adrian B. Smith, ed. *TM, An Aid to Christian Growth* (1983). Cited in ibid.

[89]Peter Spink, *A Christian in the New Age* (London: Darton, Longman & Todd, 1991).

[90]See Eileen Caddy, *The Spirit of Findhorn* (San Francisco: Harper & Row, 1979).

[91]"Centre to Centre," *Teilhard Review* 25/1 (Spring 1990): iii.

[92]George Trevelyan, *Operation Redemption: A Vision of Hope in an Age of Turmoil* (Walpole NH: Stillpoint, 1981) 46. Also see his book *A Vision of the Aquarian Age: The Emerging Spiritual World View* (London: Coventure Ltd., 1977). Trevelyan is the premier leader of the New Age Movement in the UK. N.B.: New Agers do not believe in the biblical millennium (e.g., Rev. 20:1-6).

well depend on the success or failure of the new age movement. Now we stand on the edge of a great transformation."[93]

Thompson is founder of the New Age's Lindisfarne Association, which operates out of the Cathedral of St. John the Divine in New York City, a Liberal Episcopal church often associated with New Age causes. Two of his other books, *Evil and World Order*[94] and *Darkness and Scattered Light*,[95] deal with the emerging new world order. In the latter book Thompson says that the New World Culture will be achieved through "planetization"—the implementation of a political regime brought about by a growing world consciousness of unity.[96] In Thompson's introduction to New Ager David Spangler's book *Revelation: The Birth of A New Age*, he begins by quoting Teilhard:

> A generation ago Teilhard de Chardin made a prediction that has now become a cultural reality: "Like the meridians as they approach the poles, science, philosophy, and religion are bound to converge as they draw nearer to the whole."[97]

He goes on to predict the convergence of all world religions before the dawning of the New Age, a vision shared by Teilhard:

> The new spirituality does not reject the earlier patterns of the great universal religions. Priest and church will not disappear; they will not be forced out of existence in the New Age, they will be absorbed into the existence of the New Age.

Marilyn Ferguson states that Teilhard de Chardin "prophesied the phenomenon central to [her] book: a *conspiracy* of men and women whose new perspective would trigger a critical contagion of change,"[98] leading to a new world "soul." In fact, she begins her book by quoting Teilhard: "This soul can only be a *conspiracy* of individuals," and ends her book by stating: "You are the seed, a silent promise. You are the conspiracy."

Elsewhere she refers to Teilhard's writings in which he urged for a worldwide movement, a "*conspiracy* of love."[99] She states that his essay "The Spirit

---

[93]William Irwin Thompson, *From Nation to Emancipation* (Findhorn: Findhorn Publications, 1982) 52.

[94]William Irwin Thompson, *Evil and World Order* (New York: Simon & Schuster, 1975).

[95]William Irwin Thompson, *Darkness and Scattered Light* (New York: Doubleday/Anchor Books, 1978).

[96]Ibid., 13.

[97]David Spangler, *Revelation: The Birth of a New Age* (Scotland: Findhorn, 1976) 7.

[98]Ferguson, *The Aquarian Conspiracy*, 25.

[99]Ibid., 19.

of the Earth" was inspired by his growing conviction that a conspiracy of individuals from every layer of American society was engaged in an effort "to raise to a new stage the edifice of life." She quotes him as stating: "The only way forward is in the direction of a common passion, a conspiracy,"[100] and concurs with his analysis. In 1983 a book coedited by Robert Muller was published in honor of Teilhard and contained an essay by Ferguson entitled "The Mandate of Our Collective, Real Self."[101]

A number of New Age Movement leaders have acknowledged Teilhard's influence, including Eileen Caddy,[102] Sir George Trevelyan,[103] and William Irwin Thomson.[104] In Sir George Trevelyan's foreword to David Spangler's book *Revelation on the New Age*, he begins by drawing on Teilhard's vision for the future, stating:

> Much talk there is of a New Age. Many are filled with a mounting sense of expectation. It was Teilhard de Chardin in the closing pages of *Le Milieu Divin* who wrote that "expectation . . . is perhaps the supreme Christian function and the most distinctive characteristic of our religion. . . . We persist in saying that we keep vigil in expectation of the Master but in reality many would have to admit, if they were sincere, that they no longer expect anything. The flame must be revived at all costs. At all costs we must renew in ourselves the desire and hope of *the Great Coming*."[105]

The "Great Coming" for Teilhard was "Omega Point," a new state of planetary or cosmic consciousness. Sri Aurobindo (1872–1950), the Indian philosopher and "mystic" with whom he shares many similarities in outlook, was another to prophesy a coming planetary consciousness. He called it the "Supermind"—*Sacchidananda*—the absolute being, the consciousness and bliss of traditional Hindu

---

[100]Ibid., 50.

[101]Zonneveld and Muller, eds., *The Desire to Be Human*.

[102]Caddy, *The Spirit of Findhorn*, 29.

[103]Trevelyan, *Operation Redemption: A Vision of Hope in an Age of Turmoil*, 144-45, 170, 172, 188.

[104]William Irwin Thomson, *Passages About Earth: An Exploration of the New Planetary Culture* (San Francisco: Harper & Row, 1981) 144-45, 170, 172, 188; *At the Edge of History*, USA ed. (New York: Harper & Row, 1971).

[105]Spangler, *Revelation: The Birth of a New Age*, 13. Teilhard's statement draws upon the New Testament teaching of the return of Christ and imagery related to this event, e.g., "The flame must be revived at all costs" (cf. Matt. 25:1-13: the parable of the five wise and five foolish virgins).

philosophy as reinterpreted by Aurobindo's vision of human evolutionary development.[106]

Aurobindo, an evolutionary pantheist, formulated a spirituality supposedly based on the Hindu Scriptures, independently of Teilhard. He stressed that if humanity is to survive, a radical transformation of human nature is indispensable. For Aurobindo "it is only the full emergence of the soul, the full descent of the native light and power of the Spirit and the consequent replacement or transformation and uplifting of our insufficient mental and vital nature by a spiritual and supramental supernature that can effect this evolutionary miracle."[107]

Unlike Teilhard, who stressed the need for the transformation of humanity as a whole, Aurobindo's chief concern was for personal transformation. He saw the transformation of the future as the work of a few gifted individuals, the "gnostic beings," the supermen, who contribute to and bring about the descent of the Supermind. In articles written in 1949–1950 and published under the title *The Mind of Light* there is a suggestion that his vision of the future is ultimately an eschatological one. He writes of man's transformed divine body and the divine life come to earth when man "will live in God and with God, possess God."[108] He not only gave a new theoretical image of the future man, but claimed to be a representative realization of this image himself.

Professor Ernst Benz has pointed out the "amazing agreement" of Aurobindo's reinterpretation of the theory of evolution with similar European conceptions. "This shows," he states, "the universal character of the transformation of religious anthropology which takes place under the influence of the doctrine of evolution."[109] Professor R. C. Zaehner, who devoted an entire book to comparing the two thinkers, has highlighted the many striking resemblances between the two.[110] He points out that both were obsessed with the theory of evolution and yet unlike most other evolutionary thinkers, they interpreted the ultimate meaning of evolution as being spiritual.

In contrast to the New Age "eschatological" doctrines concerning "planetary consciousness" and the coming "Supermind," all of which are born of the cult

---

[106]R. C. Zaehner, *Evolution in Religion: A Study on Sri Aurobindo and Teilhard de Chardin* (Oxford: Clarendon Press, 1971).

[107]Sri Aurobindo, *The Future Evolution of Man—The Divine Life Upon Earth*, comp. P. B. Saint-Hilaire (Pondicherry: Sri Aurobindo Ashram, 1963) 55.

[108]Sri Aurobindo, *The Mind of Light*, ed., R. A. McDermott (New York: Dutton and Co., 1971) 85. Cited in King, *The Spirit of One Earth*, 171-72.

[109]Ernst Benz, *Evolution and Christian Hope: Man's Concept of the Future from the Early Fathers to Teilhard de Chardin*, trans. Heinz G. Frank (London: Victor Gollancz, 1967) 190. See chap. 11, 190-206, "Sri Aurobindo's Doctrine of Evolution and the Future of Man."

[110]Zaehner, *Evolution in Religion: A Study on Sri Aurobindo and Teilhard de Chardin*.

of evolutionism and gnosticism; orthodox Christianity teaches the return of the Lord of Glory. The Church has always affirmed and believed that the Scriptures teach the personal return of the glorified Head of the Church, Jesus Christ, who will judge the living and the dead. For example, the Nicene Creed, developed from the Council of Nicea around AD 325, states: "He [Christ] shall come again, with glory, to judge both the quick and the dead; Whose kingdom shall have no end."[111]

## 4.4 Teilhard's "New Age" Vision

Ferguson reports that in 1967 Barbara Marx Hubbard, a futurist inspired by Teilhard's prophetic vision of an evolution in planetary consciousness,[112] invited a thousand people from around the earth, including Abraham Maslow's network, to form a "human front" of those committed to belief in the possibility of transcendent consciousness. Hundreds responded, including Thomas Merton. From this developed a newsletter and later a loose-knit organization, the Committee for the Future.[113]

In 1982 Hubbard began the process of establishing the World Good News Network (WGNN) which seeks among other things to communicate the positive, expand our perception of the human experience, and demonstrate creativity. President and cofounder of WGNN, David L. Smith, has produced a television special called "The Evolving Earth: Teilhard de Chardin's Hope for a Human Future."[114] In his paper to the United Nations 1983 Teilhard Colloquium, Smith affirmed a direct link between Teilhard and the New Age Movement, when he stated:

> [A] new way of seeing is imperative if we are to survive. Teilhard's ideas can help to bring about this shift in perception.
>
> The specific nature of this change in outlook has been expressed in Marilyn Ferguson's book, *The Aquarian Conspiracy*, which suggests that a paradigm shift is in fact occurring.[115]

Another colloquium contributor referred to the "conspiracy" highlighted by Ferguson:

---

[111]The Nicene Creed is an expansion of the Apostles' Creed which was used in the very early Church. Gerald Bray, *Creeds, Councils, and Christ* (Downers Grove IL: InterVarsity, 1984) 204-207.

[112]See Barbara Marx Hubbard, *The Evolutionary Journey* (San Francisco: Evolutionary Press, 1982).

[113]Ferguson, *The Aquarian Conspiracy*, 57.

[114]Film for public television. David Smith, project director and executive producer.

[115]Zonneveld, ed., *Humanity's Quest For Unity*, 99.

[T]here is a swelling tide of people who believe they see, beneath the wreckage of an old, decaying world, the first flowering of a newer age, as if witness to the ancient belief in resurrection, in the eternal return, in the Phoenix, in Osiris and Christ. . . . They say [that] a "third wave" is sweeping over humanity, that "an 'Aquarian conspiracy' has been effected. . . . The death of the old is imminent or has already occurred, they say, and rebirth is here."[116]

Hubbard, like Ferguson, argues that we must embrace "spiritual futurism" which she claims is compatible with "evolutionary futurism" (the hope for radical evolutionary change), and she views evolution itself as "a consciousness-raising experience."[117] Hubbard's vision of a "human front" was derived from Teilhard's attempt to set up a similar group. In his essay "Human Energy" (1937) he described how forces hidden in the earth must one day be deployed in the achievement of his hoped-for "Human Front."[118]

In *Building the Earth* he refers to "a spiritual Human Front" consisting of "'technicians' solely concerned with defining and propagating the concrete goals, ever more lofty, upon which the efforts of human activities should be concentrated."[119] He even persuaded a few men of good will to form such a group, but it proved to be short-lived.[120] He saw its aim as being similar to that of the one world government movement: "namely to develop a kind of spiritual medium in which a number of varied tendencies are bound to converge toward a general drift in the direction of a constructive peace and human feeling."[121]

To a friend he wrote: "what strikes me is the necessity to bring about a general reorganization of forces, not on a "population front," but on a "Human Front," and according to the following program: faith in a Future, faith in Universalism, faith in the priority of the Personal . . . [these] must replace or complete the old slogan that stirred our fathers, 'Liberty, Equality, Fraternity'."[122]

Some have suggested that Teilhard's ideas, if not properly understood, can evoke the shadow of a rather terrifying "Brave New World," as brilliantly portrayed in Aldous Huxley's book. Teilhard denied any link between his vision

---

[116]Jerome Perlinski, "Hoping For Peace: Teilhard in the History of Ideas," Ibid., 117.

[117]Barbara Marx Hubbard, "The Future of Futurism," *The Futurist* (April 1983): 52. Cited in Douglas Groothuis, *Unmasking the New Age* (Downers Grove IL: InterVarsity, 1966) 30.

[118]Teilhard de Chardin, *Human Energy*, 113-62.

[119]Teilhard de Chardin, *Building the Earth*, 37.

[120]René d'Ouince in Teilhard de Chardin, *Letters to Two Friends*, 10

[121]Letter of 14 February 1949, in ibid., 199.

[122]Letter of 30 October 1936, in ibid., 91.

and this caricature,[123] and yet the parallel remains valid.[124] For him, man was incomplete, so the means, the product, and the goal of evolution, must be the advancement of man to a completed state, *by whatever means.*

Like Teilhard, Hubbard and her respondents see themselves as spearheading a new evolutionary wavefront towards a new planetary consciousness, and a new species of spiritual man, progenitors of a Master Race or "élite" (Teilhard's term). Hubbard, a convinced evolutionist, even claims that we can expect to see a new suprahumanity emerge shortly, a new species "as superior to present-day humanity as we are to the apes."[125]

A number of other authors have predicted such an emergence, seeing themselves as contributing to an irresistible tide of evolutionary progress. Such authors generally assume that the rapid social evolution witnessed over the past few hundred years will be paralleled in biological evolution. However the latter, involving supposed morphological and physiological changes, has no essential link to social changes.

In his book *The Global Brain: Speculations on the Evolutionary Leap to Planetary Consciousness*, Peter Russell, a Teilhardian, expounds Teilhard's vision of evolution at the stage of "noogenesis" (the genesis of mind). "He saw this stage," writes Russell, "as the 'planetization of Mankind . . . [into] a single, major organic unity.' The fulfillment of the process of noogenesis [being] 'Omega Point,' the culmination of the evolutionary process, the endpoint toward which we are all converging."[126]

After discussing Sri Aurobindo's concept of the "Supermind," Russell refers to the possibility of "the emergence of something beyond a single planetary consciousness or Supermind: a completely new level of evolution, as different from consciousness as consciousness is from life, and life from matter." He believes that this "new order of existence will be the *ultimate effect* of the continued integration of humanity" and "it will be happening at the planetary level, to Gaia." Just as reflective consciousness arose (according to Teilhard) as the *ultimate effect* of the complexification of spirit-matter within the hominid line, so a new reality beyond consciousness would emerge from the involution of the noosphere—the birth of a "world-soul" as Teilhard called it.

Russell has coined the term "Gaiafield" to refer to this new order of existence "emerging from the combined interactions of all the minds within the social superorganism."[127] The awakening of Gaia would, in his view, come about through patterns of coherence built up through the billions of information ex-

---

[123]Teilhard de Chardin, *The Appearance of Man*, 255n.

[124]Lukas and Lukas, *Teilhard: A Biography*, 141.

[125]Hubbard, "The Future of Futurism," 55.

[126]Russell, *The Global Brain*, 98-99.

[127]Ibid., 100. For other references to Gaiafield see 231, 235.

changes shuttling through the global networks. Today terms like "information superhighway" and "INTERNET" have been coined to describe such worldwide computer information links.

Teilhard too, saw the emergence of global telecommunication links and the development of computer systems as integral to the birth of "planetary consciousness." In Man, he wrote, "heredity . . . becomes primarily 'Noospheric'—transmitted, . . . by the surrounding environment."[128] He applied the term 'noospheric' to refer to the transformation of the use of tools by Man as a mere extension of the body, into a "mechanized envelope . . . appertaining to mankind" on a global scale.[129] He referred to the "extraordinary network of radio and television communications which . . . already link us all in a sort of 'etherized' universal consciousness."[130] He saw in this example and in the growth of computer technology elements which contributed to the formation of the Noosphere.

In April 1991, at the Eleventh International Teilhard Conference, Russell's video "The Global Brain" was screened. In the report on the conference in *The Teilhard Review*, it is noted that the audience was "held spellbound" by the video which described the concept of "global consciousness" and the "sense of being a planetary citizen." Russell is reported as having spoken about the focus of evolution now being the human mind: "We have moved beyond biological evolution to the evolution of human consciousness." He predicted "a period of inner awakening which would be crucial in the linking of humanity into an integrated society as we become aware of our potential individually and collectively."

The present crisis, in his view, is "a crisis of consciousness." "We need to tap into our inner wisdom, to experience a greater oneness with ourselves and with our world."[131] He believes the practice of Transcendental Meditation (as taught by Maharishi Yogi) is the best way people can advance the evolution of the "Global Mind" and "collective consciousness." Enlightenment, in his view, "means more than being particularly wise, aware, or well balanced; it denotes a clearly defined state of consciousness."[132] It is of interest that Leo Zonneveld, an influential leader in the present-day Teilhardian network, gave an address entitled the "Renaissance of the Global Mind," at the 1988 residential conference of the Teilhard Center.[133]

---

[128]Teilhard de Chardin, *Activation of Energy*, 163.

[129]Ibid., 166.

[130]Ibid., 167.

[131]Eoghan Callaghan, Conference report: the Eleventh International Teilhard Conference at London Colney 26-28 April 1991, *Teilhard Review* 26/2 (Summer 1991): 63.

[132]Russell, *The Global Brain*, 154.

[133]Leo Zonneveld, "Renaissance of the Global Mind," *Teilhard Review* 23/2 (Summer 1988): 45-53. This paper was delivered at the Wantage Residential Conference in 1988.

In 1969 a leading French political writer, Jean-François Revel, predicted that the United States would experience a "second great world revolution, led by the emergence of *homo novus*, a new human being."[134] In 1973 New Age biologist the late Jonas Salk (discoverer of the polio vaccine), in his book *The Survival of the Wisest*,[135] described the same new evolutionary vanguard of humanity. William I. Thompson extolled this vision of the emergence of a new spiritual man in 1976.[136]

New Age leader Donald Keys, cofounder of Planetary Citizens[137] and a former United Nations advisor, has written of the need for "a new kind of person, a person with a planetary perspective" for the New Age.[138] In his book *Earth at Omega: Passage to Planetization*, he quotes Teilhard as predicting that this development will be accompanied by "the formation of an organicosocial super-complex . . . the planetization of mankind."[139]

More recently, New Ager John White has predicted the emergence of a "more advanced form of humanity" which he names *Homo noeticus* (from the Greek *nous*, meaning to know).[140] He predicts that evolution will produce a "new species" of humanity, stating:

> We are witnessing the final phase of *Homo sapiens* and the simultaneous emergence—still quite tentative because of the nuclear threat to all life—of what I have named *Homo Noeticus*, a more advanced form of humanity.[141]

John Randolph Price, another New Age Movement leader, confided to his followers that "a new species of man is coming forth to lead us out of the dark-

----

[134]Jean-François Revel, *Without Marx or Jesus*, cited in Ferguson, *The Aquarian Conspiracy*, 58.

[135]Jonas Salk, *The Survival of the Wisest* (New York: Harper & Row, 1973).

[136]Introduction by W. I. Thompson in Spangler, *Revelation: The Birth of a New Age*, 7-11.

[137]This organization was originally headquartered at the UN (where it was founded in 1970) and has been relocated in California. Its key goal is public education and it seeks to transform the world's political systems. It sponsored the Planetary Initiative for the World We Choose, which operated in many countries.

[138]Donald Keys, *Earth at Omega: Passage to Planetization* (Boston: Branden Press, 1982) iv.

[139]Ibid., 69.

[140]John White, "Channelling, A Short History of a Long Tradition," *Holistic Life Magazine* (Summer 1985): 20. It is noteworthy that Edgar Mitchell, who was the lunar module pilot on Apollo 14, in October 1972 founded the Institute of Noetic Sciences to study human consciousness.

[141]Ibid. Also see John W. White, *Frontiers of Consciousness: The Meeting Ground between Inner and Outer Reality* (New York: Julian Press, 1974).

ness into a new dimension."[142] He believes 1987 marked the beginning of the end for the old race of man and that we are seeing the dawning of an age of Cosmic Consciousness—divinity for a collective humanity.[143]

This view is widespread among New Agers who describe the process as "conscious evolution"—man voluntarily participating in the work of his own evolution. Willis W. Harman, a professor at Stanford University and one of the founders of the Association for Humanistic Psychology, has founded and is now president of a group called the Institute of Noetic Sciences. He believes that by following "The Plan," man will eventually spiritually evolve into a new species, *Homo Noeticus*, replacing *Homo sapiens*. He believes that "The Plan" has already been revealed through ancient mystical religious writings and arises from what Carl Jung called the "collective unconsciousness." Harman states:

> Mind exists in coextensive unity with the world. . . . There seems no reason to doubt that my creative/intuitive mind might "have in mind" a "plan." . . . This idea of a "plan" coming from beyond consciousness seems implausible. . . . Yet there is impressive testimony . . . in a vast literature on mysticism and religious experience.[144]

The cooperative effort to effect "The Plan" involving many groups and individuals has been named the "Aquarian Conspiracy."[145] This vision of a planetary consciousness is sociopolitical and amounts to an attempt to supplant the existing culturally dominant worldview of secularism and traditional religion.

In *Man's Place in Nature* (1948) Teilhard spoke of the "curve of corpuscularization" evident in the growing complexity of the inorganic world. He reasoned that it leads to the gradual emergence of new, higher, and more flexible forms of freedom, spontaneity, and the ability to respond to an environment evident in the evolution of the central nervous system (cerebralization), and culminates in the social and cultural convergence of mankind. Teilhard's optimistic vision for the future of man was summed up in the following quote from his work *The Phenomenon of Man*:

> [E]vil on the earth at its final stage will be reduced to a minimum. Disease and hunger will be conquered by science and we will no longer need to fear them in any acute form. And, conquered by the sense of

---

[142]John Randolph Price, *The Superbeings* (Austin TX: Quartus Books, 1981) back cover.

[143]John Randolph Price, *The Planetary Commission* (Austin TX: Quartus Books, 1984) 29.

[144]Willis W. Harman, "Rational for Choosing," *Journal of Humanistic Psychology* (Winter 1981).

[145]Barry McWaters, *Conscious Evolution* (Los Angeles: New Age Press, 1981) 27-28.

the earth and human sense, hatred and internecine struggles will have disappeared in the ever-warmer radiance of Omega. Some sort of unanimity will reign over the entire mass of the noosphere. The final convergence will take place *in peace*.[146]

Teilhard's "prophetic" vision of a "convergence . . . in peace," as the evolutionary destiny for mankind, has been widely acclaimed. Scholars, leaders within the United Nations, and many within the New Age Movement claim that his religiophilosophical writings provide the framework within which peace can be achieved in our generation. Teilhard has become a patron saint of those attempting to effect "The Plan"—the Aquarian Conspiracy.

## 4.5 New Age Luminaries

### Robert Muller

As noted, Robert Muller, a "true Teilhardian" and ex-assistant secretary-general of the United Nations, has emerged as one of the most influential New Age leaders of our time. Muller, who was born in Belgium and grew up in Alsace-Lorraine, considers himself to "have never been a deeply religious person" and "was raised in a good Catholic family."[147] Prior to his commitment to Teilhard's theory of evolution, he admits: "The religion taught me during my youth had largely given way to rationalism, scientism and intellectualism so prevalent in our time. I was not at all concerned with spirituality and religion [while I worked] in the United Nations."[148]

In 1970, at the age of forty-six he was appointed director of Secretary-General U Thant's office. He states: "From then on I really had to have a total view and I often heard myself being described as a "Teilhardian.""[149] It was during the 1970s that he began to receive his "Teilhardian enlightenments," as he calls them.

He largely credits U Thant, a practicing Buddhist, for his own development into a "spiritual being." A background in rationalism, scientism and intellectualism, and Roman Catholicism, provided the "fertile" soil for his ready absorption of Teilhard's theory of evolution. Under the influence of U Thant he made a serious study of Buddhism and, as he recalls, also "began to read the mystics and understand more about this new dimension of life consciousness."[150] Of this experience he writes:

---

[146]Teilhard de Chardin, *The Phenomenon of Man*, 288.
[147]Muller, *New Genesis*, 169.
[148]Ibid., 163.
[149]Ibid., 160.
[150]Ibid., 171.

> I could seek, know and feel in myself the entire universe and Godhead,
> for I was part of them and they were part of me; it could not be other-
> wise; and last but not least I was the master of my cosmos, it was up
> to me to guide it, to uplift it, to give it confidence and joy, to keep it
> in an endless, wondrous, inquisitive, searching, loving and hopeful
> mood.[151]

His conceptions of morality and spirituality have little in common with Christian
teaching, for he has written:

> Morality is simply the expression of the highest interest of the
> group—this time of the entire humanity living in a limited biosphere.
> Spirituality is the perennial search for total consciousness and union
> with the cosmos, the infinitely large, the outer reaches of the heavens,
> the conjunction of inner and outer space.[152]

In April 1985 he delivered the keynote address at the annual convention of
the National Catholic Education Association (NCEA) in St. Louis. The theme of
the St. Louis convention was "Gateway to Global Understanding."[153] As one conservative Catholic writer noted, the theme was that society (including religion)
must be restructured "to conform to a 'global model' which will ensure peace
and justice and perfect harmony in the New Age toward which humanity is inevitably 'evolving'."[154] Other speakers included the professor of astronomy and
atheist Carl Sagan, New Age networker Robert Theobald,[155] and several other
promoters of Global New Age Education.

Muller commented in the NCEA's glossy journal *Momentum* that "we know
so much we are probably of divine character," adding that as "cosmic beings,
divine beings," we find evolution grants us a cosmos becoming aware of itself

---

[151]Ibid., 166.

[152]Muller, *Most of All They Taught Me Happiness*, 194.

[153]The NCEA launched its "Peace Education" program in 1972. Its aim was to seek
to develop a global consciousness among its member educators, thus laying a planetary
framework for integrated curricula development. See Gerald and Patricia Mische, *Toward
a Human World Order* (New York/Ramsey NY: Paulist Press, 1977) 308.

[154]Helen Hull Hitchcock, "Catholic Education Goes Over the Rainbow: The NCEA
and the New Age," *Fidelity Magazine* 4/9 (August 1985): 26.

[155]Economist-educationist Robert Theobald is involved in a group called Communications Era Task Force and he calls himself a "futurist." He is known for his work in
setting up Action linkages, a continental network of people concerned with social transformation. See Ferguson, *The Aquarian Conspiracy*, 59, 191, 205, 218-20, 224, 353. A 1987
edition of this book contains some new material.

as God.[156] This is his constant theme. As main speaker at a convention in San Diego in 1983, he stated: "the earth and, ultimately the cosmos are becoming self-conscious through Networking and the evolution of humankind."[157]

Concerning the doctrine of evolution, Muller has stated: "I believe the most fundamental thing we can do today is to believe in evolution."[158] In his address to the NCEA in 1985, he said that there was "a need to design a core curriculum for every Catholic school on this planet" and that he had written such a "global core curriculum."[159]

*The Robert Muller School: World Core Curriculum Manual* (published by Robert Muller School, Arlington, Texas),[160] is in effect an eighty-five-page school brochure, incorporating a long passage on the philosophy of Global Education, ascribed to Robert Muller, and a detailed description of a curriculum that arises out of that philosophy. This philosophy is clearly expressed in the International Teilhard Compendium *The Desire to be Human*, of which he is coeditor:

> We must now administer our planet well, learn the art of fulfilled living, practice justice, love and tolerance, and celebrate the miracle of life through individual peace, happiness, joy, altruism and harmony. . . . "The World Core Curriculum" is an overview of the working out of that philosophy in a school dedicated to Muller's principles.[161]

Eleven pages of the *World Core Curriculum* are devoted to a paper produced by Muller for a convention in 1981 on the theme "Catholic Education, A World of Difference." The goal of education he defines elsewhere is "to make each child like a king or queen in the universe, an expanded being aggrandized by the

---

[156]R. Muller, cited by Hitchcock, "Catholic Education Goes over the Rainbow: The NCEA and the New Age," 25-26.

[157]Dean Halverson, "Transformation Celebration," *SCP Magazine*, (January 1984): 4. Cited in Tal Brooke, *When the World Will Be as One: The Coming New World Order in the New Age* (Eugene OR: Harvest House, 1989) 206-207. Muller's address was to the Ninth Annual Mandala Conference at the Town and Country Center in San Diego, August 1983. An audience of 2,200 were present.

[158]Kristin Murphy, "United Nations' Robert Muller . . . A Vision of Global Spirituality," *The Movement Newspaper* (September 1983): 10. Cited in Miller, *A Crash Course on the New Age Movement*, 53.

[159]Robert Muller, cited by Randy England, *The Unicorn in the Sanctuary* (Rockford IL: Tan Books, 1991) 47. England attended the conference and the keynote address.

[160]Robert Muller Unit School (accredited from "birth to twelfth grade") received certification from UNESCO as "A Participating Institution in the UNESCO Associated Schools Project in Education for International Cooperation and Peace."

[161]Zonneveld and Muller, eds. *The Desire to be Human*, 17-20, 302-10.

vastness of our knowledge."[162] There is now a growing network of "Robert Muller Schools" teaching the World Core Curriculum.[163]

Muller defines a good spiritual life as having "spiritual exercises of interiority, meditation, prayer and *communion with the universe and eternity or God*."[164] He has called for the publishing of a worldwide New Age bible which would both implement the divine commandments of the Bible and "show how the United Nations is a modern biblical institution." He argues that this should be done for the Christian, "as well as all great religious or sacred books, such as the Koran, the Grant Sahib, etc."[165]

Like Teilhard, he envisages a World Religion transcending doctrines and creeds which is focused on the "Cosmic Christ," supposedly found in all religions. He believes that the exclusive claims of Christianity must be abandoned, for he has written: "Religions must actively cooperate to bring to unprecedented heights a better understanding of the mysteries of life and of our place in the universe. 'My religion, right or wrong and My nation, right or wrong,' must be abandoned forever in the Planetary Age."[166]

Muller's Teilhardian vision is to see Catholic education merge science and religion. This, he believes, would prepare children for the coming of an interdependent, planetary age, which he suggests has been foretold by all the leading prophets throughout history.[167] Like Teilhard, he believes humanity is evolving toward a single consciousness which he explains by the use of the metaphor "planetary brain."

He sees every person as an important neuron in this brain, which is constituted by the myriad "networkings" among people.[168] In a lecture entitled "A Cosmological Vision of the Future," he stated:

---

[162]R. Muller, *The Beacon* (New York: Lucis Publishing Co., July/August 1982) 299. Cited in England, *The Unicorn in the Sanctuary*, 48.

[163]*World Goodwill Newsletter* 3 (1992): 8. Other schools listed which implement the same "visionary educational initiatives" include the worldwide Waldorf School movement based on the teachings of Rudolf Steiner, the schools based on the ideas of Juddi Krishnamurti, the global network of peace studies centres, and Atlantic College schools. Schumacher College based in the Devon countryside of southern England, which caters to adult education, is based on the same principles. Fritjof Capra, David Bohm, James Lovelock, and other New Age leaders lecture at this residential establishment for a five-week-long course.

[164]Muller, *The Beacon*, 332.

[165]Muller, *New Genesis*.

[166]Ibid., 183.

[167]Ibid., 8.

[168]Jessica Lipnack and Jeffrey Stamps, *Networking* (Garden City NY: Doubleday, 1982) 193.

You, as cosmic and earth cells, are part of a vast biological and evolutionary phenomenon which is of first importance at this stage, namely,
Humanity as a whole, the whole human species, has become the brain,
the heart, the soul, the expression and the action of the Earth. We have
now a world brain which determines what can be dangerous or mortal
for the planet: the United Nations and its agencies, and innumerable
groups and networks around the world, are part of this brain. We are a
world heart. . . . All this is a manifestation of the fact that on this planet
after having evolved from protozoas to metazoas, we are now becoming
what one could call terrozoas.

. . . I am predicting that we are rapidly moving into a cosmic consciousness . . . each of us is a cosmic unit, that we have the ingredients
of the total cosmos in ourselves. . . . the religions are trying to tell us:
"Be in tune with the Universe. Be in union with eternity. Remember
that your temporary lives have a message, a duty to fulfil."[169]

That mankind's evolutionary destiny is linked to experiencing "cosmic consciousness," is a central tenet of New Age Movement thought. The concept is rooted
in pantheism, gnosticism, and monism, and was expounded in detail well before
Teilhard's publications by R. M. Bucke and J. Lonsdale Bryans (the latter
author's work is dealt with in detail in §5.2 below).

*The Beacon*, a bimonthly publication of the openly occult Lucis Trust,
disseminates Muller's views on education. The goals of Lucis Trust include the
establishment of a "New World Order," a new world religion, and a new world
leader.[170] The New Age "World Core Curriculum" designed by Muller is used
at the Robert Muller School of Ageless Wisdom (Arlington, Texas), an
accredited private institution certified as a "UN-Associated School." Among its
teaching materials are books and computer diskettes with such titles as "Education in the New Age," "Toward a World Religion for the New Age," "Teaching
the Gaia Hypothesis" (that planet earth is to be regarded as a living organism),[171]
and "Whole Brain" teaching.[172] It is noteworthy that Maria Montessori's concept
of "cosmic education" has similarities to Teilhard's vision.

---

[169]Robert Muller, "A Cosmological Vision of the Future," *Teilhard Review* 25/2
(Summer 1990): 41-42.

[170]England, *The Unicorn in the Sanctuary*, 51-52.

[171]James E. Lovelock, *Gaia* (New York: Oxford University Press, 1979). The earth
is named "Gaia" after the Greek goddess of the earth. For a discussion of the original
myth of Gaia see Charlene Spretnak, *Lost Goddesses of Early Greece* (Boston: Beacon
Press, 1981).

[172]Steichen, *Ungodly Rage*, 244.

Muller claims that he discovered "spirituality" in the religions of Buddhism and Hinduism and he presents a view of God as a force, a "cosmic" force that is indistinguishable from the universe as a whole. The propulsive thrust of evolution, in his view, is to bring mankind to the realization that it is divine. Muller sees "no compelling reason" for people to switch religions and advocates syncretism, for he states:

> Our planet, all life on it, and in particular human life, is a manifestation of cosmic or divine forces of the universe. Within us therefore resides a basic cosmic force that impels us to respond to our evolutionary duties. . . .
> Humankind is seeking no less than its reunion with the "divine," its transcendence into ever higher forms of life. Hindus call our earth Brahma, or God, for *they rightly see no difference between our earth and the divine.* This ancient simple truth is slowly dawning again upon humanity.[173]

> We must elevate ourselves again as light, cosmic beings in deep communion with the universe and eternity. We must reestablish the unity of our planet and of our beings with the universe and divinity. . . . We must see our planet and ourselves as cells of a universe which is becoming increasingly conscious of itself in us. That is our royal road out of the present bewilderment.[174]

Randy England, who has documented the infiltration of the New Age Movement within the Roman Catholic Church, describes such statements as "syncretistic groping" which "gives us a 'cut & paste' system in which Christianity puts in only a cameo appearance."[175]

One chapter of Muller's book *New Genesis: Shaping a Global Spirituality*[176] is called "The Reappearance of the Christ." It is a transcript of an address he gave at a conference sponsored by the theosophists. The footnote for the chapter heading indicates that the material was delivered to an Arcane School conference. Located in the UN Plaza, New York City, the Arcane School[177] is one of the

---

[173]R. Muller, cited in England, *The Unicorn in the Sanctuary*, 50.

[174]Ibid.

[175]Ibid.

[176]The book contains 25 addresses and contributions given on different occasions by Muller. For a review by Ursula King, see *The Teilhard Review* 18/1 (1983): 24-25.

[177]The Arcane School, 866 United Nations Plaza, Suite 566-567, New York NY 10017. According to one of its brochures, the school is nonsectarian, and respects the right of each student to hold his or her own views and beliefs. It does not rely upon an authoritarian presentation of any one line of thought or code of ethics. Material used in

major Lucis Trust divisions and was founded by theosophist Alice Bailey in 1923.

One of three fundamental requirements of the training in the School is "occult meditation" and disciples are taught to "cooperate with the Plan of Hierarchy" elaborated in the writings of Alice Bailey. Serving "the Plan" by serving humanity is central to the esotericism which forms a practical way of life for disciples and prepares them for "service in the Aquarian Age."[178]

In the conclusion of *New Genesis*, Muller declares that through the divinization of the earth Man will "have brought heaven down to earth" and God and man will be united as the *Alpha* and *Omega*. Instead of Jerusalem as the throne from which the millennial reign of Christ will be based, the United Nations building in Manhattan, New York, will become the focus of world peace.[179] In the chapter on his "Teilhardian Enlightenments," Muller wrote:

> I have come to believe firmly today that our future peace, justice, fulfillment, happiness, and harmony on this planet will not depend on world government but on divine or cosmic government, meaning that we must seek and apply the "natural," "evolutionary," "divine," "universal" or "cosmic" laws which must rule our journey in the cosmos. Most of these laws can be found in the great religions and prophecies, and they are being rediscovered slowly but surely in the world organizations.
>
> Any Teilhardian will recognize in this the spiritual transcendence which he [Teilhard] announced so emphatically as the next step in our evolution. He had arrived at this conclusion both from his archaeological and theological studies. I had arrived at mine through three decades of observation and endeavors in our planet's first universal government.[180]

Teilhard's visionary jargon, so evident in Muller's statements, became so widely quoted during the 1960s and 1970s by influential leaders such as President John F. Kennedy, that his ideas have become common coinage in the West. Teilhard's books have sold in the millions and have been translated into all major

---

the lesson courses is drawn from a variety of sources. The knowledge, insight, and wisdom, and capacity to wield spiritual energy resulting from work and training with the Arcane School should be expressed and applied in daily living service in helping to materialize the Plan of God and to aid in solving the problems of humanity.

[178]From Arcane School brochure supplied by the Triangle Center, PO Box 25, Paekakariki, Wellington NZ. The Aquarian Age is the "New Age" issued in under the astrological sign Aquarius.

[179]Muller, *New Genesis*, 190-91.

[180]Muller, "My Five Teilhardian Enlightenments," in Perlinski ed., *The Spirit of the Earth*, 124. Repr. in Muller, *New Genesis*, 159-68.

languages in the world. Those who have never read his books become aware of him through the popular press. Here his ideas are often presented with a seductive appeal. On 11 October 1981 the *Los Angeles Times* described Teilhard's vision of the noosphere. Teilhard's writings, it stated, argue for "the coming of a deeply moral superhumanity ennobled by the universal spirit of the cosmic Christ [as human consciousness evolves through] the "noosphere" . . . the converging-but-distinctly-individual spirits transcend space and matter and mystically join god-Omega at the Omega point."

Teilhard's influence has continued unabated in the popular press and within the NCEA. Those attending recent NCEA conventions have often been exposed to neognosticism packaged under the alluring labels of "global transformation," "revolution in consciousness," or similar jargon.

Through the continuing efforts of Robert Muller, Teilhard's calls for a convergence of religion and science, a new universalism, and the "birthing" of a new, living planetary system, are being delivered. Muller delivered this message in the first plenary address, "Interfaith Understanding," at the 1993 Parliament of World's Religions, an eight-day convocation (28 August-4 September), held in Chicago's Palmer House Hilton Hotel. The eight-day convocation was held to promote understanding and collaboration among the world's religions. There were 6,500 in attendance from about 250 religious traditions. Muller called for a new spiritual world order and the setting up by the United Nations of a global Parliament of the World's Religions to work together with its other United Nations global agencies.

Roman Catholicism was well represented at the conference. Archbishop of Chicago Joseph Cardinal Bernardin participated in the opening and closing ceremonies. In a major presentation, Archbishop Francesco Gioia, a Vatican official, presented the official position of Rome on religious dialogue. Numerous lay and religious Catholics made presentations and participated in dialogue. Also present were representatives from seemingly every school of Hinduism and Buddhism; Jains, Sikhs, Confucianists, and Taoists; Zoroastrians, Jews, Muslims, and Baha'is; representatives of numerous indigenous religions, especially native American traditions; Mormons; Rastafarians, witches, and other neopagans; Theosophists and numerous other New Agers; liberal Protestants, and even a number of evangelicals (present only as observers).[181]

As the *Christian Century* observed: "A century ago Jews and Catholics looked to the Parliament to find greater recognition and acceptance in American life: at this year's event religious movements such as the Fellowship of Isis, the Covenant of the Goddess, and the Lyceum of Venus of Healing sought attention

---

[181]Elliot Miller, "The 1993 Parliament of the World's Religions, part 1: Interreligious Dialogue or New Age Rally?" *Christian Research Journal* (Fall 1993): 8, 10-15.

and respectability alongside older, more established traditions."[182] The original World's Parliament of Religions—held in conjunction with the Columbia Exposition of the Chicago World's Fair (1893)—did indeed have a profound affect on twentieth-century religion. Although the gathering was predominantly Christian, both in terms of its themes and delegates, it was not truly global, since the majority of the world's religions were not represented. However, it provided an avenue for the favorable introduction of certain Eastern and Near Eastern religions to the West, including Hinduism, Buddhism, and the Baha'i faith.[183]

New Age researcher Elliot Miller, an evangelical observer, reports that the 1993 Parliament called on all present to accept all religions as true. It went beyond the call to show tolerance, compassion, understanding, and respect to followers of other religions. It called for a commitment "to a particular metaphysical view on no other grounds than that it has become the politically correct view." Miller adds:

> This metaphysical view is a religious relativism which states that truth is partially grasped by all religions but cannot be fully (exclusively) possessed by any. Such a view of truth presupposes that a special, uniquely authoritative revelation by God cannot or has not been given. Thus, it excludes at the outset the claims that provide the historic foundation for theistic religions such as Judaism, Christianity, and Islam. On the other hand, it fits in quite well with pantheism or even panentheism (God is *in* everything), since the underlying oneness of all reality in pantheistic/panentheistic systems allows for all religions to have a partial but incomplete grasp on truth.[184]

Leading New Age political figure Robert Muller, a thoroughgoing Teilhardian, is committed to this metaphysical view of religious relativism as the basis for global ecumenism. He is captivated by the astrological myth of the "dawning of the Age of Aquarius" which provided the initial basis for New Age optimism. In his address to the 1993 World's Religions Parliament he could not resist citing astrological support for believing that the Parliament would help usher us into the New Age. He advised the delegates of the Parliament that their collective recommendations be submitted to the United Nations as a contribution to the thinking being done on the "New World Order."[185]

---

[182]Leo D. Lefebure, "Global Encounter," *Christian Century* (22-29 September 1993) 887.

[183]Miller, "The 1993 Parliament of the World's Religions," 1: 10.

[184]Elliot Miller, "The 1993 Parliament of the World's Religions: part 2, The Fundamentalism of Tolerance" *Christian Research Journal* (Winter 1993): 16, 18-19, 32-35; quote is from 35.

[185]Miller, "The 1993 Parliament of the World's Religions," 1:12.

To emphasize the cosmic urgency of becoming involved with the Parliament, a range of New Age networkers and activists presented workshops and lectures promoting Teilhardian/New Age themes. New Age visionary and activist Barbara Marx Hubbard shared her concept of "conscious evolution." According to this New Age scenario, the current world "megacrisis" is of an evolutionary order, for the crisis is actually the birth of a new, living planetary system (that is, a Global Being, or "Gaia"). She claimed that in each of the world's religions there exists a seed, pattern, or blueprint of what is coming next in evolution. Our task is to speed up this process of "conscious evolution."[186] In the same fashion, in her New Age "Manifesto," *The Aquarian Conspiracy,* Marilyn Ferguson, after reminding her coconspirators that they are coconspirators with Teilhard de Chardin, closes by saying: "You are a seed, a silent promise. You are the conspiracy."

*Jean Houston*

Through her [Jean Houston] Teilhard has entered into the Human Potential Movement, the Omega Institute and different New Age workshops.[187]

Another New Age luminary to influence the NCEA is Jean Houston, who addressed the 1982 and 1984 NCEA conventions and opened the Chicago convention. She makes it widely known that she was strongly influenced by Teilhard in her youth.[188] In her public lecture I attended at Victoria University, Wellington (25 August 1992), she spoke passionately about an old Frenchman "Mr. Thayer" who befriended her in Central Park, New York, and shared with her his spiritual/evolutionary vision of the cosmos.

When she finally named him as Teilhard de Chardin, there was an audible gasp of delight that swept across the audience of almost 500 people. It was as though the name struck a deep resonance with the crowd, the majority of whom were already in tune with Teilhard's spiritual vision.[189] "Through her" [Houston], as theologian Thomas M. King SJ has noted, "Teilhard has entered into the

---

[186]Ibid., 14.

[187]King, "The Milieux Teilhard Left Behind," 95.

[188]Perlinski, ed. *The Spirit of the Earth*, 167-68. Also see "Jean Houston, *New Realities Magazine* 5/4 (San Francisco 1983). Houston tells of her childhood memories of conversations she had with a man during long walks in Central Park. A poignant account of her encounter with Teilhard is told in her book *God Seed: The Journey of Christ*. It is reprinted in a foreword to the book *Meditations with Teilhard de Chardin* (Santa Fe NM: Bear & Co.) by Blanche Marie Gallagher IBVM.

[189]Two of the organizers of the lecture I spoke to, who stated that they knew many in attendance, agreed with my perception of the crowd response.

Human Potential Movement, the Omega Institute and different New Age workshops."[190]

Houston's Wellington lecture entitled "Breakthroughs in Social Transformation: Fractals" was advertised in a brochure as "Toward Higher Levels of Civilization." It described her as having "the vision of a high-level civilization—a planetary culture in the birth process—the new millennium." She says, "Something stupendous is happening in our time because of crosscultural fertilization through the media and the migrations of people. We have the potentials beyond our wildest dreams."

Houston, one-time Catholic, codirector of the Foundation for Mind Research (founded in 1964 in Pomona, New York), and past president (1978–1979) of the Association for Humanistic Psychology, is a leading voice of the "human potential movement." She pioneered research into determining the effects of LSD on human personality, and is considered an expert on nontherapeutic and educational applications of nondrug induced altered states of consciousness.[191]

She is listed in the closed membership U.S. Association for the Club of Rome (November 1979), which includes some of the world's leading industrialists, scholars, and financiers.[192] Among other activities, she has chaired or been keynote speaker at national and international conferences, such as the United Nations Conference on the Unity of the Human Spirit, the U.S. policymakers' symposium on the Possible Society, Practical Policy Alternatives.[193]

She is also described as an internationally known futurist, philosopher, scientist, psychologist, charismatic, dynamic leader, master teacher, explorer, one who consults heads of state, and is promoted as "one of the most remarkable women of our time" who is on the "cutting edge in the development of human capacities."[194] Her seminars listed in an advertising brochure include the following: "The Meaning of Being Human on the Eve of Millennial Change," "Myths of the Future/Dreaming The Future," "Empowering Us to Become Sacred Stewards of

---

[190]King, "The Milieux Teilhard Left Behind," 95.

[191]Robert Masters and Jean Houston, *Mind Games* (New York: Viking, 1972). Information from dust jacket of book.

[192]Constance Cumbey, *A Planned Deception* (Shreveport LA: Huntington, 1983) 185, 216. The full listing of USA membership is found on 213-22.

[193]Listed from seminar brochure. She has also conducted workshops for organizations such as the Hong Kong Institute of Personnel Management, American Association for Training and Development, and American Society for Public Administration. She has been a consultant to companies such as AT&T, IBM, Hewlett-Packard Europe, Wilson Learning, Xerox Corporation, and Shell (Netherlands).

[194]Advertisements in *Evening Post* (19 August) and in *Contact* (20 August) for lecture at Victoria University, Student Union, Wellington NZ, 25 August 1992.

Aotearoa—The Earth,"[195] and "Beyond Your Wildest Dreams: Exploring the Creative Imagination."

Houston has been reported as being an advocate of rebirthing techniques which encourage people to regress into their past evolutionary lives as animals.[196] It is noteworthy that Robert Muller credits her with having launched his speaking career, and they often address the same conferences.[197]

Like all New Age leaders, she has an unbiblical perception of Christ, for she claims that he taught that "God indwells every person . . . [and] that the indwelling God, expressed as God-Son, Logos, Christ, or Chalice of Life, is a unique expression within us of the universal parent-being."[198] She has referred to sin as "unskilled behavior" which can be transcended through sacred rituals which enlighten participants to the Christ within us all.[199] In an interview she stated in 1983: "I predict that in our lifetime we will see the rise of essentially a New World Religion. . . . I believe a new spiritual *system* will emerge."[200]

American Catholic bureaucracy has been infiltrated by New Age propaganda beyond the sources of NCEA convention speakers. For example, its influence can be found in reports on a "Catholic Education Futures Project" in which the NCEA participated between 1985 and 1988, summarized in the September 1988 issue of *Momentum*. In one article the importance of creation-centered spirituality in educating for "global citizenship" is stressed and the bibliography of the "Planning Phase" includes a number of New Agers including Thomas Berry and physicist Fritjof Capra.[201] As Donna Steichen observes, in NCEA workshops "futuring" is "a lengthy, repetitious, groupthink process, having less to do with designing for the future than with redesigning the participants to think along the New Age lines suggested by the reading list."[202]

The NCEA is clearly taking seriously the subjectivist theories of humanist and transpersonal psychology, despite the fact that these ideas are not taken seriously by leading academic and professional psychologists. Jean Houston's "pop

---

[195]*Aotearoa* is the name given to New Zealand by the indigenous people (Maoris) of the country, and now promoted as an alternative name by some Maoris and non-Maoris. Some seek to have Aotearoa as the only official name.

[196]Bob Larson, *Straight Answers on the New Age* (Nashville: Thomas Nelson, 1989) 238.

[197]Steichen, *Ungodly Rage*, 244.

[198]Jean Houston, *Godseed: The Journey of Christ* (Amity NY: Amity House, 1988), 54.

[199]Ibid., 21.

[200]"Jean Houston: The New World Religion," *The Tarrytown Letter* (June/July 1983): 5.

[201]Steichen, *Ungodly Rage*, 244-45.

[202]Ibid., 245.

psychology" is either unknown or viewed with disdain by many legitimate psychologists. Professor Paul Vitz, a psychologist at New York University, states that it is "a sign of the pathological condition of most of our educators that they would buy this stuff. It's Shirley MacLaine [a New Age film star/writer] in textbook form. It's embarrassing."[203]

Through a host of New Age luminaries, "futurists," and global networkers like Jean Houston and Robert Muller, Teilhard's religiophilosophical ideas and "prophetic" vision are being effectively disseminated throughout the world. The "conspirators" have an "agenda" which has become more clear as the movement has become more "visible." In the next chapter we examine "The Plan" that is being followed by those who are assuming "cosmic leadership" within the movement. Many of them are aware that their teachings are incompatible with the philosophical underpinnings of the Judeo-Christian heritage upon which the Western world has developed. The "conspiracy" is being waged by many gifted and alluring personalities whose charm and "mystique" disguises the insidious nature of their message. While the Aquarian Conspiracy has been described by some commentators as a benign movement promoting the transformation of inner consciousness to effect a new "global consciousness," great discernment is required in the assessment of its teachings. While many New Age Movement aspirations are good, it is the overall orientation of its teachings, with its mixture of truth and error, that is of concern.

---

[203]Paul Vitz, cited in ibid., 247.

# Teilhard in the New Age

I am predicting that we are rapidly moving into a cosmic consciousness
. . . each of us is a cosmic unit, that we have the ingredients of the total
cosmos in ourselves. . . . the religions are trying to tell us: "Be in tune
with the Universe. Be in union with eternity."[1]         —*Robert Muller*

## 5.1 The "Wisdom" of the "Ascended Masters"

Many New Age Movement leaders today claim to either follow or "channel"
messages from a select group of "Ascended Masters" who impart Ancient Wisdom. According to theosophical doctrine, which forms a significant part of the
philosophical underpinnings of New Age thought, specific individuals from the
human species have evolved, spiritually (rather than biologically), to a place of
cosmic leadership. A formative influence on New Age thought has been the
writings of theosophist Alice A. Bailey (1880–1949), founder of the Arcane
School.[2] She claimed to have channeled the distilled wisdom of the Tibetan spirit
entity Djwhal Khul (D.K.) and many decades ago wrote about a coming "New
World Order."

The influence of the "wisdom of the spiritual Masters" is pervasive among
Teilhardians. In 1991, the late Claude Curling, a leading Teilhardian, stated in
his address at the World Goodwill Seminar in London:

> We now have within our reach a universal vision of the cosmos that can
> unify the human race as it is drawn forward to nonseparability by the
> power of relation. The new model of reality, evolved from within
> science itself, is not tied to a particular race, culture or religion. It
> frames the value of humanity within the scale of the dynamic system of
> the cosmos, a cosmos which has given birth to consciousness, and

---

[1]Robert Muller, "A Cosmological Vision of the Future," *Teilhard Review* 25/2 (Summer 1990): 41-42.

[2]The Arcane School is one of the major Lucis Trust divisions located in New York
city. Lucis Trust is a nonprofit tax-exempt educational corporation founded in 1922. It
derives its income from voluntary donations.

carries us forward within its network of light. Each of us stands at a new threshold within the convergent evolution of humanity.

All things are being drawn into unity by the power of the spirit. All that we are, all that is within, and all that is without, flows forward towards that unity, pulled by a kind of spiritual gravity as compelling, as incessant, as the force of physical gravity that holds us to the Earth. Ordinary physical gravity acts on matter through space. Spiritual gravity acts on consciousness through time, pulling us forward. To serve the planet and its future we must go with that flow, and ourselves act as channels. Our approach to the unity is therefore evolutionary and progressive. This gravitational pressure changes us day by day. . . . We live with a dynamic directed to the future. *The wisdom of the spiritual Masters is our guide to this future, and through the evolution of consciousness seeks to awaken us to an awareness of the reality these Masters knew and share with us.*[3]

Curling refers to the same eclectic group of "spiritual Masters" referred to in the writings of Alice Bailey. This is not surprising, as World Goodwill is a division of Lucis Trust which actively disseminates Bailey's occultic writings. Curling's address is thoroughly Teilhardian in its content, which is not surprising since he was a council member of the Teilhard Center (UK).

In 1991 Curling presented a paper to the Eleventh International Teilhard Conference entitled "Convergence, the Universe and Ourselves." According to the conference report, he used Teilhard's injunction "Make your way towards what is most interior in the soul and most new in the future" to investigate "the god ahead and the god within." Using what he called "computer poetry," he "ingeniously transformed images, bringing Alpha and Omega together on the screen, resulting in the formation of the human heart."[4]

Fritjof Capra has described the ultimate state of consciousness sought by New Agers in his book *The Turning Point*, as the one "in which all boundaries and dualisms have been transcended and all individuality dissolves into universal, undifferentiated oneness."[5] In this state of "cosmic consciousness" as New Agers call it, reality is viewed as a *gestalt*, a continuous whole, in which all conceptual opposites such as good and evil disappear. New Agers regard this as a classic

---

[3]An address by Claude Curling given at the World Goodwill Seminar in London on 21 December 1991 celebrating the Festival Week of the New Group of World Servers. The full paper is available from Sydney Goodwill Unit of Service Ltd., PO Box 627, Caringbah NSW 2229, or the Triangle Center, PO Box 25, Paekakariki NZ.

[4]Conference report by Eoghan Callaghan, the Eleventh International Conference at London Colney, 26-28 April 1991. *Teilhard Review* 26/2 (Summer 1991): 61.

[5]Capra, *The Turning Point*, 371.

presentation of Taoism, unaware of Nasr's warning regarding recent "works seeking to relate modern physics to Oriental esoteric doctrines," that: "Not all of these studies have displayed a full grasp of the Oriental doctrines involved and many deal with traditional teachings from a profane point of view."[6] Paradoxical descriptions of the Ultimate Reality may mislead when applied out of context. They may lead to, often inadvertently, the creation of bizarre caricatures of Oriental doctrines.

Such cautions also apply to the path to *prajna* called *satori* (enlightenment) taught in Zen Buddhism. *Satori* is the perception of Reality itself in its wholeness, a firsthand experience. One who has experienced *prajna* is supposed to have infallible assurance: "I am absolute knower." *Prajna* involves gaining direct knowledge through the overcoming of all subject/object divisions. It is contrasted with rational or conceptual knowledge (for example, doctrines) based on analysis and differentiation (such knowledge is called *vijnana*).

Frithjof Schuon, while acknowledging such a higher faith, warns that:

> This higher faith is something altogether different from the irresponsible and arrogant taking of liberties so characteristic of the profane improvisors of Zen or Jnang, who seek to take a "shortcut" by stripping themselves of the essential human contact of a realization, whereas in the East, and in the normal conditions of ethical and liturgical ambience, this context is largely supplied in advance. One does not enter the presence of a king by the back door.[7]

Like Teilhard, Capra argues that the inadequacies of the mechanistic Cartesian paradigm forced him to embrace a new paradigm which is holistic.[8] He argues that Western philosophy and religion, being based on a dualistic and immobilist worldview, are less compatible with the new findings of science. The view Capra expounds was first comprehensively formulated in the 1930s by Austrian-born biologist Ludwig von Bertalanffy (d. 1975), the father of General Systems Theory.[9]

This theory proposes that several natural laws determine the functioning of *all* systems including those studied in the physical and biological sciences. It can be summed up in the statement "the whole is more than the sum of the parts," which has been attributed to Aristotle[10] and also to Hegel.[11] This statement is re-

---

[6]Seyyed H. Nasr, *Knowledge and the Sacred*, Gifford Lectures (Edinburgh: Edinburgh University Press, 1981) 116.

[7]Schuon, *Logic and Transcendence*, 206n.12.

[8]Capra, *The Turning Point*, 59, 77-78.

[9]For a good introduction, see Gerald M. Weinberg, *An Introduction to General Systems Thinking* (New York: John Wiley & Sons, 1975).

[10]Ludwig von Bertalanffy, "The History and Status of General System Theory," in

garded by the authors of the book *Systems Thinking*, as expressing "the essence of the general systems theory."[12] Capra considers aspects of the "new physics" to be very close to the general systems theory, in that it emphasizes relationships rather than isolated entities, and perceives these relationships as being inherently dynamic.[13]

Capra and Teilhard applied this approach, unaware of its present sophisticated status. As a consequence of this approach, both were dynamic-minded, and both were convinced that the creation was an ongoing process in the present world. New Agers, like Capra, reiterate the notion implicit in all these works, that there is a self-organizing force behind the universe, with an inherent bias toward promoting higher and higher levels of organization and complexification. More recently they have begun to invoke the work of Nobel Prize Laureate Ilya Prigogine on nonequilibrium thermodynamics[14] and dissipative structures to bolster this argument.[15] Marilyn Ferguson argues that the very instability of these structures is the key to transformation, and applies this to society.

In his presentation to the 1983 United Nations Colloquium, David L. Smith, a Teilhardian, wrote: "The work of systems theorists, most notably that of Nobel-prize-winning physicist Ilya Prigogine, demonstrates that in fact human history is not necessarily destined to entropy." Such statements from New Agers are speculative assertions. Their reliance on avant-garde science to promote a view similar to Teilhard's theory of "complexity-consciousness" is an attempt to side-step the implications of the Second Law of Thermodynamics.[16] This Law teaches

---

*Trends in General Systems Thinking*, ed. George J. Klir (New York: John Wiley & Sons, 1977) 21.

[11]John P. van Gigch, *Applied General System Theory* (New York: Harper & Row, 1974) 49.

[12]Nic J. T. A. Kramer and Jacob de Smit, *Systems Thinking* (Leiden: H. E. Stenfert Kroese B.V., 1977) 3.

[13]Capra, *The Turning Point*, 267. The similarity is especially shown in the "bootstrap" approach in the new physics. Capra states: "Systems thinking is process thinking; form becomes associated with process, interrelation with interaction, and opposites are unified through oscillation" (267).

[14]Thermodynamics is the science of relations between heat and other (mechanical, electrical, etc.) forms of energy. Nonequilibrium thermodynamic theory applies to open systems such as those in which life would have arisen (according to evolutionists), in which there was a continual supply of raw energy (e.g., the sun).

[15]See Russell, *The Global Brain*, 61-64, self-organizing systems; 64-66, dissipative structures.

[16]The effect of the second law under classical thermodynamic theory (applied to a closed system) is to make biochemical evolution (life from nonlife) "highly improbable" according to Prigogine.

that, although the total energy of the cosmos remains constant, *the amount of energy available to do useful work in the cosmos is always diminishing.*

In simple terms it means that entropy, the thermodynamic characteristic of randomness or disorder within a system, will always increase in an isolated system (where there is no energy flow). Even when there is energy flow (defined as an open or nonequilibrium system), it does not produce organizing work or increased information content without a "converting mechanism" (such a mechanism is the chlorophyll molecule in photosynthesis which utilizes the raw energy of the sun to do useful work). Just burning gasoline, for example, does not produce organizing work or increased information without the "converting mechanism" of a complex engine. Prigogine has admitted that the principle underlying the *decrease* in entropy in some open systems (for example, crystal formation) "cannot explain the formation of biological structures."[17]

New Agers view the Christian church as a spiritual dinosaur heading for permanent extinction, as well as being responsible for division, war, injustice, hatred, mistrust, and bigotry. Many, like Capra, blame Christianity for the present global ecological crisis, because of its supposed emphasis on dualism and patriarchy.[18] Ferguson states that above all else dualism must be abandoned if we are to gain a sense of the connectedness of all life and bring about transformation.[19] It is ironic that in her attempt to proselytize the "new paradigm," she constantly contrasts the "old paradigm" with the new, creating an immediate dualism. Rather than transcend either/or distinctions (dualism) she perpetuates the "mindset" she most vigorously attacks.

For many New Agers, the answer to the world's crises is seen to lie with a return to a deification of nature and the worship of the cosmos as God immanent. However, some have problems with such a view since it contradicts their belief in a spiritual factor in man and inner human development.[20]

---

[17]Ilya Prigogine, Gregoire Nicolis and Agnes Babloyantz, "Thermodynamics of Evolution," *Physics Today* (November 1972): 23-28.

[18]Capra, *The Turning Point*, 41. Terrence McKenna, a New Age leader from California, expresses the problem in blunt terms: "The Judeo-Christian ethic is that man is the lord of creation, and can do as he wishes. The pagan, archaic-revival point of view is biological, ecological, and stresses coadaptive relations. We are in a global suicide crisis—and Christianity has a lot to answer for." McKenna, quoted in the *San Francisco Chronicle* (25 April 1990). As John Drane points out: "Such a view is at best naive and uninformed. Quite often it is deliberately malicious." See John Drane, *What Is the New Age Saying to the Church?* (London: Marshall Pickering, 1991) 163-67.

[19]Ferguson, *The Aquarian Conspiracy*, 131.

[20]Writing in *Gnosis* magazine, Richard Smoley points out the problem of viewing Man as embedded in nature: "There is a danger, I believe, in equating God with nature . . . man is not fundamentally of nature. The truest, deepest part of him is beyond the cycle of reproduction and survival. To deify nature is to forget this and to put man at the

In his book *New Age Politics*, Mark Satin maintains that the New Age Movement has its roots in Western paganism, and will lead to the emergence of a new "planetary consciousness," a phrase used by Teilhard de Chardin. Satin's New Age Society is one that is androgynous and feminist, neooccult and paganistic, tribal and cooperative, and fully and globally planetized.[21] He has stated:

> Planetary consciousness recognizes our oneness . . . with all life everywhere and with the planet . . . the interdependence of all humanity. . . .
>
> Planetary consciousness sees each of us as "cells in the body of humanity," as Planetary Citizens. . . . we are beginning to see the emergence of a new *collective* consciousness. . . .
>
> Planetary events are, in a sense, *conspiring to inspire* us to recognize our oneness and interdependence.[22]

New Age literature is infested with a plethora of buzzwords such as *interconnectivity, connection making, collective unconscious, global ecumenism, global village,*[23] *divinization of existence, networking, synchronicity,*[24] *synergistic,*[25] *centering, psychic justice, holistic,* and *planetary vision.* Some of these terms, products of current pantheistic/neopagan trends, are symptoms of the emerging pop culture associated with the New Age Movement. They are coined to express the "paradigm shift" that New Agers believe Western culture must undertake to reach a new level of "spiritual evolution."

Central to New Age thought is the belief that our thinking on reality needs to be radically restructured and that we need to gain access to a domain that transcends time and space for Man to fulfil his evolutionary destiny. Develop-

---

mercy of this cycle rather than to help him transcend it." See R. Smoley, "Fundamental Differences," *Gnosis* 14 (Winter 1990): 50-51. Cited in Drane, *What Is the New Age Saying to the Church?*, 166.

[21]Satin, *New Age Politics*, 90, 94, 96, 99.

[22]Ibid., 11, 148, 149.

[23]In his book *Understanding Media* (New York: McGraw-Hill, 1964), Marshall McLuhan described the coming world as a "global village," unified by communications technology and the rapid exchange and dissemination of information. He claimed that mankind would be remade by the flood of new knowledge.

[24]The theory of synchronicity states that nothing is accidental and it is invoked in the use of divination tools such as reading Tarot cards and I Ching. Tarot cards, which are sold in occult shops, are supposed to provide a way of seeing within rather than of foretelling the definite future.

[25]The term synergy is used particularly in reference to "transformative relationships," which Ferguson describes as: "a whole that is more than the sum of its parts. It is synergistic, holistic." Ferguson, *The Aquarian Conspiracy*, 392. Also see 156, 215, 332-37.

ments in technology such as space travel and holographic theory,[26] have enabled us to actually conceive of a dimension beyond space and time. Theoretical physics and cosmological research has also assisted and caused us to question the nature of reality in a new way.

David Bohm is a physicist widely quoted by New Agers. His starting point is the concept of "unbroken wholeness," and he seeks to investigate the order he believes to be inherent in the cosmic web of relations at a deeper level. He calls this deeper order "implicate," or "enfolded," and expounds the concept using the analogy of a hologram. In his view, like the hologram, the real world is structured in such a way that the whole is enfolded in each of its parts.

Capra notes that Bohm "sees mind and matter as being interdependent and correlated, but not causally connected. They are mutually enfolding projections of a higher reality which is neither matter nor consciousness."[27] Such concepts are promoted as being in tune with the intuitions of mystics and philosophers from bygone eras. These "truths"—the so-called "wisdom" of the "Spiritual Masters"—which have resurfaced in New Age thought, are promoted with such an intensity by New Age leaders, that it suggests they have become the new dogma.

In the colloquium to honor Teilhard held at the United Nations in New York in 1983, the link between Teilhard's work and so-called "new physics" was defined by the colloquium organizer. He argued that Teilhard's concept of "seeing," so central to his book *The Phenomenon of Man*, implies a symbiotic relationship between the interpretation of the inner and outer world. More importantly, he claimed that it leads to the conclusion that the outer physical world has no reality *independent* of the observer's inner perception, and that the "new physics" supports this view:

> Modern physicists agree with Parmenides, Whitehead, and Bishop Berkeley that consciousness is at the root of the material universe. The physical universe does not exist independent of the awareness of the participator; we construct ourselves, as we construct each other. *Seeing*, then, means to reconstruct and cocreate the world according to one's own image and after one's own likeness.[28]

Teilhard believed that our mental processes are in effect made up of the same "stuff" as the organizing principle of the cosmos. Man is seen to have unlimited evolutionary potential since he embodies the organizing principle of the cosmos. Mind, he said, was inherent in matter, and Man was only a description of matter having become conscious of itself. These philosophical views have

---

[26]Ibid., 177-87.
[27]Capra, *The Turning Point*, 96.
[28]Zonneveld, ed. *Humanity's Quest For Unity*, 11.

hardened into a new dogma which was evident throughout the 1983 United Nations colloquium publication. Reflecting on Teilhard's belief that "fuller being is closer union," the editor wrote:

> I may add to his [Teilhard's] words: a change in the quality of seeing, is a change of the Self, is a change of the Universe—or, to put it even more boldly: any attempt toward the perfection of the quality of seeing is an attempt to perfect, re-create and unite the Self, and to perfect, co-create and unite the Universe.[29]

For Teilhardians, as with devotees of the New Age Movement, the term *God* is the evolutionary drive to higher levels of consciousness. God is the sum total of consciousness in the universe, expanding through human evolution. Teilhard referred to a universe of *monads* linked to the Universal *Monad*. It was, as we have noted, the seventeeth-century philosopher and mathematician G. W. Leibniz, who had first postulated a universe of *monads*—units that incorporated the information of the whole. Teilhard conceived of the human person as nature's attempt to create a self-developing framework of introspective thought, wrapping the earth and the universe in a blanket of cocreative reflection.

Teilhard spoke of God as a "center of centers"[30] at the heart of matter. His concept of God should be distinguished from the Eastern concept of the *ekayanam*, or the point at which all centers converge. The latter is found in the *Brihadaranyaka Upanishad*, where it is part of an elucidation of the Self (*atman*) as that which is loved in everything that is loved. Accounts throughout the centuries of transcendental experience often described it as a mysterious "center," the penetration of some unknown but central realm. Ferguson notes: "This transcendent center is in the lore of all cultures, represented in mandalas, in alchemy, in the king's chamber in the pyramids ('fire in the middle'), the sanctum sanctorum, the holy of holies."[31]

For New Agers, the transcendent center is "God" *within*, the uniting of heart and mind in the soul through enlightenment. Harvard theology professor Gordon Kaufman defines the paradigm shift he and New Age followers endorse: the rejection of a God separate from His Creation is replaced with a concept of "serendipitous creativity"—a creative force that reveals itself throughout history and throughout the universe.[32] In such a system the distinction between the Prin-

---

[29]Ibid.

[30]Teilhard de Chardin, *Human Energy*, 68: "God can be defined as a *center of centers*. In this complexity lies the perfection of His unity—the only final goal logically attributable to the developments of spirit-matter."

[31]Ferguson, *The Aquarian Conspiracy*, 81-82.

[32]*US News and World Report* (23 December 1991): 56-64.

ciple as Being (God the Creator) and His Creation (derived, secondary, contingent and participating being) is destroyed.

Central to New Age teaching is the concept of self-transformation, the exploration of what Teilhard de Chardin referred to as the "within of things." To be transformed is to be aware of your mind, conscious of your own consciousness. By entering the "fourth dimension" of consciousness, New Agers believe they are empowered to comprehend the other three dimensions from a new perspective. Self-knowledge is enhanced even further if they go beyond this dimension. Marilyn Ferguson expressed it as follows: "The fourth dimension is not another place; it is *this* place, and it is immanent in us, a process."[33] This teaching is fully compatible with the vulgarized representations of Eastern mysticism which characterizes much of the New Age Movement's approach.

New Agers devotees heap scorn on any suggestion that Man's problem is rooted in his sinful nature. While conceding that man is alienated, he is only seen to be alienated from his "Higher Self" due to excrescential thinking patterns, reflecting ingrained patriarchy, and dualistic notions learned from childhood. The "solution," as in New Age representations of Eastern mystic healing, is seen to lie in readjustment to the cosmic energies. New Age "enlightenment" is seen by many New Age leaders to be the awakening to the Truth of being—that the Higher Self of each individual *is* the Christ.

The "New Age" message is that the reason most of us fail to recognize that we are God is due to our lack of "spiritual evolution." Such a view posits that the goal of evolution is towards Unity with the One Person. The entire race must rise to a higher awareness of God before all things that are possible with God (including Unity), become actual. Cosmic evolution directed by the "Cosmic Christ" is seen to be the means by which this is achieved. In this scheme, as Teilhard stated: "Evolution is Holy" and "Evolution makes Christ possible."

## 5.2 Cosmic Consciousness

As a child and a young man, Teilhard had a number of "mystical" experiences which he described later as a realization of cosmic consciousness. The term "cosmic consciousness" was coined by R. M. Bucke in 1901[34] to mean a state of enlightenment where a person discovers that he is part of the cosmic whole, one in being with all reality, and one with the Godhead. This path to "enlightenment," is central to the teachings of the New Age Movement today. Teilhard's "mystical" experiences of the fundamental oneness, beauty, and divine quality of nature predisposed him towards monism and pantheism, a nature mysticism that

---

[33]Ferguson, *The Aquarian Conspiracy*, 101.
[34]R. M. Bucke, *Cosmic Consciousness* (New York: Dutton, 1901).

remained with him for all his life, although it was later significantly modified at several points.

In a book entitled *The Curve of Fate*[35] (1941) written over a decade before any of Teilhard's major works were published, J. Lonsdale Bryans expounded in considerable detail within the framework of the doctrine of emergent evolution, the concept of cosmic consciousness. He also elaborated many of the main ideas that are central to Teilhard's religiophilosophical writings. Teilhard has been widely hailed by scholars as an original thinker who developed a synthesis of science and religion which showed that evolution has a definite goal. He is also credited with having dissolved the dualism created by the matter/spirit and body/soul distinctions of philosophers. However, Bryans had developed all these concepts well before Teilhard, and quite independently of him.

Christ, wrote Teilhard is "the end supernaturally but physically marked out as the consummation of humanity."[36] Bryans argued that "Christ" represented the "penultimate approximation to the evolutionary goal of humanity."[37]

> Jesus Christ thus claims and accomplishes [he wrote] by returning to life again after his death, the goal of evolution. **He starts as man *and* finishes as God** [emphasis added], the Christ-anointed Sovereign of the Universe, One with Divinity, the evolutionary 'son' of man who is the Son of God.[38]

In contrast to Bryans's perverse doctrine, orthodox Christian teaching states that Jesus Christ, the Word of God (*Logos*), has always possessed the Divine nature, being coequal, coeternal, and consubstantial with the Father, and the third eternal Person of the Holy Trinity (see John 1:1-3).

Bryans wrote that Jesus "attained to and lived upon a plane of transcendental perfection and *cosmic consciousness* unknown before or since."[39] He was "foremost" among the world's "illuminated beings, the flower of the genius of the race" and "the world's transcendent luminary."[40] By the term "cosmic consciousness"[41] he meant a state of "mystical" enlightenment as taught by R. M. Bucke

---

[35]J. Lonsdale Bryans, *The Curve of Fate* (London: Andrew Dakers, 1941). This work of over 300 pages is a précis of a longer treatise that involved more than a decade's research. The only review of this book I have located is one from *Punch* 202 (7 January 1942): 18-19. The reviewer describes the book as "turbid . . . but not without interest as a sign of the times."

[36]Teilhard de Chardin, *Activation of Energy*, 23.

[37]Bryans, *The Curve of Fate*, 23.

[38]Ibid., 92.

[39]Ibid., 108. Italics added.

[40]Ibid., 76, 80.

[41]Bryans refers to this term many times. Ibid., 49, 165, 172-173, 178, 180-92, 194-97,

(1901). Man achieves "cosmic consciousness," or what Bryans termed "Christ-hood," through the evolutionary process—"full man grown to full God."[42] "Christhood" is "the inevitable goal of evolution which is reached . . . [through a] process of acceleration in the tempo of the evolutionary phases [of] anthropol-ogy."[43] "Consummated Christhood," wrote Bryans, is the same as "consummated Evolution."[44] "The historic Christ stands forth revealed once more to twentieth-century man as the goal of mankind, evolution, and the future."[45]

The "Key to the secret of the Universe," according to Bryans, was recogni-tion that "all cosmic parts [are] equal to the whole," a concept central to the pan-theism of New Age thought. "Each part of infinity," wrote Bryans, "is thus not only equal to the whole but is, in reality, the whole. . . . This Infinity is only another word for Truth, for God, and for the actual Universe we live in. . . . man is God—and God is MAN."[46] "The particle, in fact, *is* the whole: coequal, co-eternal, [and] consubstantial with it."[47]

This metaphysical position, while being in full harmony with Teilhard's, is incompatible with biblical Christianity. It denies God's essential character, that of self-subsistent being (God's ipseity), denies the contingency of the creation to the Creator, and destroys the doctrine of God's transcendence. It also denies the ontological priority of Spirit over matter. Teilhard's conception of spirit and matter being two faces of the "cosmic-stuff" can no longer be viewed as an original contribution, for Bryans wrote:

> Matter, in short, is no more and no less than the outward and visible sign of the inward and spiritual Essence of the Universe—the UNKNOWN GOD. It is, therefore, essentially found to resemble much more closely that which we have always looked upon as "mind" than that which the fatuous Victorians were pleased to label "matter." [In conclusion] . . . matter = mind.[48]

Such a metaphysics denies the ontological priority of Mind to Matter, and denies the doctrine of a "first cause." Indeed, Bryans wrote:

> [F]or it is in that false idea [of a "first cause"], that false presentation of the fact, that lies the whole error of orthodox dualist theology. Cause

---

290, 304. He used the term "Cosmic-Ego" as a synonym.
[42]Ibid., 108.
[43]Ibid., 38-39.
[44]Ibid., 47.
[45]Ibid., 109.
[46]Ibid., 214.
[47]Ibid., 215.
[48]Ibid., 142.

is in effect—*Creator Spiritus* indeed—and effect is in cause. Both are one Eternal Cosmic Process—Eternal Incarnation, the Everlasting Word of God made Flesh: "Before Abraham was, I AM."[49]

Both Teilhard and Bryans subscribed to the erroneous doctrine of panpsychism. Matter and mind, wrote Bryans, "like every other thesis and antithesis, are seen to be as inseparable as they are distinguishable." By this reasoning, he perceived that all "dead" matter was "mind at its lowest dynamic. . . . All things one Universe of Matter-Mind."[50]

The birth of the "new cosmic consciousness," Bryans wrote, lies in a "physical sense of unity between the ego and the nonego of so-called inanimate nature." "In the thrall of cosmic consciousness we feel that they are *we*—the mountain and the mere, the sea and sky—and we are *they*. But we feel further that ours is the controlling mind in command."[51] In a chapter headed "Nirvana" in a section entitled "Cosmic sense of power," he wrote:

In a flash, we realize this infinity of matter as *mind*, the cosmic mind, and yet that "mind" that is most intimately *our* mind. [The peace it brings] springs from an intimate sense of physical unity with everything—a sense of having nothing and possessing all things, of *being* nothing, yet at the same time of *being* all things.[52]

He referred to this as an experience of the "Brahmic Splendor"[53] of Hinduism. It is identical to the pantheistic flights of fancy that embellish much of Teilhard's writings.

Central to Bryan's religiophilosophical thesis is the perverse teaching that "true Man is God," a rerun of the subtle lie which Satan used to deceive Eve (Gen. 3:5), and a teaching central to the New Age Movement. He attempts to substantiate his case by arguing that the *Atman*,[54] the SELF, of "ancient Hindu theology," is the Cosmic Ego, and "is thus the Johannine Logos in both its aspects, static and dynamic."[55] "*Atman* is thus the revelation," he wrote, "of MAN to man, of SELF to self. It is the apocalypse of the 'God within.' In terms of evolution it is the revelation of MAN to man in Man—of MAN, God the Son,

---

[49]Ibid., 143.

[50]Ibid., 144.

[51]Ibid., 189. Italics in original.

[52]Ibid., 187. Italics in original.

[53]Ibid., 176, 182-83, 185-86, 191, 198.

[54]In the words of the Hindu Scriptures (the *Upanishads*), the ATMAN is "the Inward Ruler, the Deathless." For references to *Atman* see Bryans, *The Curve of Fate*, 78, 109, 154, 163, 165, 222, 270, 272, 284, 303, 319.

[55]Ibid., 270.

to present-day man in the street."[56] However, the Johannine *Logos*,[57] according to orthodox Christian theology, is the Word of God, Jesus Christ, Who self-subsists within the plurality of Persons we call the Trinity or Godhead.

The preexistence of Jesus the Christ as *Logos*, the Word, the idea, in the mind of God lies behind the notion of "very God of very God, begotten, not made, being of one substance with the Father, by whom all things were made." The traditional doctrine, summarized in this creedal formula, presupposes a transcendent God and *Logos*, not an immanent God whose diaphany breaks through the very heart of matter as "Christ his heart, a flame"—the words of Teilhard.

The New Age Movement cannot understand that the true Transpersonal Self of the regenerate believer is Christ (Gal. 2:20). The old "self" has died and the true life "is hid with God in Christ" (Col. 3:3). It is in the "inmost self" (Rom. 7:22) that the regenerate man is in union with God, not in the carnal "self" or "flesh" (Rom. 8:9-10). The Self which does not sin (1 John 5:18) and has no need of teaching (1 John 2:27), is not of the world (John 17:16) and is not the unregenerate lower ego. As the Apostle Paul wrote: "It is no longer I that live, but Christ that liveth in me" (Gal. 3:20), or as Catherine of Genoa expressed it: "My Me is God, nor do I know my selfhood save in Him."[58]

Both show the true meaning of "deification," which is never simply a matter of blasphemously and mechanically deifying the finite and creaturely lower ego of unregenerate man, the inversion and caricature of orthodox reality. The created finite self of each man is contingent to the Godhead. It is not identical to Godhead as Bryans teaches. As the Apostle Paul stated: "In Him [God] we live and move and have our being" (Acts 17:28 NKJV; see also Eph. 4:6).

The doctrine of the *Atman*, according to Bryans, "embodies at once that dynamic point in time when man comes into his own, which is his true cosmic self . . . together with the static element of Godhead in man—'God the Son,' the Second Person of the Christian Trinity."[59] He claims that the true conception of the SELF, as DIVINE gives rise to "Cosmic consciousness." It involves conceiving the ATMAN "SELF" as "an individual not separate from other individuals, from the Individuality of the Universe, but as an ego-thesis fused with the nonego antithesis in Synthesis of Truth. A compound coalescence of universal confraternity."[60]

---

[56]Ibid.

[57]For a detailed discussion of this term in its biblical and historical context, see my article "John's Gospel and the *Logos* Enfleshed," *Apologia* (Journal of the Wellington Christian Apologetic Society [Inc.]) 3/2 (1993): 18-36.

[58]Quoted in Gerald Vann OP, *The Water and the Fire* (1953; repr. London: Collins, Fontana Paperbacks, 1966) 39.

[59]Bryans, *The Curve of Fate*, 270.

[60]Ibid., 154.

Such ideas are reminiscent of Teilhard's reference to Jesus Christ as a "mysterious Compound" formed by the synthesis of the Universe and God. This is a distortion of the doctrine of the Incarnation derived from his pantheistic bias. Well before Teilhard's theology of the "Cosmic Christ" was published, Bryans wrote:

> [Jesus Christ] is, in his short life and sudden death, the "tentative superman" *par excellence* and the closest approximation to the evolutionary objective of the ages that the world has known. . . . And in His Cosmic capacity as Risen Christ, He is at once the static all-pervading Logos and the dynamic climax of that fullgrown MAN coming in the dawn-flushed clouds of Promise and Planet Evolution—Apocalyptic Rider, He of the countless crowns, Lord King of Kings, set on the snow-white steed of Sovereignty![61]

Like Teilhard, Bryans distorts the doctrine of the Incarnation by supposedly transposing it to a transhistorical dimension, yet in fact embedding it within the naturalistic evolutive process. The whole evolutionary sequence (inanimate chemicals—slime—"ape-man"—"subman" [i.e., present-day man]—Christ) is seen as the INCARNATION of the LOGOS. Like Teilhard, Bryans replaced the New Testament concept of *Logos* with the "*neo-Logos*" of modern philosophy—the evolutive principle of a universe in movement.[62]

Christ, according to Bryans, is the "Logos Life of Evolutionary Biogenesis,"[63] and "the God of Evolution,"[64] allegedly "corresponding to the Siva aspect of the Hindu Trinity."[65] In "Christ" the "Cosmic Logos" was "incarnate to a superlative degree" for he "attained [through the evolutionary process] penultimate approximation to anthropological climax, the full Divinity, a man, the 'Son of Man'—the Forerunner of the Future Final Full MAN, GOD THE SON."[66] Bryans' redefinition of the doctrine of the Incarnation is compatible with Western heresies purporting to be derived from Hinduism and with New Age thought, for he wrote:

> The human individual will evolve at last into the Incarnation of the BRAHMA, the Universal LOGOS, Who is the Living Christ "in Whom all things were made." This mystic "change" of crowning evolution will take place in him for the very reason that he will have taken up his psy-

---

[61]Ibid., 91-92.
[62]See Teilhard de Chardin, *Christianity and Evolution*, 180-81.
[63]Bryans, *The Curve of Fate*, 141.
[64]Ibid., 61.
[65]Ibid., 64.
[66]Ibid., 101.

chological "cross." He will have most literally denied his "self." He will have repudiated his entire self-existence—name, nationality, class, creed. . . . He will become the All-Pervading for precisely the same reason that He will have arrived at the quintessence of the truly Personal. . . . The man Who attains to MAN—which we have seen to be the same as to say to Christhood, to BRAHMAN, or to the GODHEAD—is the final incarnation of the Logos, which is the Cosmic Ego, which is the Universe, which is also Humanity.[67]

Bryans argued that the conception of a "God" and of a human "soul" had to be reinstated in the light of modern science, "not only as a feasible hypothesis nor yet as a mere subjective necessity of human nature . . . but as an *objective necessity* and as the *only possible hypothesis consistent with the facts.*"[68] He advocated a synthesis of science and "mysticism" as the vehicle to assist man experience "Cosmic Consciousness the beginning of Godhead, that full Divine Consciousness."[69]

Like Teilhard, he embedded man's nature within the stream of "rising consciousness." "Whatever evolution really is," he wrote, "it is definitely our nature, since we are part of it. We are it and it is we."[70] Bryan's conception of man was thoroughly Teilhardian, for he wrote:

It is no more than reasonable, therefore, to assume that present-day man is in the process of producing something at least as far ahead of himself in beauty of form and power of intellect and scope of enterprise as he is ahead in these respects of the ancestral prehistoric monkey. . . . We are the transition stage, ourselves the "missing link," between the MAN of tomorrow and the ape of yesterday . . . future MAN . . . is . . . Himself the Incarnation of the Universe, the "fellow" of Almighty-hood. . . . Man is not MAN as yet—but in terms of anthropological time . . . He is about to burst his cocoon. . . . we still are, no more than sublimated monkeys—shaved, washed, and clothed, admittedly; nevertheless no more than anthropoid-transition apes. . . . we are most certainly not yet MAN. . . . We have got too much of our recent ape-ancestry in us to be able to lay claim to such a title as that of MAN. . . .

Present-day man is . . . himself the long-sought "missing link" between subhuman and superman, the monkey-man of yesterday and the Christ-Man of tomorrow. He is the center of creative evolution, the

---

[67]Ibid., 308, 317.
[68]Ibid., 17-18. Italics in original.
[69]Ibid., 183.
[70]Ibid., 16.

focus point of planetary gestation. . . . Evolution becomes conscious in man.[71]

Teilhard was convinced that present-day man was deficient, for he wrote of a coming "Ultrahumanity," in which the personal would find its highest form of expression, or as Bryans put it, the "quintessence of the truly Personal."[72] Bryans referred to present-day man as "the dwarf of himself"[73] and used the term "Superman" to define the crowning glory of evolution—Man as God. He referred to the historical Jesus of Nazareth as that "Superman who came to be known as the world's first Christ"[74] and as the "Apostle *par excellence* of Evolution."[75] He was perceptive in detecting an emerging paradigm shift, for he wrote:

> By an irony of fate it is science, and not orthodox religion, that has been chosen as the final mouthpiece of God and the organ of His eschatological Apocalypse.

Like Teilhard, Bryans rejected the Christian doctrines of the special creation of man and the Fall and presented man as the natural product of evolution:

> Evolutionary man has ceased to present the anomaly of a divine animal, exiled from his Eden, fallen from grace, created *ex nihilo* and married, by special license, to one of his ribs upwards of some 6,000 years ago. He is seen today—no less miraculous for being a reasonable proposition—as the evolutionary emergence of countless creative aeons; and the Humanity of God, the Divinity of Man is shown to be the *Leitmotif* of twentieth-century interpretation of creative evolution.[76]

He regarded the story of the virgin birth of Christ as on "a psychological par with creation stories." "Evolutionarily speaking," he wrote, "both theories, in their literal interpretation, present no more than an intellectual form of infantile paralysis."[77] Teilhard showed the same disdain towards the traditional doctrine of creation.

Teilhard is acclaimed by his supporters for enlarging our understanding of Christ in his "Cosmic dimensions," as the "Alpha and Omega" of the Apocalypse (Revelation). However, Bryans advanced these ideas well before Teilhard's work, incorporating them within his eschatological vision. "The alphabet of planet

---

[71]Ibid., 23-25, 28, 71, 305.
[72]Ibid., 308.
[73]Ibid., 62.
[74]Ibid., 76-77.
[75]Ibid., 78.
[76]Ibid., 18-19.
[77]Ibid., 97.

evolution," he wrote, "has come full circle, and the Omega is reunited with the Alpha."[78]

By Omega he meant that which emerges from the evolutionary process, namely, the "Universe Itself grown SELF,"[79] and Alpha is the "self" or unrealized Godhood. This coincidence, or convergence of "self" with "SELF," was seen as a cosmic necessity: "Alpha must coincide with Omega. No goal, therefore, less than Godhead could suffice."[80] Bryans, like Teilhard, envisaged a reincarnation of Alpha into Omega via a "mystic change," for he wrote:

> [F]rom the earliest floodlit molten aeons of the past, there is one unswerving purpose which streamlines through evolution to that final spearhead of time, that lightening metamorphosis . . . the moment when the *Logos Spermatikos*—first cause and last effect—involved in the beginning is evolved in the end. And the Alpha is reincarnated in the Omega.
>
> It is here that the mystic "change" from man to MAN, from humanity to "Godhead," takes place . . . [referred to] in the First Epistle to the Corinthians (xv, 51, 52).[81]

Teilhard made famous the French phrase "Le Milieu Divin," (the Divine Environment), the title of one of his well-known books. His supporters have applauded the originality of his thought in his explication of this concept. However, Bergson and Bryans elaborated this idea within the framework of emergent evolution well before Teilhard. Bryans wrote:

> Ever-present there remains around us, outside us and within, the Universe of infinitely great and of infinitely small, by telescope and microscope, extending into One Limitless Eternal . . . there is no word at once comprehensive enough, and exact enough, to meet the case. "Essence" is the only possible expression to supply the want, since the word means literally BEING—I AM BECAUSE I AM—the Hebrew verb *jahweh*, "to be"—the God JEHOVAH. This is the Divine environment indeed. . . . This "environment" is found to be none other than the Cosmic Ego.[82]

He stressed that the truth concerning the divine environment lies in a middle point, the synthetic mean:

---

[78]Ibid., 266.
[79]Ibid.
[80]Ibid., 323.
[81]Ibid., 58-59.
[82]Ibid., 33-34.

This truth is simply that nothing could exist, could BE, were it not for infinity (an infinite environment) in which to put it; yet, at the same time, no thing could be a thing (implying, and opposed to, other "things"), if it were not entirely finite, in the sense of being *definite*. Therefore all things, collectively and separately, must contain both these two necessary elements at once in simultaneous synthesis of the infinite and the definite.[83]

Well before Teilhard redefined and subsumed evil within the evolutionary process, Bryans wrote that "the entire so-called 'problem of evil' stands revealed as the mere 'growing pains' of evolution, or rather as the birth pangs themselves of MAN."[84] In "the same sense that dirt is said to be matter misplaced," wrote Bryans, "sin" is "energy misdirected."[85] Consistent with this distortion of the doctrine of sin and moral evil, he, like Teilhard, rejected the doctrine of the Atonement, opting instead to redefine it in evolutionary terms. He wrote:

The whole doctrinal importance attached to the execution of the man Jesus, together with his consequent role of race "redeemer," stressed so heavily by the Church throughout the ages, is no more than a reversion to those primitive cults of sacrifice, human and otherwise, which played such an important part in the barbaric worship of tribal deity. It is the ancient law of blood sacrifice.

The crucifixion was, in historical reality, no other than the outcome of a tactical error of the first magnitude on the part of a young man of genius unique in the annals of anthropology who had not yet reached his prime and who, by his own confession, had still to be "perfected."
. . .

In a word, the entire myth of a vicarious atonement is reactionary. In terms of psychological evolution it is a hark-back to the dim atavistic past of animistic fear which is the seed-ground of all superstition. Like devil-worship, its roots lie in the primeval slave-instinct of placation, the placation of evil spirits rather than the worship of that Father God to Whom sacrifice and burnt offering are anathema. . . . we do not genuinely any of us believe in being "saved" by anybody's blood.[86]

---

[83]Ibid., 211.
[84]Ibid., 158.
[85]Ibid., 154.
[86]Ibid., 80-81, 83. Cf. Acts 20:28; Rom. 3:25; 5:9; Eph. 1:7; 1 Pet. 1:18-19.

Bryans, like Teilhard, conceived of the human race as the "spearhead of evolution"[87] and subscribed to the notion that white races were privileged to be on the very growing tip. "It is we," he wrote, "who are the heroes of the evolutionary hour—we, the white races of Indo-European origin, we who are the heirs of aeon-accumulated promise—twentieth-century We, Spearhead of Evolution."[88]

Teilhard tried to show that the universe was not closed, for there was an escape route at Omega Point—the point of evolutionary maturation of the planet. Bryans addressed this problem, concluding that "we are living in an infinite, unchanging box which it is impossible to get out of, even by death . . . for the good reason that the 'box' is everywhere and 'nowhere'—its center everywhere, and circumference nowhere—at once the 'nothing' and the everything, the cipher and the sum total of all things."

The universe was eternal, in his view: "It must, therefore, stand without beginning and without end, always the same, always its SELF—the same yesterday, and today, and for evermore."[89] In contrast, Christianity teaches that God alone is eternal, the universe had a beginning, and it will have an end. Scripture affirms that all of creation was made through the eternal Word,[90]—"Jesus Christ—the same yesterday, and today, and forever."[91]

The escape route Bryans proposed was identical to Teilhard's, namely, the consummation of personal being at Omega Point—the apex of a "cone of consciousness" (Teilhard's terminology). Bryans wrote:

> [T]he epoch-inaugurating implications of the new theory of "emergence" in biology [are "of such a kind" that] when that evolutionary "tomorrow" shall flush the skies of time with rosy-fingered dawn, then shall we consummate that correspondence with universe-infinity that spells eternal youth. This is that Christ-prophetic dawn foretold when MAN shall at long last emerge out of ape-embryo-man, present-day "man" so-called. This is that Christ-prophetic dawn of MAN on earth, the literal, full physical and evolutionary son of man.[92]

Among the many quasiscientific terms and neologisms that Teilhard is purported to have invented is "cosmogenesis." Scholars have claimed that they reflect the originality of his mind and convey deep philosophical and theological insights. However, it is hard to support these claims. In 1941, for example, Bryans stated in his work *The Curve of Fate*:

---

[87]Ibid., 35.
[88]Ibid., 36.
[89]Ibid., 32.
[90]John 1:1-3; Col. 1:16.
[91]Heb. 13:8. Cf. Psa. 90:4.
[92]Bryans, *The Curve of Fate*, 38.

We are living, therefore, today in the last *cosmogenetic* [emphasis added] throes of planet pregnancy and it is unto us of the twentieth century that the agelong awaited "child" of prophecy is to be born. This final phenomenon of evolutionary growth will consist in the psychophysical fruit of that "second birth" . . . of MAN in man.[93]

We can conclude that there is little in Teilhard's writings that has not been said before. His general thesis is in full harmony with the writings of those like Bryans and New Age scholars who have constructed a pantheistic version of Christian doctrine. Once the doctrine of emergent evolution becomes the grid through which Christian truth is reinterpreted, we have serious distortions of the truth.

## 5.3 Aquarian Roots and Christology

Many New Age Movement leaders consider Christ to be a "*Bodhisattva*," an enlightened one among a pantheon of enlightened beings. The Dalai Lama Tenzin Gyatso, venerated today by Tibetan Buddhists, is believed to be the fourteenth in the line of the reincarnations of the *Bodhisattva* of Compassion, Chenrezig. The Dalai Lama, a Nobel Peace Prize recipient, considers himself a god-king and believes that Jesus Christ is the highest *bodhisattva*. He has become an apostle for a new creed which has great appeal among New Agers, a Buddhist-based universalism integrating important parts of Christianity. Largely due to his influence and charisma, more than forty-one centers of Buddhist teaching—*Dharma* Centers—have sprung up in pluralist Britain alone in the last ten years.

David Spangler, widely regarded as a New Age leader, has made contact through "channeling" with several higher spiritual entities, one who bears the name "Limitless Love and Truth."[94] He claims to have received the following message from this entity:

Am I God? Am I Christ? Am I a Being come to you from the dwelling places of the infinite? I am all these things, yet more. I am revelation. I am the Presence which has been before the foundations of the Earth.
. . .
   I am all those recognizable thought forms which you have formed of God and of Christ and of great Beings, but I am also more. *I am aspects of Divinity of God which you have not learned to recognize but which will be revealed to you in this New Age.*[95]

---

[93]Ibid., 282.
[94]Spangler, *Revelation: The Birth of a New Age.*
[95]Ibid., 150, 152, 153.

Spangler states that Christ was a human being who progressed and evolved to such an advanced state that "he achieved a position of mastership at a time when humanity as a whole was still in its infancy; and this being traveled a path which in the Orient would be called the path of the *Bodhisattva*."[96] In an editorial in the *Beacon* magazine, a Lucis Trust publication, we read:

> *Christ is the archetype of the true Aquarian*; he is cooperative, inclusive, intelligent, and active. His motive is love of humanity; his keynote is service. He is . . . the guarantor of ultimate spiritual achievement.[97]

But is this New Age perception of Christ consistent with the historical facts and what is recorded in the testimony of Scripture? Is Christ merely a harbinger of a New Age, a highly spiritually evolved being who provides us with an example of how to evolve to higher levels of consciousness? While it is true that Christ preached that the Kingdom of God had come among men through His ministry, which can be viewed as the advent of a New Age, this "New Age" is centered on God Incarnate, not on man's attainment of Godhood.

We need to address the question, Is Christ just one among a host of Masters, yogis, gurus, or shamans who have manifested facets of the perennial truth? Popular New Age teacher Emmet Fox, formerly a prominent liberal Christian minister, asserts that whatever one thinks of Him, "Jesus Christ is easily the most important figure that has ever appeared in the history of mankind."[98] All true Christians of course would agree with this view, but the issue surely hinges on the *nature* of His claimed uniqueness, namely, did He differ *qualitatively* from the "enlightened" ones revered in other faiths, and if so how? Emmet Fox does not accept any *qualitative* distinction between Jesus Christ of Nazareth and Buddha, for Fox states:

> The Christ is not Jesus. The Christ is the active presence of God—the incarnation of God—in living men and women. . . . In the history of all races the Cosmic Christ has incarnated in man—Buddha, Moses, Elijah, and in many other leaders. . . . However, in his New Age, the Cosmic Christ will come into millions of men and women who are ready to receive it. This will be the second coming.[99]

---

[96]David Spangler, *Reflections of the Christ* (Forres, Scotland: Findhorn Publications, 1981) 12.

[97]*The Beacon* (November/December 1978).

[98]Emmet Fox, *The Sermon on the Mount* (New York: Harper & Bros., 1938) 1.

[99]Emmet Fox, *Diagrams for Living: The Bible Unveiled* (New York: Harper & Row, 1968) 158, 159.

Here we have two key New Age doctrines: (1) the distinction drawn between "the Christ" and Jesus (involving the denial that Jesus is the Christ); and (2) the belief that "the Cosmic Christ" was incarnated in the man Jesus, as well as in Buddha, Moses, Elijah, and other leaders. Both beliefs find no biblical support.

Jesus Christ is identified in Scripture as the unique and eternal Son of the God[100] sent from the Father (John 5:36-38). He stated: "He who has seen Me has seen the Father" (John 14:9). He alone has dwelt with the Father from all eternity (John 1:1-2) and through Him all things were created (v. 3). He is the very fullness of Deity come in the flesh.[101] For Paul states: "in Him all the fullness of Deity dwells in bodily form" (Col. 2:9). Jesus is the only sinless man to have ever lived.[102] He is called the "unblemished spotless Lamb of God Who takes away the sins of the world."[103] The resurrection of Jesus Christ from the dead is testimony to all these unique qualifications.

For New Age writers like John White, Christ's unique place in history is based "upon his unprecedented realization of the higher intelligence, the divinity, the Ground of Being incarnated in him."[104] Like Emmet Fox, he distinguishes the historical person of Christ from "the Christ"—a "transpersonal condition of being to which *we must all someday come.*"[105] He asserts that we too can reach the same "unprecedented realization" of higher intelligence or consciousness possessed by Christ (that is "Cosmic Consciousness" or "Christ Consciousness").

The uniqueness of Christ, the only Savior of Mankind (Acts 4:12) and the eternal Word of God (John 1:1-3) is incompatible with White and Spangler's view. Christ did not come as one of many revelations ("avatars" in Hinduism)[106]

---

[100]E.g., John 4:34; 5:23-24, 30; 6:38-40, 44, 57; 7:16, 18; 8:16, 18; 9:4; 10:36; 11:42; 12:45, 49; 14:24; 15:21; 16:5; 17:3, 18, 21, 23, 25; 20:21).

[101]John 1:14; 3:34; Col. 1:15-20; Heb. 1:2.

[102]See 2 Cor. 5:21; Heb. 4:15; 7:26; 1 John 3:5; Acts 3:14.

[103]John 1:29; 1 Pet. 1:22

[104]John White, "Jesus and the Idea of a New Age," *The Quest* (Summer 1989): 14.

[105]Ibid. Italics in original.

[106]"Avatara," or avatar (as it is usually spelled in English), means literally a downcoming, from Sanskrit *avatārah* (*ava*, down, plus *tarati*, he crosses [over], and [by extension] attains, or saves). The term is a relatively recent one, not occurring in the classical *Upanishads* and only a few times in some later *Upanishads*. Geoffrey Parrinder, in his book *Avatar and Incarnation* (New York: Barnes & Noble, 1970), has listed twelve characteristics of the Hindu avatar doctrines. These have been summarized by Bruteau as (1) the avatar is real, not a mere appearance, even a genuine historical person, who is born of human parents and dies upon the completion of his/her particular divine purpose; (2) the avatar displays both human and divine qualities and demonstrates the reality of the world and the value of action by setting an example of moral and religious significance; (3) the avatar brings God into direct communication with men by delivering a

of some partial representation of the impersonal Absolute (for example, Brahman). Instead He came as the personal revelation[107] of the personal God.[108]

Spangler refers to "the Christ" as an "individual being beyond individualized selfness . . . a being, who quite some time ago lost or moved beyond that aspect of experience which we call the isolated or individualized self. The consciousness of the Christ, the life of this being, is completely planetary in scope."[109] Like Teilhard, Spangler transposes the historic incarnation of Christ to a transhistorical level, replacing it with a "mass incarnation" of human souls seeking enlightenment at Omega point. The ascended glorified Christ who intercedes for sinners[110] is replaced with a universal "spirit" embracing all religions.

Spangler believes that "the Christ" is manifest through the experience of "connectedness" with the universe or any part of it,[111] and he is opposed to any form of dualism. He believes Christ is a cosmic principle, for he states:

> Any old Christ will not do, not if we need to show that we have something better than the mainstream Christian traditions. It must be a cosmic Christ, a universal Christ, a New Age Christ.[112]

He does not consider Christ so much a religious figure, but rather "a cosmic principle, a spiritual presence whose quality infuses and appears in various ways in all religions and philosophies that uplift and seek unity with spirit."[113] Like Teilhard, Spangler considers the traditional biblical teaching on Christ deficient. The Incarnation and the sacrifice of Christ on the cross for sinners are seen as avenues by which the Cosmic Christ entered the evolutionary process to pursue the enlightenment of Mankind. He refers to Christ's blood as:

> [T]he life-energy . . . released within this relative world of form as never before, stimulating the increased revelation of the divine immanent within the world. . . . Here the seed is the inner divinity, the nourishing blood is the Christ life and awareness poured into the earth, and

---

special revelation of the God of grace who loves men dearly. Parrinder concludes that the avatars are not adequately conceived as genuine human beings, i.e., incarnations. They lack historicity, their personalities comprise a montage of legends in which they are either too supernatural or too abstract or (rarely) all-too-human. See Beatrice Bruteau, *Evolution Toward Divinity: Teilhard de Chardin and the Hindu Scriptures* (Wheaton IL: Theosophical Publ. House, 1974) 65, 76-77.

[107]Heb. 2:9; 4:14-15.

[108]Mark 9:37; John 14:7-9; 12:45.

[109]Spangler, *Revelation: Birth of a New Age*, 14.

[110]Heb. 7:25; 1 Tim. 3:16.

[111]Ibid., 129.

[112]Ibid., 107.

[113]David Spangler, *Conversations with John* (Middleton WI: Lorian Press, 1983) 5.

the harvest is the New Age, when man as a more collective unity will realize and experience the birth of God immanent.[114]

Christian researchers have responded to the faulty Christology advanced by leaders of the New Age Movement.[115] The errors endemic in this false theology are best confronted by first gaining a clear picture of the true biblical view of Christology before exploring their counterfeit.[116] The Christ of New Age thought is essentially a gnostic Christ, a revealer or a "Way shower," not a personal Savior from sin. The New Age counterfeit is hailed as a revealer of the hidden or esoteric "knowledge" that we were divine and will return to divinity. Such thinking can be traced back to the gnostics of the first century, whose errors the apostles refuted in their writings.

Neo-Gnosticism,[117] a present-day manifestation of New Age thought, is extremely eclectic and syncretistic in its approach to truth. It is a form of New Age Esoteric Christianity, a perverted version of Christian doctrine which draws on the occult, mystical theology and inner or hidden meanings of biblical passages.

Its roots have been historically traced by a number of authors to the writings of Theosophists (for example, Helena Petrovna Blavatsky [1831–1891],[118] Alice A. Bailey[119] and Annie Besant[120]); German Goethe scholar Rudolf Steiner (d. 1924),[121] who founded the Anthroposophical Society in 1912; and American seer

---

[114]Ibid., 28.

[115]E.g., Ron Rhodes, *The Counterfeit Christ of the New Age Movement* (Grand Rapids MI: Baker Book House, 1990).

[116]See Douglas Groothuis, *Confronting the New Age: How to Resist a Growing Religious Movement* (Downers Grove IL: InterVarsity, 1988).

[117]A resurgence of interest in Gnosticism took place with the discovery of Gnostic texts like the *Gospel of Thomas*, the *Gospel of Philip*, the *Gospel of Truth*, and others found at Nag Hammadi, Egypt, in 1945. They were all originally written in Coptic and English translations appeared in the 1950s. The entire Nag Hammadi Gnostic library is now available in English translation. These published works have proved to be a phenomenal success in terms of sales.

[118]H. P. Blavatsky, *The Key to Theosophy* (Pasadena CA: Theosophical University Press, 1972); *The Secret Doctrine* (Wheaton IL: Theosophical Publ. House, 1966). In a 1,200-page book entitled *Isis Unveiled*, Blavatsky set out the aims of her Theosophical Society. She claimed this was a channeled document "dictated by the Masters of Wisdom via astral light and spirit guides." She believed in reincarnation, stating: "It is owing to this law of spiritual development that mankind will become freed from its false gods and find itself finally—*self-redeemed*." Cited in Mark Albrecht, *Reincarnation: A Christian Appraisal* (Downers Grove IL: InterVarsity, 1982) 21.

[119]Alice A. Bailey, *The Externalization of the Hierarchy* (New York: Lucis, 1957).

[120]Annie Besant, *Esoteric Christianity* (Wheaton IL: Theosophical Publ. House, 1953); *The Ancient Wisdom* (Wheaton IL: Theosophical Publ. House, 1954). Annie Besant (1847–1933) was the most prominent of all the British Theosophical luminaries.

[121]Rudolf Steiner was born in Kraljevic Croatia, of German ancestry and educated in

Edgar Cayce (1877–1945),[122] whose books are among top sellers in Bantam's New Age paperback series. Other esoteric cults and religious movements which have provided fertile soil for the present New Age Movement include the Rosicrucians (of which the late Max Heindel was a follower), Christian Science (founded by Mary Baker Eddy), and Swedenborgianism[123] (the Church of the New Jerusalem).

The American Transcendentalist movement which formed in 1836, with its emphasis on personal and social transformation, also provided fertile soil for the seeds of the New Age Movement. These transcendentalists, including Henry David Thoreau, Ralph Waldo Emerson, and Walt Whitman, reacted against the sterile intellectualism of the day and sought the unseen dimension of reality, which some of them called the Oversoul. They believed that mind and matter were continuous and their sources for understanding included direct experience, intuition, the Quaker idea of the inner Light, the German Romantic philosophers, historian Thomas Carlyle, poet Samuel Taylor Coleridge, Swedenborg, and the English metaphysical writers of the seventeenth century.[124]

Added to this potpourri were the influences of Hindu religion, as presented in the *Upanishads*, the *Bhagavad-Gita*, and the *Vishnu Purana* from India. These in particular have been misused to undermine the concept of a transcendent deity,

---

Vienna. Steiner's major works include *Philosophy and Freedom* (1896); *Goethe's Worldview* (1897); *Knowledge of the Higher Worlds* (1923). Steiner taught that Jesus was separate from the Christ, that Christ came upon Jesus at his baptism, that Christ is the higher self of all people, and that reincarnation is a reality. Steiner claims he gained his revelations from the *Akasha Chronicle*. See R. Steiner, *From Buddha to Christ* (Spring Valley NY: Anthroposophic Press, 1974); *The Reappearance of the Christ in the Etheric* (Spring Valley NY: Anthroposophic Press, 1983).

[122]His work is reviewed in detail by Gary North, *Unholy Spirits* (Tyler TX: Dominion Press, 1986) 193-225. Cayce did much to popularize belief in reincarnation. He was a therapist who specialized in psychic diagnosis of medical conditions, and one of his main healing techniques is now referred to as past-life recall. He was a channeler for an entity who claimed to provide scientific and metaphysical insights. He taught that Jesus had been incarnated many times before "becoming the Christ." In his book *Occult ABC*, Kurt Koch has documented Cayce's many false doctrinal teachings. Cayce also believed in a theory that thousands of years ago, there existed two great continents and races, Atlantis and Lemuria. The Lemurian race was peace loving and dedicated to the good of all humanity, while the Atlanteans were warlike and separative. He said that the future of man belonged to the higher-consciousness Lemurian race. See Edgar Cayce, *Edgar Cayce on Atlantis* (New York: Paperback Library, 1968).

[123]Founded by Swedish-born Baron Emmanuel Swedenborg (1688–1772), a professor and dean of the University of Upsala. He had a brilliant mind and was a noted mathematician, mining expert, engineer, and inventor. During the years 1749–1756 he published in London his *Arcana Coelestia*.

[124]Ferguson, *The Aquarian Conspiracy*, 47; also see 120.

a residue in Western culture of the Judeo-Christian worldview. The transcendentalists linked mysticism to the Romantic quest. To penetrate the secret world of "things in themselves" or the true essence of things, required deep intuition, mystical mind states, or some meditative epiphany. Ecstatic self-absorption into the mystical oneness with or through nature, illustrated in the works of Wordsworth, Shelley, and Whitman—became almost a conventional form of religious experience.

A crucial factor in the collapse of historic Christianity in the West and the regression into forms of Neo-Gnosticism, has been the adoption of the theory of evolution, which is not compatible with any of the historical Eastern or Western religions. In particular, the acceptance of the doctrine of "spiritual evolution" espoused by Teilhard de Chardin and many nominal Christians has made them very vulnerable to the deceptions of New Age thought. The "Christ" proclaimed by New Age leaders is a counterfeit Christ.

The New Age Movement is therefore a subtle enemy to Christianity for it perverts the truth of Scripture in exchange for a lie. Instead of worshiping the eternal Creator (God in three eternal Persons) they have "changed the glory of the incorruptible God into an image made like to corruptible man" (committing idolatry) and "changed the truth of God into a lie" (Rom. 1:23,25). The idols of the New Age Movement are consciousness itself and the evolutionary process by which adherents believe it rises to higher levels of existence.

## 5.4 Teilhard and the Emerging New World Order

> The age of nations is passed. Now, unless we wish to perish we must shake off our old prejudices and build the earth.[125]

> It is, indeed, the mysterious Divinity that "possesses" and stirs up nations at the turning points of history; *it is* once again *that same Divinity, it is Evolution.*[126]

Since Teilhard de Chardin's death in 1955, an international network of Teilhard study groups and organizations have been formed. In January 1989 delegates from Belgium, French, Italian, German, and British Associations met in the Jesuit Adult Education College outside Zurich, to agree on a charter for the collective body at the European level. They succeeded in that purpose and the official signing of the European Teilhard Charter took place on 22 September 1989, at the

---

[125]Teilhard de Chardin, "The Spirit of the Earth," in *Human Energy*, 37. Italics in original.

[126]Teilhard de Chardin, *Writings in Time of War*, 78. Italics in original.

headquarters of the European Parliament in Strasbourg, in the presence of members of that parliament and other dignitaries.

Strasbourg, seat of the Council of Europe, was chosen in the belief that Teilhard's vision has an essential significance for the building of the new Europe. It was in Strasbourg that much of Teilhard's work was conceived. The question of what qualifies an association to be admissible as Teilhardian, is dealt with in article 2a of the charter, and states:

> [A]ny Association adhering to the Charter must have as its primary objective, duly written into its constitution, the study and propagation of the work of Teilhard de Chardin and *the promotion of his vision of evolution*. It should be required that they endeavor to expand Teilhard's thinking in a manner that is consistent with contemporary developments in all fields of knowledge.
>
> Lastly, as Teilhard de Chardin's work combines Cosmic, Human, and Christic aspects, it is essential that a Teilhard Association be open to people concerned by all of these aspects or only by one or another of them. But the Association itself can be admissible among the signers of this Charter only if its activities effectively include all three aspects and if these three aspects are at least implicitly endorsed by its constitution.[127]

Put simply, Teilhard's vision of evolution, in its Cosmic, Human, and Christic aspects, is the common ground of "fellowship" for Teilhardians seeking to promote a unified Europe.

Testimony to the ecumenical nature of Teilhardism and its influence among distinguished intellectuals, is found in the composition of the recent leadership of the London-based Teilhard Center. The presidential and vice presidential officers in the last ten years have included at least ten professors, two bishops, a lord, and a lady.[128] The founding president was Joseph Needham FRS FBA, an

---

[127]News from Abroad, *Teilhard Review* 24/1 (Spring 1989): 9.

[128]Recent vice presidents include Bishop George Appleton, Lady Collins, Lord Craigmyle, Paul Davies (prof. of Theoretical Physics at Newcastle University), Prof. Robert Faricy SJ, Prof. Roger Garaudy (a Marxist theoretician), Errol Harris (emeritus prof. of Moral and Intellectual Philosophy, Northwestern University, USA), David Jenkins (Anglican bishop), Prof. William Johnston SJ, Robert Jungk, Margaret Mead, Robert Muller, Raimundo Panikkar (prof. of Comparative Religion, University of California), Prof. Henryk Skolimowski, Rupert Sheldrake, Prof. William Thorpe, Bernard Towers (prof. of Pediatrics and Anatomy, University of California, Los Angeles and first chairman of the Teilhard Center), M. Francois-Règis Teilhard de Chardin, and Renée-Marie Croose Parry (founder). The British Teilhard Association (formerly the Teilhard Center) is a founder-member of the European Teilhard de Chardin Center. The secretariat is located in

Anglo-Catholic who professes to being an "honorary Taoist."[129] Until her recent resignation, for work and personal reasons, Dr. Ursula King[130] was president (an honorary function without any executive responsibility).

In his book *The Mission of Mysticism*,[131] Richard Kirby classifies the Teilhard Center as an esoteric society, fitting the same category as the Druids, Glastonbury Zodiac,[132] and the Emin. The common bond shared by all officers of the Teilhard Center is a commitment to propagating Teilhard's vision.

The theme of the twelfth International Teilhard Conference held in London 24-26 April 1992, was "World without Frontiers." The conference proceedings, like those in 1991, took place under the twelve gold stars, representing the twelve member- and soon-to-be-member-nations of the E.E.C. This was intended as a symbol of "unity-in-diversity," a theme underlying much of Teilhard's philosophy.

Members of the European Teilhard Charter are committed to promoting Teilhardian spirituality, not only as the basis of a unified Europe, but as the basis of the world community. As the conference report for 1989 stated: "Constructing Europe (the present-day task) is part of wider developments of the planetization of humanity."[133] (The European Teilhard Center is a registered educational charity.)

In his opening address to the 1992 International Teilhard Conference, John Cowell, vice president of the European Teilhard Center (Bad Schonbrunn, Switzerland) and chairman of the Teilhard Center (London), introduced "a sense of

---

Beaumaris (U.K.).

[129]Joseph Needham, foreword, in King, *Towards a New Mysticism*, 8.

[130]King was born in Cologne, Germany. After studying theology and philosophy at universities of Bonn, Munich, the Institut Catholique, Paris, and the Sorbonne, she took her STL in Paris in 1963. She went on to earn her PhD at the University of London. She is a founding member of the Teilhard Center and since 1971 has worked at the University of Leeds as senior lecturer in the Department of Theology and Religious Studies, before accepting her present appointment at the University of Bristol.

[131]Richard Kirby, *The Mission of Mysticism* (London: SPCK, 1979) 61.

[132]This esoteric group is associated with Glastonbury Abbey (Cornwall, England). This Abbey was originally a Celtic monastic establishment probably dating from the seventh century. It became a Saxon monastery in the early eighth century, was destroyed by the Danes in the ninth century, and in the tenth century was revived as a Benedictine foundation that acquired much fame for religion and learning. It is reputed to contain the tombs of King Alfred and Saint Dunstan, and has become a famous place of pilgrimage. It became associated with the search for the "Holy Grail" (the sacred chalice used at the Last Supper). See R. F. Treharne, *The Glastonbury Legends* (London: Cresset, 1967).

[133]Conference report 2 by Francis O'Kelly, the European Teilhard Meeting at Strasbourg, 22-23 September 1989, *Teilhard Review* 24/3 (Autumn 1989): 108.

urgency as he related the Conference to current events in Europe, where an effort is being made to reconcile ancient enemies within a new and greater union."[134]

Noting that the emphasis of the union had been primarily economic, he stressed that "it is vital that such a community of nations should become ecological, social, and ethical, avoiding the dangers of 'seeking to have rather than to be'." "Teilhard's insights into convergence," he maintained, "are of great relevance here: differentiated union is the only way forward."

In another talk, Richard Brüchsel, who assisted in the founding of the European Teilhard Network, stated that for Teilhardians to build up Europe within a world without frontiers, "we need to listen to poets, thinkers, and visionaries like Teilhard. They know what cosmic consciousness and the universal element mean and can help us to develop a common soul." The final talk, "The Spiritual Rebirth of Europe," was given by Jean-Pierre Ribaut of the Council of Europe at Strasbourg. He spoke of the Council's role, independent of the economics-oriented European Community, to bring nearer a Europe truly without frontiers.

At the 1991 International Teilhard Conference, John Cowell reminded those present that in keeping with Teilhard's injunction, they had "a coresponsibility for the future of evolution on a human, planetary, and cosmic scale."[135] In his address, the Jesuit theologian and Scripture scholar John Russell SJ spoke of Teilhard's views on our position and vocation in this world, and his visions of the future in which the whole cosmic process converges to a single human society—the Omega Point. "Can we achieve this comprehensive world community?," he asked. "The unique dilemma and glory is ours!."[136]

While this Teilhardian "spirituality" is officially defined as "Christic," the question remains as to whether it is Christian. In an article on "Ecological Spirituality" published in 1992 in the *Teilhard Review*, Prof. Henryk Skolimowski, a former vice president of the Teilhard Center (London) stated:

> When we reflect on the lives of *the Illustrious Ones, such as Jesus* and Buddha, and in our times such as Gandhi and Mother Teresa, we see that their lives were an active prayer of healing, of helping, of nourishing, and of nurturing. This is what the living spirituality is all about, has always been, and will always be. . . .
>
> Each form of spirituality is the realization of our inner being, of our deepest potential, *of the god within*. The idea of spirituality as the reali-

---

[134]Conference report by Evelyn Woodcock: "World without Frontiers," the Twelfth International Teilhard Conference at London Colney, 24-26 April 1992, *Teilhard Review* 27/3 (Winter 1992): 85-87.

[135]Conference report by Eoghan Callaghan, the Eleventh International Teilhard Conference at London Colney, 26-28 April 1991, *Teilhard Review* 26/2 (Summer 1991): 61.

[136]Ibid.

zation of *our inner divinity* does not clash with the conception proclaiming that spirituality is an articulated essence of the human condition of a given time. . . . *There are many roads leading to Rome, many roads leading to the inner god, many roads which actualize our spiritual potential. . . .*

The act of the will to transcend, this inner discipline to tune one's soul to receive the subtle melodies of the universe may be considered as an act of god making, an act of actualizing the inner god. However, many of the *Illustrious Ones* speak of an intervention of the outside God which, as it were, begins to dwell in them. *Yet with an amazing consistency those who were seemingly "chosen by God" [e.g., Jesus] are the very ones who have worked on themselves incredibly hard, and who have exhibited an enormous will power to actualize their inner potential.*[137]

Here we see an emphasis on the discovery of "the god within," "the inner god" or the "inner divinity"; an outright denial of the transcendence of God. As Prof. Swolimowski states, in Teilhardism, transcendence is a concept restricted to the plane of phenomena, the purely natural and organic aspect of reality:

Transcendence is therefore the formative force of the universe. Transcendence is the longing of the universe to make something of itself, and the will of the universe to do so. Transcendence is the primary expression of God's creative will. Transcendence (as the vehicle of all creative change) may be conceived as God itself. . . . Spiritual life is the blossoming of the force of transcendence. . . . Spirituality as the flowering of life makes all life a divine phenomenon. To accept this conception of life is to accept the *evolutionary conception of divinity.* Yes, life had to reach out to the realm of the spiritual because it had the divine potency in it. *Within this perspective, God can be seen as a crystallized essence of the process of transcendence—finally leading to divinity.*[138]

The term "transcendent" when applied to God has always meant "existing apart from, not subject to the limitations of the material universe, the opposite of immanent" (*Concise Oxford Dictionary*). God the Creator is therefore "over, above, and beyond" the space-time-matter continuum since His existence is not contingent to the created order and the realm of phenomena which are subject to change. However, in Teilhardism this *relational* concept of transcendence is lost and replaced with one which bears no relationship to the word's true meaning.

---

[137]Henryk Skolimowski, "Ecological Spirituality and Its Practical Consequences," *Teilhard Review* 27/2 (Summer 1992): 50-51.
[138]Ibid., 51.

Instead, transcendence is conceived of as a process in which "God" evolves with the universe. Wilber, as noted, begins his book *The Atman Project* with the words: "development is evolution, evolution is transcendence, and transcendence has its final goal Atman, or ultimate unity." Thus, in Teilhardian and New Age terms, transcendence is "the formative *force* of the universe"—Evolution.

The ranking of Jesus Christ, by Skolimowski, as an "Illustrious one" along-side Buddha, Gandhi, and Mother Teresa is a feature of much Teilhardian "theology," and is common to "New Age" beliefs. Christ is not seen as the eternal and unique Son of God, the very fullness of Deity in human form. Instead, He is only seen to be one among a pantheon of enlightened "gurus," either of a higher order, equal to, or inferior to other manifestations of "Deity," who has merely discovered in fullest measure His own "inner divinity."

The quest for the "god within" found in Teilhardism, is the basis of all "New Age" philosophies and religions which draw heavily on concepts of "spiritual evolution," pantheism (literally "Everything [is] God"), monism (the idea that all of reality is one), and elements supposedly drawn from Eastern mysticism. We find in Teilhardism an emphasis on the "actualiz[ation] [of] our spiritual potential" or "inner potential"; beliefs common to the many branches of "New Age" thinking, including the Human Potential Movement.

The attraction of Teilhardian "spirituality" to a post-Christian Europe and indeed as the basis for a one-world religious body is immense. Here we have a New Age religion which has the potential to be truly ecumenical and provide the "unity-in-diversity" sought after by New Age leaders. This was exactly Teilhard's dream, a convergence of all world religions and the flowering of a spirituality in tune with a the ultimate evolutionary convergence of humanity. This religion, an amalgam of "mysticism" and science and a hybrid of pantheism and "Christiani-ty," has become an integral part in the growing Aquarian Conspiracy.

## 5.5 A Decisive Judgment

As yet, the impact of the writings of Teilhard de Chardin upon New Age Move-ment thought has not been analyzed. New Age leaders[139] and specialists on Teil-hard[140] have acknowledged his significant influence and we have seen how his religiophilosophical writings have been used to form much of the philosophical underpinnings of the New Age Movement. At the heart of New Age thought are the philosophies of pantheism, monism, gnosticism, and emergent evolution, all of which were repackaged in "Christian" garb by Teilhard. The quest for the "god within"—god immanent—and "cosmic consciousness" are also central to New Age thought, as well as to Teilhard's philosophy.

---

[139]E.g., Ferguson, *The Aquarian Conspiracy*, 50, 420.
[140]E.g., King, "Science and Mysticism," 8.

Teilhard has been elevated to the status of a sort of "patron saint" by many New Agers, not because their ideas necessarily stem from his, but because he gives a supposed level of academic respectability to their movement. His merger of science and "mysticism" is fully compatible with New Age thought including the so-called "new physics." His "religion of evolution"—in its Cosmic, Human and Christic aspects—has been embraced by many New Age leaders in the belief that it will foster "planetary consciousness" within the convergent evolution of humanity leading to Omega Point. Such ideas were elaborated by J. Lonsdale-Bryans, R. M. Bucke, and others, decades before Teilhard's main works were published.

In passing a decisive judgment on Teilhard's writings, I do so fully aware that many may be deeply offended. If Teilhard has been a beacon of light to them and truly assisted in moving them closer towards Christian faith, or even embracing it, then I rejoice with them. However, in my view, the devastating impact of his erroneous "theological" fictions far outweighs any morsels of spiritual truth that can be gleaned from his writings. These fictions have been instrumental in undermining the faith of many sincere Christian believers, as many scholars have noted. A warning needs to be sounded, loud and clear (see Jas. 5:16) against the deceptions, ambiguities, and errors which are rife in his writings.

Dom Aelred Graham, professor of Roman Catholic Theology at Ampleforth Abbey, York, and author of many works on Catholic theology, described Teilhard in 1965 as: "the author of a unique brand of theological science fiction which many people find exciting and even satisfying."[141] Clearly one cannot assess the spiritual value of a message by the extent to which people are excited or satisfied by it.

Sadly, many will continue to extol Teilhard's religiophilosophical writings despite the fictional nature of much of his "theology," the erroneous nature of his metaphysics, and the speculative nature of his "science." His overly zealous supporters as well as his enemies who have been overanxious to condemn him, need to recognize that, as Maritain wrote: "At the very root of Teilhard's thought there was . . . a poetic intuition—extremely powerful."[142]

Like a poet who seeks to express the incommunicable, Teilhard endeavored to communicate his cosmic vision which was born of a peculiar kind of spiritual experience. However, when "we remove the element of myth from Teilhard," Maritain maintains, "there remains of his personal contribution little more than a powerful lyrical impulse, which he himself has taken for a sort of prophetic an-

---

[141]Dom Aelred Graham, "The Pathos of Vatican II: Some Comments on 'Catholic Disarray'," *Encounter* 25/6 (December 1965): 16-22.

[142]Jacques Maritain, *The Peasant of the Garonne: An Old Layman Questions Himself about the Present Time*, trans. Michael Cuddihy and Elizabeth Hughes (London: Geoffrey Chapman, 1968; orig. French, Paris: Desclée de Brouwer, 1966) 118.

ticipation."[143] While Maritain concedes that fertile ideas and lofty aspirations can open minds to the flame of *living faith* which burns in the soul of the poet, in Teilhard's case, he concludes that it was a "travesty,"[144] a science-fiction theology born of "the cult of evolution."[145]

Whatever was the tenor of authenticity of Teilhard's religious experience or the illusions it may have fostered, his confused insights expressed in "mysticophilosophical imagery"[146] have aroused much admiration among his followers. Many claim to see at the center of his thought the bright luminous flame of the Risen Christ and claim that the speculations he indulged in all remain within the Christian orbit.

However, the question remains: Can such a channel which has been judged by leading Christian scholars to be "theology-fiction," light the flame of true Christian faith, or guide spiritual seekers into the path of Truth? We should expect the writings of a true Christian prophet to elicit such responses through the grace of God.

Nasr concluded that Teilhard "caters to certain of the antitraditional and even countertraditional tendencies of this world."[147] His writings can be admired for their beauty and boldness, but since his work is essentially born of "a poetic intuition" and is built on pseudometaphysical speculations, one should not expect it to convey knowledge, be it scientific, philosophical, or theological.[148] As Burckhardt concludes, Teilhard's thesis "expresses no particle of transcendent truth."[149] Gilson's assessment is fair-minded:

> Scientific illumination and the cult of evolution, in a manner somewhat similar to the confused evolutionism of Julian Huxley, invited [Teilhard] to conceptualize, in a language that was imprecise although it wore a scientific look, a religious experience of whose depth there can be no doubt.[150]

It is the unfathomable quality of a "religious experience" which has struggled with scientific dreams that shines through Teilhard's work. It is this and not the Teilhardian doctrine that has moved seekers in the direction of

---

[143]Ibid., 269.

[144]Ibid., 126.

[145]Gilson, "Le cas Teilhard de Chardin," cited in Maritain, *The Peasant of the Garonne*, 120.

[146]Maritain, *The Peasant of the Garonne*, 125.

[147]Nasr, *Knowledge and the Sacred*, 241.

[148]Maritain, *The Peasant of the Garonne*, 125.

[149]Titus Burckhardt, *Mirror of the Intellect: Essays on Traditional Science and Sacred Art*, trans. and ed. William Stoddart (Cambridge: Quinta Essentia, 1987) 99-100.

[150]Gilson, "Le cas Teilhard de Chardin."

"faith." But faith in what? Was it the faith in the dazzling primacy of science Teilhard promoted? Was it faith in the "Christ-Omega" who emerged from the evolutive process as the crowning glory of man's cooperative efforts? Or was it faith in the world and in the ultimate triumph of human reason? It is difficult to see how it could have been faith in Jesus Christ *as Redeemer and Savior.*

To those who would protest that Teilhard's philosophies, and those of the New Age Movement which has embraced them, must contain elements of value, however diluted, which must surely have something of value for priest, teacher, politician, artist, and poet, one must respond in the words of 1980 Nobel Prize for Literature recipient Czeslaw Milosz:

> With the law of hierarchy goes the law of travesty and parody. There is no inspiration, no idea, or discovery that, when mirrored in a lower intelligence, at a lower level of the "interhuman church," does not lose proportionately in value. If only something of the original, however weakened, however dimmed, would endure! But since the difference of degree is often one of absolute quality, the diluted version becomes a parody of the higher. Inspiration, its parody, and the parody of its paro-dy: they surround us in constant and clamorous collision. Or, to use another metaphor, everything of substance is undermined, hollowed out by the termites of inferiority. By endowing masks and facades with a real existence, we find ourselves one day the victims of an illusion. A priest nurtured on the Freudian-Marxian-Chardian dregs will be a priest in name only; a teacher, though able to read and write, an illiterate and a corruptor; a politician, an outlaw; artists and poets, the helpers of cir-cus managers who stage spectacles with real blood and live copulation, exactly as in those Roman circus-theaters described by Tertullian.[151]

My critical judgments of Teilhard's thought concur with that of a good num-ber of world-class scholars including Dietrich von Hildebrand, Étienne Gilson, Jacques Maritain, Titus Burckhardt, Martin Lings, Frithjof Schuon, and Seyyed H. Nasr, to name but a few. The Cistercian monk and well-known author Thomas Merton, while generous in his praise of aspects of Teilhard's writings, agreed with Frithjof Schuon that there was a "naïve infatuation with Teilhard de Chardin." "I think there is much that is good in Chardin," he wrote in 1964, "along with some grave illusions."[152] A year later he wrote of "a rather irre-sponsible and fantastic progressivism à la Teilhard."[153]

---

[151]Czeslaw Milosz, *The Land of Ulro* (Manchester: Carcanet Press, 1985) 88.

[152]Thomas Merton, letter of 10 December 1964 to Marco Pallis, in *The Hidden Ground of Love: The Letters of Thomas Merton on Religious Experience and Social Con-cerns*, ed. William H. Shannon (New York: Farrar, Straus, Giroux, 1985) 468.

[153]Letter of 24 April 1965 to Martin Lings, in ibid., 454.

I cannot agree with Teilhard's supporters such as Henri de Lubac, that his theological fiction is a "possible" addition to Christian revelation. Rather, there is compelling evidence that as Philippe de la Trinité OCD, one of the consultors of Vatican II put it: Teilhard's "theology" is "a deformation of Christianity, which is transformed into an evolutionism of the naturalistic, monistic, and pantheistic brand."[154] (These are conclusions I propose to endorse in a forthcoming more comprehensive analysis of Teilhard's thought.)

If for the sake of charity we concede that Teilhard may have *inadvertently* overstepped the bounds of Christian orthodoxy, but always remained faithful "in heart" to the Christian beliefs he was nurtured in; we must still issue a strong warning concerning his writings. While the writer accepts the limitations of all "formulations" of Christian doctrine, it is his conviction that all truth is in God and in Christ, that God has His own system, a system infinitely vaster than that of all thinkers, orthodox and heterodox.

In Jesus Christ, who is the "radiance of God's glory and the exact representation of His nature" (Heb. 1:3) are found "hidden all the treasures of wisdom and knowledge" (Col. 2:3). "He is the one whom God exalted to His right hand as a Prince and a Savior" (Acts 5:31), and to whom "God has bestowed the name which is above every name" (Phil. 2:9).

He identifies Himself with the title of the Lord God: "I am the Alpha and the Omega, the first and the last, the beginning and the end" (Rev. 22:13).[155] When all things are subjected to God the Father who will ultimately "fill all things" (Eph. 4:10), those who truly know Christ will fully know the One who is the Truth.[156] What matters in the end is whether we truly know him who to know is life eternal (John 17:3).

---

[154]Philippe de la Trinité, *Rome et Teilhard de Chardin* (Paris: Arthème, Fayard, 1964) 38. This work has the imprimatur of five Roman Catholic censorship authorities.
[155]Cf. Rev. 1:8; 21:6; Isa. 41:4.
[156]1 Cor. 13:12; John 14:6.

# Name Index

# Subject Index

transtheistic mysticism, 31

Nag Hammadic Gnostic Library, 162
National Catholic Education Association (NCEA), 127, 133, 135
National Council of Churches, 91
natural selection ("survival of the fittest"), 39, 64-65, 69
    Darwinian selection, 66
Neanderthal Man, 10
Neo-Darwinism: Neo-Darwinian explanation of the General Theory of Evolution, xi
neo-humanism, 54
neologisms (of Teilhard), xi, 3
    New Age Movement, vii, 36, 100-107, 120, 126, 131, 139, 169, 172
    apostate Christian roots, vii
    beliefs, 100
    "consciousnes-raising" groups, 96
    leaders, vii, ix, 100, 105
    link to Teilhard, x, xiii
    subtle enemy to Christianity, 164
New Age Jesus, 80
New Age of Enlightenment, 104
New Age thinking, ix, 36, 69, 99, 101-102, 139, 144, 147, 170
    New Age Bible, 129
    buzzwords, xiii
    Christology, 137, 162
    networks (SPINS), 101
    New Age ideology, 112
    pantheistic version of Christian doctrine, 157
    Teilhard's influence on New Age thought, x, xiv, 106
    vision of "unity-in-diversity," 98
new spirituaity, x
New York City, ix
Nicene Creed, 120
noogenesis, 38, 53, 95, 122
noosphere, xi, 3, 8, 47-48, 51, 62-63, 107, 109, 111, 123, 126, 133
    noospheric structures, 3
nucleic acids, 35

occult meditation, 132
Old Testament: references from Teilhard's writings, 67
Omega Institute, 135-36, 161
Omega Order, 116
Omega Point, 5, 33, 47, 49-51, 53, 56, 66, 69, 71, 79, 83, 110, 122, 133, 167, 170
    Alpha and Omega, 5
    Christ-Omega, 171
    god-Omega, 133
    Omega, 48, 52, 91, 124, 126
    Omega, the point of convergence, 91
    Omega united with Alpha, 155
Oriental Christianity, 90
Oriental doctrine, 141
    Oriental esoteric doctrines, 141
Original Sin (doctrine), xi, 58, 73, 80, 84
    reformulation of doctrine by Teilhard, 81
orthogenesis, 61-62, 65

paganism, 144
paleoanthropology, xii
panentheism, vii, 59, 134
    dipolar (or bipolar) theism, 59
panpsychism, 150
pantheism, vii, xii, xiv, 31, 68-69, 91, 115, 134, 147, 149
    Christian pantheism, xiv
    evolutionary pantheism, xiv, 119
    false pantheism, 73
    monistic pantheism, 32
    of the New Age Movement, 130
    pantheisms, 72
    pantheistic deity, 55
    Stoic pantheism, 68
    Teilhard's pantheism and monism, 169
    Teilhard's pantheistic fights, 150
Paris, 5
    Centre Sèvres, 6
    Paris Press, 68
Parousia, 20, 66, 72-73
Peking, 35
    Peking man, 9, 10
phenomenology, 60, 109
physics, new, 142, 145, 170

# About the Author

David H. Lane is a graduate of Victoria University, Wellington (N.Z.) where he gained his M.Sc. (Hons.) degree in Zoology in 1984. He has wide interests in biology, including entomology, evolution theory, and ecology. He has published work in the fields of biology and theology in New Zealand and North America. He had been actively researching the fields of human evolution, speciation theory, and theology for more than twenty years. His interest in the work of Teilhard de Chardin has led to six years of research culminating in the present book and its sequel.

David lives with his wife, daughter, and son in Wellington. He is currently president of the Wellington Christian Apologetics Society (Inc.) and editor of the Society's journal *Apologia* which seeks to provide a reasoned defense for the Christian faith.

*The Phenomenon of Teilhard: Prophet for a New Age.*
by David H. Lane

ISBN 0-86554-498-0. Catalog and warehouse pick number MUP/P131.
Mercer University Press, 6316 Peake Road, Macon, Georgia 31210-3960.
Text, interior, titles, and cover designs, composition and layout
    by Edd Rowell.
Camera-ready pages composed on a Gateway 2000 via WordPerfect
    dos 5.1 and wpwin 5.1/5.2, and printed on a Lasermaster Typesetter 1000.
Text font: TimesNewRomanPS. Display and titles font: Mistral.
Printed and bound by McNaughton & Gunn, Inc., Saline, Michigan 48176.
Printed via offset lithography on 50# Natural Offset (500 ppi)
    and perfect bound in 10-pt. c1s printed PMS 476 (red-blue-yellow-black)
        and black with lay-flat film lamination.
Individually shrinkwrapped and bulk packed in cartons on skids.

[ First printing June 1996 1m ]